MOVING
ORGANIZATIONS

MOVING

ORGANIZATIONS

How to use agile transformation
to make your business crisis-proof

Frank Boos
Barbara Buzanich-Pöltl

Aldine
Publishing

ISBN 978-1-7398092-0-1 (print)
e-ISBN 978-1-7398092-1-8 (ebook)

Original German language edition:

Frank Boos / Barbara Buzanich Pöltl: *Moving Organizations. Wie Sie
sich durch agile Transformation krisenfest aufstellen.* 1. Auflage 2020.
(ISBN: 978-3-7910-4661-7) originally published by Schäffer Poeschel
Verlag für Wirtschaft Steuern Recht GmbH, Stuttgart, Germany.

This edition has been translated and published in English by
Aldine Publishing, 2022
Aldine Publishing, Stroud, UK
Typeset by Newgen Publishing UK
Aldine cover illustration: courtesy of Benjamin Ben Chaim

British Library Cataloguing in Publication Data
A catalogue record for this book is available from the British Library

www.aldinepublishing.com

Contents

1 Moving organizations

1.1 On the goal of remaining flexible and crisis-proof

This book is about the transformation of companies and organizations—a transformation that is becoming necessary in order to keep pace with the complex demands of the market and society. Until now, organizations mostly operated in largely stable environments and were able to anticipate developments. This enabled them to buy, produce, sell and plan and to become more and more efficient in all of this. Efficiency was their focus. Like a competitive athlete who sets the bar higher and higher or runs the same distance faster and faster, organizations were able to become better and better, that is, more efficient, over many decades. This is why today we purchase products and services that are much faster, cheaper and more efficient than decades ago.

But the world has become more unpredictable and complex. The big challenge for organizations today is to cope with a high degree of uncertainty and complexity. Instead of being able to devote themselves primarily to improving and increasing the efficiency of their services or products, they must now primarily try to get to grips with this uncertainty and complexity and work with it. Digitalization has driven these changes, and the Corona crisis has accelerated them enormously.

Crises are, by definition, turning points. The great crisis triggered by the Corona pandemic has presented the world with completely new challenges. Such crises cannot be mastered without well-functioning organizations, which have to bring their full potential to bear, often reaching and even extending beyond their limits. Organizations that already knew how to use digital media sensibly during the Corona crisis were at an advantage, others tried to follow suit as quickly as possible. In the meantime, modern digitalization strategies have become part of the basic equipment of every organization and continue to drive change within it.

Some organizations proved able to act even in the middle of the crisis. They had already planned buffers in advance, established stable processes and prepared their staff. They were resilient, that is, prepared for the problem and able to survive the crisis largely unscathed. We will discuss the characteristics of resilient and thus crisis-resistant organizations in more detail later.

The digitalization of processes is accompanied by an increase in complexity within organizations. More and more options are available in ever less time, and at the same time there are hardly any routines and empirical values to fall back on in individual cases. This increase in complexity is a major problem, especially for decision-makers. They have to decide on a multitude of options in a short time without being able to fall back on tried and tested decision-making aids. This shifts their focus and the focus of the whole organization. A huge change!

This book is about how such a transformation can succeed. It is about the transformation from "efficiency" mode to "agility" mode. Because if organizations want to be crisis-proof, they must above all be able to make decisions quickly despite complexity, and they can do that if they are agile. In the time of the Corona crisis, it was easy to observe which companies were able to change quickly and adapt their services—including state organizations. Which is not to say that agility automatically has to come at the expense of efficiency—one does not exclude the other. But it is primarily agility that guides a company through uncertain times.

"Agility" is another word for playability. Agile organizations focus on staying playable. This objective determines how they work, what tools they use, how they decide and distribute power. The term "agility" thus encapsulates all the initiatives that organizations develop to capture complexity.

The process, the transformation to get there, is a challenging journey and this book is a travel guide for all organizations that want to go down this path of transformation. We want to show you how such transformations can succeed. Walk through the different stages with us: We report directly from our practice and embed it in theory in such a way that you can deepen your understanding. We will demonstrate why it is especially important now to use a good framework to make good decisions. We invite you to take short excursions into history and explain how and when some concepts originated. You may also be surprised where ideas first originated, why they were forgotten for a while, and why they resurface today. We also introduce you to our practical tools and instruments.

More than ever, organizations are exciting places. Places where important things can happen for people and society, but only if this is wanted and if the right skills are developed for it. We would like to contribute to this. We would like to invite you to do so.

We are particularly concerned with connecting the steps, with painting the big picture. You use a tool differently when you know the associated model and have thought through the context and theory in which everything is embedded. Too often we have seen processes fail because their primary focus was on the use of tools and the overall context was lost. But if you know the context, if you learn to climb from the lowlands of practice to the heights of the models and abseil down again, if you know what the assumptions behind the approaches are, you will be much more successful and will enjoy the path of agile transformation.

The starting point of our journey is described in six hypotheses in the first chapter. These are assumptions about how we understand digitalization, agilization, crisis resilience and change in organizations today and how organizations relate to society. Then, in a separate step, we derive the special requirements for transformation processes and show how these differ from earlier procedural models. An example from our consulting practice illustrates how we proceed.

The second chapter begins with the example of a service team in crisis and describes the capabilities that organizations need in such situations. For decades, resilience research has been investigating what distinguishes robust organizations, that is, organizations that cope better with crises. However, the results were long overshadowed by the debates on agility until the Corona crisis suddenly made them red-hot. Surprisingly, the two concepts of organizational resilience and agility are not very different. We compare both approaches and offer the Tension Square as an orientation framework to help you locate your own organization. This will help you find the starting points that you can practice so that your organization is equipped for a successful journey. Furthermore, this second part describes agile tools for project work and the model of an agile organization: the holacracy. The chapter is rounded off with the systemic perspective, that is, how much the systemic view will benefit you in times of crisis and high complexity. And as in the first chapter, we conclude with a case study from our consulting practice.

The third chapter is dedicated to the nine levers of agile transformation. These have proven to be particularly important for us in the context of the transformation of organizations. The fields of transformation, such as working in teams, culture, role design, skills of individuals, leadership, power and purpose are examined in more detail. Our way of working is also explained here by case studies.

The fourth chapter is about the process of agile transformation. Here it becomes clear how we work in transformation, how interventions are planned and used. For this we use models, also called power tools, which have a strong impact and show what difference they make for us compared to common practice. Our concern is to place concrete procedures in a larger context and to link tools to the process and effects.

Finally, the last chapter is devoted to tools. Practitioners and counsellors will find over 40 tools here that we have successfully used in transformation processes. The purpose, the conditions for use and a direction are described for each tool and cross-referenced to the corresponding chapters in the book. We recommend reading these before using the respective tool.

1.2 What *moving organizations* is all about

The title of this book, *Moving Organizations*, owes much to the fact that organizations today are on the move more than ever before. By organizations we mean not only companies but also public authorities, non-profit organizations or associations. The movement varies depending on the sector or area of society, but standing still is no longer an option. Organizations and their employees have to cope with it and make sense of the movement. Moving organizations are able to move, touch and engage employees. Organizations can be places that create meaning, that help to develop people and that contribute to social development. We find it desirable to create moving organizations that are mobile and also crisis-proof.

Crisis resilience—especially when viewed in the light of recent history—is a primary goal if organizations are to survive for long. In order to survive, organizations have to perform, but the conditions under which they do so have changed massively. We have, therefore, chosen the term "moving organizations" for those organizations which

- work on their agility and resistance to crises, and thereby become resilient;
- give special priority to the development of employees; and
- consciously take on their social role.

Moving organizations are organizations that keep moving by changing many things at once. They know that this is not just a phase of change followed by a period of calm and stability, but that the next, as yet unknown change is already waiting. The basic idea of change management was quite different: unfreeze, change, freeze again. Instead of thinking of change in phases, it is now important to understand it as a movement, as a swarm of individual changes that influence each other.

Moving, that is constant movement makes different demands on the members of an organization and influences their relationship to the organization. In order to be able and willing to participate in these movements, more is needed than just a purely factual relationship along the lines of "service for remuneration". It also needs an emotional agreement between the employees and the organization, their relationship has to get out of the end-means logic, where employees or the organization are means for the ends of others. This is also the thinking behind the strange expression: "work-life balance". Does that mean that we work for money but our lives take place in our free time?

In a moving organization, we want a different quality of encounter. In this sense, organizations must be able to touch employees and they must open up and get involved. Only then can the trust and security arise to cope with this mixture of opportunities and excessive demands. Moving thus creates some security in change.

1.3 Six theses that move organizations

Most of us spend a large part of our lives in organizations and they are of great importance for our development and well-being. We are born in hospitals, learn in schools and universities, work in companies, authorities or NPOs, get involved in associations. Have you ever thought about which and how many organizations have been really relevant for you in your life so far?

Organizations inspire us. We think this "institution" is great and believe that we and society owe a lot to it. We ourselves found our dream job in an organization that specializes in the development of organizations. As a result, we know many very different types of organizations and also the challenges they face. The starting point and the motives are very different, but they all face a big challenge: They need, more than ever, to transform themselves. Digitalization, increasing complexity and crises are forcing them to do so. It is time for the transformation. For this, it is important not only to work *in* them, but also *on* them.

We believe that working on organizations is important not least from a societal perspective. Good organizations are important not only for the individual, but also for the community, because much that is socially relevant arises in organizations: Scientific research, new vaccines, film and music services, care and support services, platforms for finding partners. Practice shows that new ideas only become relevant for society when organizations take them up. We see this with the environmental movement, which had to found associations and parties in order to become effective. From these assumptions we derive our credo: Organizations are hugely important and we can shape them. This is our motivation, our purpose for writing this book.

To work with organizations, one should understand them and the current context in which they operate. From our point of view, the most important theses for moving organizations today are:

1. Digitalization is forcing organizations to find new responses to cope with greater complexity.
2. Agility is a social innovation that organizations use to counter increasing complexity. One of the ways they do this is by acquiring virtual competences.
3. In transforming organizations, one of the biggest hurdles is the redistribution of power.

4. More and more people want to work differently and develop in the process. Moving organizations need exactly that and are responsible for creating the space for this development.
5. Preparing for and managing crises is part of the daily business of organizations.
6. The likelihood of crises increases due to greater interconnectedness and rising interdependencies, and organizations will be increasingly called upon to make their contribution to social development (common good).

1.3.1 Thesis 1: Digitalization is forcing organizations to find new answers[1]

In 1890, electricity replaced the steam engine as the power source in factories. Engineers bought the largest electric motors available on the market and replaced the steam turbine, which was in the middle of the machines, with the new motor. Little changed in the production process: The space concept, the way of working and productivity remained similar. Thirty years later, factories were unrecognizable. Instead of one big machine standing in the centre, there were many small electric motors. The spatial concept had changed completely. The work units were divided and women workers were divided according to material flow and workflow.

A new form of organizing was needed. Factories needed the arrangement of machines in the form of production lines, which analytically broke down work processes into their individual steps in order to structure them according to economic aspects. This would have been unthinkable in a factory run by steam engines. The new arrangement required a different way of thinking and was a social innovation. It was this that made effective use of an electrified factory possible in the first place. This form of social innovation is called Taylorism, which in its extreme application also had many negative social effects. Consequently, the technological innovation of electrification needed the social innovation to become effective. It then took another almost 100 years before electrification could fully develop its actual effect.

The change brought about by digitalization is no less profound. Digitalization is an innovation that necessitates social change in a co-evolutionary process. We call this social innovation agility. It is related to and dependent on the technological innovations of digitalization. Agility develops new forms of cooperation, but also creates new conflicts. It requires other social mechanisms and a new distribution of power (see also thesis 3 in Section 1.3.3 and lever 7 in Section 3.7).

---

1   Produced in collaboration with Gregor Tobeitz.

Therefore, it is worthwhile to better understand social innovations: "Social innovations are new practices for coping with societal challenges that are adopted and used by affected individuals, social groups and organizations" (Hochgerner, 2013). The challenges posed by technological change, therefore, need new social action, different patterns of behaviour, new types of communication and cooperation so that the potential of technological innovation can fully unfold. Social innovation is thus at the same time a prerequisite, a concomitant and a consequence of technological innovation.

Technical and social innovation are thus closely linked. Many things are not clearly defined, such as sequence, boundary and allocation. A prime example of this is the emergence of the World Wide Web: To enable women scientists at CERN to communicate and research more efficiently and globally, they sought new solutions. The development of the World Wide Web satisfied diverse social communication, relationship and cooperation needs through networked websites and thus through the networking of knowledge and information. The explosive spread of the World Wide Web, along with its technical development, came about in a co-creative and co-evolutionary process of social and technological innovation.

The most far-reaching innovations are those that target communication and knowledge in a society and bring about profound social changes. So far, we can reconstruct four such epochal innovations in human history (Baecker, 2007):

1. **Language:** The development of language enables a community to organize itself in tribal structures.
2. **Writing:** The invention of writing enables people to organize themselves into city-states and kingdoms.
3. **Printing:** The invention of printing enables the enlightenment of broad sections of the population and leads to the formation of nation-states and democracy.
4. **Computer:** The development of the computer and its networking through the internet enables a global society, new possibilities of communication and cooperation.

Digitalization is another far-reaching innovation that deeply intervenes in our society in many ways. The effect of this intervention could be clearly seen during the no-contact period in the Corona crisis. Where physical contact was not possible, there was a switch to virtual communication. Those who could not but needed contact with others had a problem. All those who had to work from home set themselves up according to their technical possibilities and, after an initial phase of shock, found new ways of communicating. Not only streaming

Fig. 1.1. Social innovations in history

services for films, podcasts or online yoga courses saw a surge in demand, but also professional contacts and meetings, even the exchange of information and decision-making meetings in management boards and government bodies took place virtually. What had only taken place sporadically before the crisis and was often viewed sceptically, suddenly took off of necessity. People and organizations took hold and began to use virtual media. However, this phase also had another side. Many were overloaded and annoyed, for example, because they were overwhelmed by the many virtual meetings, because details were very difficult to discuss and there was hardly any opportunity for informal, personal exchange. Boundaries that provided support became blurred.

We are constantly experiencing how digitalization increases the complexity around us. Our world is not only becoming more complicated, it is becoming more complex. Complicated things can be systematized and learned. In a complicated structure like the London Underground with over 400 kilometres of track and 270 stations, you can find your way around after a while. Complexity, on the other hand, cannot be deciphered and extensive study and patience are of little help. Interrelationships are no longer clear, the same causes have different effects, many things are interrelated, and yet elements act independently of each other. Predictions are difficult and long-term planning impossible. The result is a world for which a term has been coined: VUCA-World (German: VUKA-Welt). Its factors are Volatility, Uncertainty, Complexity, Ambiguity. VUCA refers to a world in which many things are constantly changing, unpredictable and ambiguous. The VUCA world is a different "game" and requires different responses from organizations.

In the crisis, digitalization showed that it opens up new possibilities that would not exist without it, while at the same time increasing complexity.

Organizations that had made sure in time that their IT infrastructure was well positioned by enabling cloud-based working, video conferencing and the necessary line capacity were more resilient in the crisis. In the wake of the Corona crisis, the proof was in the pudding: Digitalization helped make organizations more resilient.

While organizations in recent decades have strived to improve their efficiency above all else, today the focus is on agility and resilience. In a complex, unstable environment, it makes no sense to make organizations as efficient as possible, that is, to introduce routines, streamline processes and focus everything on working more cost-effectively. This means introducing routines, streamlining processes and gearing everything towards working more cost-effectively. The main thing now is to stay in the game. And to achieve this, organizations have to change from the ground up. Agility means: Playability comes before efficiency.

1.3.2 Thesis 2: Agility is a social innovation

Digitalization is a revolution, a game changer, especially for the world of organizations. They are confronted with more and more possibilities that are permanently changing. To deal with this, organizations need agility and thus social innovation. It is not primarily about the introduction of tools and methods, it is about a completely new form of organizing that replaces the system of Taylorism and the idea of efficiency, because digitalized organizations tick differently: They plan and lead in a more decentralized way, demand more from individuals and strive to renew themselves socially on an ongoing basis. Agility describes both the way there and the result—the constantly reorganizing organization. Agility, one could say, is the "new guiding idea for the restructuring of existing organizational relationships" (Schumacher & Wimmer, 2019, p. 12ff).

The guiding idea in daily activities is to deal with this uncertainty and unpredictability: Only those who learn permanently stay in the game. This new principle, which is attributed to the startup scene, is build-measure-learn. Three steps in a loop that is run through again and again: Make, measure, learn.

Loops are the model of agile working. Instead of breaking down an issue in detail, as the work breakdown structure in project management does, for example, it is about reviewing and improving the original assumptions (product). This is the essential difference to efficiency-driven logics: It is not the refinement of the product and "plan and control" that are the goal, but the review of the assumptions in the form of "sense and response" that lead to this product.

To start the process of agile working, initially only a small product is needed, a Minimum Viable Product (MVP) . In other words, the product is the answer

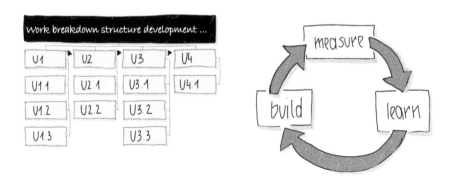

Fig. 1.2. Work breakdown structure versus build-measure-learn

and you try to clarify: Did we ask ourselves the right question? An example: A machine builder who produces electrical appliances, motors and machines comes up with the idea of bringing an electrically powered wheelchair to the market. A project team is established that works according to the basic principle "build-measure-learn". First, the market in Europe is investigated and the team discovers that insurance companies bear a significant part of the costs of purchasing the wheelchairs. So, in order to develop the market, it is necessary to win them as new customers and distribution partners. The company develops the first prototype of an electronic wheelchair and presents it to the insurers. Unfortunately, these few show interest in the new product.

The project is almost stopped, but the project team wants to learn and stays on. They make an astonishing discovery: A new group of wheelchair users that they had not seen before and recognized as relevant—the active and sporty wheelchair users. The original assumption was that women wheelchair users were people with impairments who needed to be helped and, therefore, needed support from insurers. These wheelchair users were also the insurance company's clients, which is why the project team adopted this view in its planning. The project team's new assumption turns the perspective around: What if wheelchair users like to be fit and mobile, do many things for it and do not see themselves as "sick" and dependent on "others". They might have an active interest in an e-wheely with different features like an integrated smartphone. These potential female customers are more likely to visit shops or online shops that sell, for example, mountain bikes and sports equipment than those that offer health care and nursing products. Under these conditions, completely different sales partners become interesting.

Thinking in loops has enabled this team to generate new perspectives and bring a successful product to market by having team members work on it step by step. This required the project team to change and work in a completely different way and with different methods. This radical rethinking and questioning is admittedly not easy with a product. Changing the organization to this mode of working is a Herculean task.

And that is what agility as social innovation is all about. However, attempts to transfer these methods, which are suitable for teams and startup companies, one-to-one to entire organizations regularly fail. There is a difference between working on a project with one client, clear focus and prioritization, and aligning the entire organization accordingly. But when a company makes decisions to best serve women wheelchair users, it has a clear focus. If, on the other hand, the company sells electric motors, household appliances, drills and control technology in addition to electric wheelchairs, it has different customers, distribution channels, factories and billing methods. It has to do justice to different logics and is much more complex.

Companies that want to become more agile need organizational relationships that are able to deal with complexity. Agility requires organizational relationships with different starting points. We will show which levers are effective for this. To describe and analyze these organizational relationships, we use the Neuwaldegg triangle (see Chapter 3). The challenging task of shaping the way there, that is, the process of transformation, is what we call agile transformation. This is described in Chapter 4.

1.3.3 Thesis 3: Redistribution of power is one of the biggest hurdles

A prerequisite for agility is that organizations become more open to their environments, that they process impulses from outside, from customers, suppliers, authorities, competitors and their own employees more quickly. But to be consistently open, organizations must give the external-internal relationship top priority. The most important consequence of this change is that the previously dominant top-bottom relationship loses importance. In other words, power relations change; instead of a hierarchical gradation of power, decentralized, distributed spheres of influence emerge in an agile organization (Baecker, 2017). This change in the spheres of power and influence is the biggest hurdle on the way to an agile organization. Many transformations fail because of this.

An example: We were invited by an internationally renowned machine tool manufacturer to introduce an agile organization based on Scrum principles in one area.

Scrum—term and meaning

In simple terms, Scrum is an agile project management method that handles complex development processes step by step in a loop logic.

The term "scrum" (German: Gedränge) comes from rugby, accepts the unpredictability of developments and is meant to illustrate the necessary team spirit. In Scrum, there are specific roles within a team: Product Owner, Scrum Master and the team members with their corresponding responsibilities, that is, decision-making powers. For more details, see also Section 2.2.2.

As envisaged in Scrum, there were specific roles: Product Owner, Scrum Master and the team members. In addition, the role of sponsors was established to support the transformation topics. These roles were filled from top to bottom, that is, management level 1 became Sponsor, level 2 Product Owner, level 3 Scrum Master and clerks became team members. So the existing organizational structure was transferred one-to-one to the agile roles. Despite our concerns, we could not persuade the client to change this. Over time, it became apparent that the organization was not becoming more agile and the project was soon discontinued.

This made it clear: Without a redistribution of power, organizations cannot become more agile. The classical hierarchy (from the Greek for "hierarchy") and the agile organization are not compatible. Hierarchy is based on regulating decision-making powers, that is, power, formally through superordination and subordination. Whoever sits higher up has more rights and more power. This produces bottlenecks, makes people inflexible and in many cases leads to organizations adapting to power relations and no longer ensuring effective processes. Hierarchy as a principle of power distribution has provided stability and predictability, but is becoming increasingly dysfunctional in complex environments.

Power also creates inequality and is seen as a problem in agile organizations. But power structures cannot simply be dissolved. Every organization, every system has and needs a certain distribution of power and would not function without it. Power, loosely based on Max Weber, is the ability "within a social relationship to assert one's own will even in the face of opposition" (Rudolph, 2017, p. 9). Power has an important function; it serves to reduce complexity and uncertainty. Agile organizations also need this, only here power should be more flexible and widely distributed. The change towards an agile organization, therefore, always means working on the power structure.

The change in power relations often proves to be laborious, as it is often difficult for individual previous holders of power to relinquish their power and thus also lose social significance. But even if those in power are willing and support the change, the system, the organization, initially falls into a highly unstable state because complexity and uncertainty increase enormously in the phase of change. The old rules of power no longer apply and the new ones have not yet taken hold: Many things no longer work as usual, everything is shaky and conflict-laden, power struggles break out. Exactly what the existing power structures have so far prevented, namely general insecurity, is now becoming a problem. No system can endure this state of a power vacuum in the long run and therefore many organizations quickly return to the old state.

We show how you can work on power relations in Section 3.7 (leadership, power and the transition). Most cases we know of only deal with the issue when conflicts arise. Those who deal with it proactively, on the other hand, focus on transparency and formal role descriptions. They tie power to roles and the powers of what a specific role can and cannot decide on its own, and specify exactly how these powers can be decided. For example, the Holacracy operating system uses a constitution that cannot be changed to determine the rules according to which decisions about the distribution of power can be made (see Section 2.3).

Power can be made visible and limited through rules. Similar to the separation of powers in democratic states, agile organizations rely on transparency and the distribution and formalization of power. But power cannot be completely determined by formal rules, there always remains an informal part. This can be seen, for example, in the assumption of a role: What a person responsible for designing and updating a homepage is allowed to do can be described. What is concretely done and accepted also depends on that person's experience, competence and willingness to make decisions.

This part of power that cannot be formalized is particularly relevant in the transition. For a further, quite precise description of the powers would not help. The problem, the explosive expansion of insecurity in this phase, remains. But if regulating power does not get the insecurity out of the system, what does? There is only one solution: Trust. Trust, loosely based on Niklas Luhmann, is the willingness to take the risk of assuming a good intention on the part of the other (Luhmann, 2014). Those involved must take the risk and make a leap of faith. Systems that have not learned to build trust will not survive this phase of transition, will dissolve or fall back into the old state of power.

But beware: The issue of power is too difficult to work on a change in the middle of a crisis. What everyone is longing for here is security and no questioning of one's own leadership. Closing ranks is expected. The fear that power discussions will lead to fragmentation and trench warfare, that the whole system will literally blow up in one's face, is too great. This is also the reason why the value of popular approval has risen for many government leaders in the Corona crisis, even though from the outside some have performed rather poorly. In saying this, we are in no way advocating authoritarian approaches that seek to abuse moments of crisis for their own ends. Our recommendation is:

> Work on your power relations in the so-called "normal" times when it may not seem so necessary.

1.3.4 Thesis 4: More and more people want to work differently

For many employees, organizations that are clocked for efficiency and are supposed to function like machines have become stale. This clocking contradicts the natural rhythm of humans and nature, as numerous studies have shown (Moser, 2018). The declining attractiveness of these organizations contrasts with the high appeal—despite poor pay—of the startup scene. The permanently high turnover rates of employees in clocking machines such as the large consultancies are also features of this development.

More and more people want to work differently and develop in the process— agile organizations need exactly that and are responsible for creating this space.

The need to do meaningful work and to be able to develop is growing. This longing for a different kind of organization is met by the book *Reinventing Organizations* by Frederic Laloux (2016). The book describes concrete alternatives on how to organize and work together differently today. Twelve examples from different sectors encourage meaningful practice. Although at no point is it described what is meant by organization, it meets exactly a need of people who want to shape organizations: The longing to make organizations a better place, a place where people enjoy being, meeting interested others, doing meaningful work and working on relevant issues (for our understanding see thesis 6 and Sections 3.1. and 3.2.).

Today, more than ever, employees come to organizations with this expectation. Work no longer serves the sole purpose of survival, but is also in the service of their own development and should benefit society: They no longer want to be merely a means to the ends of others. They want to experience a practice that focuses on the development of people's potential. Employees want to be the end themselves. In other words, it is necessary to think differently about the interaction between employees and organizations.

And this "thinking differently" is a particular challenge from our point of view: To open up personal resonance spaces without invading people's privacy (Rosa, 2019). By this we mean creating a space in organizations where people can open up and reflect on the impact of their actions, that is, share their feelings, irritations and thoughts. This is not about the private lives of staff. This distinction is often overlooked. It is not about "bringing your whole self to work", but about a differentiated examination of the person's role in the organization. No one wants to have to justify personal relationship problems and an organization would also be completely incapable of acting with such issues of all employees.

There are already sensible proposals for implementing this requirement, as a variety of concepts and publications on the topic show (Fink & Moeller, 2018; Pink, 2011; Kirchgeorg et al., 2019). One concept that consistently focuses on the development of employees but has not yet received much attention in this country is the Deliberately Developmental Organization (DDO; Kegan & Laskow Lahey, 2016).

A DDO has three dimensions: Home, Edge, Groove—or loosely translated home, edge and practising together. *Home* encompasses the need to belong to one or more groups that cultivate their own culture and ensure that each develops everyone—all engage in staff development. *Edge* addresses the need for people to want to grow and develop, where standing still is not an option, weakness is potential and a mistake is an opportunity. This only succeeds when contributors challenge and nurture each other, regardless of their role or status. *Groove* are the practices of co-development that help destabilize and reflect. So it is not the beat that is the goal, but the discontinuities, irregularities and gaps that need to be overcome and where learning can take place. Concrete procedures are described in the "discontinuous departures". This does not mean adapting to existing standards, but rather the break, the departure from established routines, in order to consistently dedicate oneself to the growth of the employees and the organization (see Section 3.5).

Today, this and other models are especially effective in places where competition for qualified workers is particularly fierce. You will find examples in Stuttgart, Berlin, Basel, Copenhagen, Barcelona, Vienna and elsewhere. A special place for this has been the Bay Area around San Francisco for years. There, companies like Google, Airbnb, Zappos Future Lab, Patagonia, Morning Star, Berkeley and Stanford University, among others, compete for excellent employees. Competition is fierce and turnover costs money.

The "return of the human being" to the organization is also a consequence of growing complexity. In order for organizations to become more agile, they decentralize tasks and transfer more responsibility to individuals. In classic organizations, there is more or less a "chimney effect" that delegates decisions on unregulated issues almost automatically to upper management. This knowledge that someone is responsible has a security effect in these organizations. In agile organizations, this security has to be established differently, since it can be

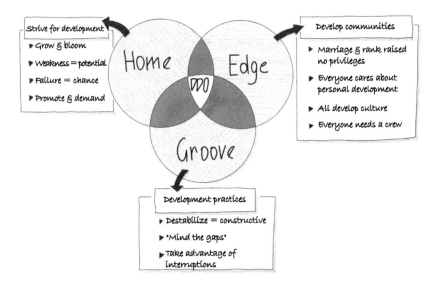

Fig. 1.3. Dimensions of Deliberately Developmental Organization (DDO) based on Kegan and Laskow Lahey (2016, p. 86)

assumed that the experts for certain decisions are not at the top of the organization, but are those who work on the respective front.

Therefore, in agile organizations, individuals are more challenged (see Section 3.6). Figuratively speaking, they have to be constantly playable and cannot easily delegate many decisions. This requires both a different willingness to participate in the organization and new skills to be able to participate. In moving organizations, it is important to combine these requirements with the employees' need for more meaningful fulfilment in their work (see Section 3.3).

The importance of the relationship between employees and the organization quickly becomes apparent in times of crisis. What is valid now and what can we rely on, the employees ask themselves and observe very closely what the leadership communicates and decides. Small groups form in a flash to compare the statements of different leaders and check their accuracy. Contradictions and lack of transparency quickly make the rounds. The question on everyone's mind in this situation: Do I still have a place in this organization and how will we be dealt with?

The organization must also be able to rely on its staff, especially in crises. Are the staff able to work and willing to take on their roles? The organization wants to feel that it is important for the staff and vice versa. It needs support, because now the staff play a big role. Sometimes, in the exuberance of this energy, the classic organizational structure is suspended: "Hey, we are here and we are all pulling together". In the process, it "forgets" its processes and roles and thus turns into a herd of startled individuals. This is where resilient organizations prove themselves; they have staff, roles and processes that are attuned to each other (see also Section 3.4).

1.3.5 Thesis 5: Coping with crises is part of day-to-day business

If you remember the Corona pandemic, you probably have images of this crisis in your mind. Like all crises, Corona probably disrupted your usual routines. It was a state of emergency, and to cope with it you needed different means than in everyday life. Uncertainty all around. This is part of the essence of every crisis. It is the state of emergency for which different rules apply than in everyday life.

In this book, we will not deal with the management of acute crises. However, we are concerned with crises here insofar as we analyze those preconditions that make organizations more crisis-resistant. The technical term for this is "resilience". Resilient organizations manage to cope with an explosion of the unexpected and uncertainty in a crisis.

An organization becomes resilient when it prepares itself in "normal time". Introducing something completely new only in a crisis seems difficult to us. We recommend that every manager and consultant study crisis research. For example, the classic study by Steven Fink, who investigated the incident at the Three Mile Island nuclear power plant in Harrisburg. There, the cooling system in the power plant failed in 1979 and a meltdown was imminent, as happened in Chernobyl in 1986. Fink was an advisor to the newly appointed governor and experienced first-hand how unprofessionally a large traditional company handled the situation despite crisis plans and media professionals. His work is considered the beginning of crisis research (Fink, 2002). This research was followed by many others, such as the classic "The Logic of Failure" (Dörner, 1989), the reading of which can still be warmly recommended today.

A current example of crisis research is the study by the consulting firm McKinsey (Pinner et al., 2020). It shows several similarities between pandemics and climate catastrophes: Crises are systemic, that is, they cannot be confined to individual areas such as the health system, but affect society as a whole. They are not linear, but spread exponentially. They reveal drastic, previously unknown weaknesses in systems, as we experienced with the dependence on important medical products from China. They predominantly affect weak and vulnerable groups of the population, who are even less able to defend themselves against the effects than others. And they are not "black swans"—the name given to unpredictable events that change society (Taleb, 2010; 2012). Pandemics and climate change are predictable because experts have been warning about them for a long time.

However, the authors also mention important differences: Pandemics have an immediate effect and pose a direct threat, whereas climate change develops gradually and cumulatively. This difference also explains why there is not nearly the same response to climate change as there is to pandemics.

At the end of their analysis, they summarize: "For companies, we see two priorities. First, seize the moment to decarbonize, in particular by prioritizing the retirement of economically marginal, carbon-intensive assets. Second, take a systematic and through-the-cycle approach to building resilience. Companies have fresh opportunities to make their operations more resilient and more sustainable as they experiment out of necessity" (ibid., p. 5).

McKinsey as well as many other experts assume that crises of all kinds will be upon us. A return to longer phases of stability seems quite unlikely to us, given the complexity and interconnectedness of the economy. So we suspect that coping with crises will be part of the daily business of organizations in the future. Organizations will always have to deal with great uncertainty and they can prepare for it. We want to show you how this can be done with the help of the resilience model (see Chapter 2).

1.3.6 Thesis 6: Organizations are increasingly required to make their contribution to social development (common good)

Organizations are special entities. Like families, couples, tribes and society, they belong to the group of social systems. They exist in many forms, for example, as companies, as non-profit organizations, as associations or as authorities. They differ from other social systems not because of the people, but because of the way they function. They tick differently than a scout camp, political parties or a family. An organization is—from a systemic point of view—a social system characterized by the temporary membership of its participants (employees), its purpose orientation and a usually hierarchical structure (see Sections 3.1. and 3.2.).

Organizations have had a stellar career over the last 150 years. They have changed our society a great deal and have spread worldwide. Organizations have been successful mainly because they have been able to focus entirely on their own logic. Organizations look at the world only from their own perspective, practically ignoring the rest and focusing only on their activities. This indifference relieves organizations and is expressed in the attitude: "I am not responsible for the whole world" (Kühl, 2017a, p. 34ff). Unlike a family, which has to take care of all the affairs of its family members, organizations do not feel responsible for much. Organizations are egoists, you could say. They devote themselves entirely to their goals and tasks and learn to pursue them ever more efficiently. It is only because of this relief that the economy and its organizations have been able to develop so dynamically (Luhmann, 1997, p. 724ff).

Since the end of the Second World War, Western societies in particular have demanded that organizations also integrate the interests of others. This led to the protection of workers, environmental regulations, consumer rights and much more. Step by step, these demands were integrated without losing their goal orientation. In this way, the organizations became more and more complex. These demands, significantly called requirements, were and are imposed on the organizations from outside by means of laws. Beyond that, that is, outside the legal framework, organizations can determine their relationship to society themselves; the relationship to society and the contribution to the common good can thus be determined by each organization itself.

This is still true and makes sense. However, we have been observing a change of mindset for some time. For example, organizations that openly display their self-centred attitude have an image problem. For their customers and for their attractiveness as an employer, organizations have to pretend, at least to the outside world, that they are interested in the welfare of others. That is why they donate and make public appearances in charity projects. The phase of exclusive task and efficiency orientation seems to be coming to an end. Organizations, one could say, are being held more accountable and asked about their contribution to the common good. An example of this was the debate on the meaningfulness of state support for airlines after the Corona crisis. What do states like Switzerland, Germany or Austria gain from having a national airline? Wouldn't it be much more necessary and sensible to invest in the climate-friendly conversion of production, the energy industry and tourism?

According to our thesis, major crises lead to organizations evaluating their contribution to the common good differently and dealing more intensively with their reason for being, their purpose. Why do we exist as an organization? What do we want to contribute to the common good?—"Purpose" is a technical term that we deal with intensively in this book, as it helps us to remain capable of acting in complex situations. Organizations that know why they exist are able to make decisions even in moments of highest crisis. For example, in September 2015, when tens of thousands of refugees flooded in overnight across the Hungarian border, only the Austrian Red Cross was one of the few large organizations able to help immediately. Their purpose "We help people in need"

mobilized the whole organization across the country without much consulta-
tion, clarification of responsibilities and budgets. Over 40 buses were rounded
up in 24 hours and brought to the border. The motto was: We know why we are
there and what to do. We'll talk about the rest later.

Organizations that know and use their purpose are more robust and better
positioned for times of crisis. But even in normal times, they will be more engaged
with their contribution to society, as it is ultimately beneficial for them as well.

1.4 Agile transformation: Why we don't talk about change management

It is obvious, at the latest after these six hypotheses, that organizational change
no longer works in eight steps according to Kotter or according to the classic
principle of "unfreeze—change—refreeze" (Lewin, 1963). When so much is
uncertain and unclear, how can a simple linear process help? For moving organizations, a classic change management process no longer fits because it does not
integrate central elements of change: It is necessary to learn how to actively deal
with uncertainty and to permanently evolve in the process. For this, organizations need another form of change: Agile transformation.

But what changes in concrete terms? As a systemically trained consultant or
manager, we always have four dimensions in mind when we accompany transformations in organizations: Factual, social, temporal and spatial (Boos, 2019,
p. 46ff). We use the four dimensions to compare classic change management
and an agile transformation so that you can see the difference and what the challenge is. Agile transformation is described in more detail in Chapter 4. The most
important changes are shown in compact form in Fig. 1.4.

Time dimension

Shorter cycles are important because things are constantly changing. In the past,
planning was done in months, today in days or weeks. The greater uncertainty is
met with shorter cycles and each cycle goes through three steps: Build–measure–
learn. So in each cycle there is also a fixed step of reflection (learn). The learning
relates to how one progresses in terms of content (matter) and how the cooperation runs (social).

Social dimension

On the social level, too, more complexity is expected of the participants. All participants have to endure more uncertainty and insecurity, because the openness of

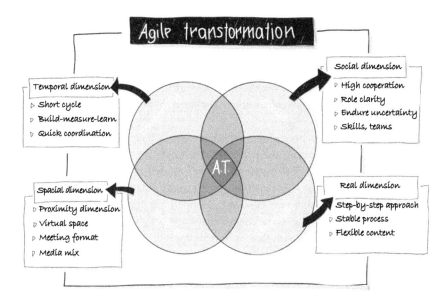

Fig. 1.4. Dimensions of interventions (Boos, 2019, p. 46; Luhmann, 1984)

the process and the higher transparency are challenging for the individuals. It can only be managed by well-functioning teams. All those who want to actively drive the change process need additional social skills, group dynamic experience and a constant and high readiness to send and receive. In addition, they must be able to handle digital tools competently. This higher density of cooperation is exhausting in the long run. Defining roles helps those involved to cope better.

Factual dimension

On the factual level, the uncertainty is absorbed by the fact that there is a clear process design. For this, rigid process steps are defined that are run through again and again. The process and the roles are rigid so that the content can be flexible. Instead of detailed planning, there is a step-by-step approach, so that the planning only emerges in the course of the process. The necessary orientation does not come from thinking everything through in detail at the beginning, but from a stable process.

Spatial dimension

Spatially, virtual communication and its peculiarities bring a completely new dimension into play for many. We have been used to resolving particularly delicate moments in transformation through personal proximity and elaborate spatial arrangements. In a real space, we hypothesize, we have learned to read and deal with social differences. In a virtual space, different rules apply to some extent, differences are coded differently and have to be used differently. Not everything that is possible in real space works in virtual space and vice versa. Therefore, a transfer to a virtual setting is challenging, but also opens up opportunities to learn.

Especially in the last three years, there have been plenty of opportunities for us to learn. Our clients and our projects have made this possible and we are grateful to them for that. The assumptions and models of systems theory have helped us again and again in the agile context and in the crisis and have given us orientation. Some things we have also dropped. So don't be surprised if we subsequently stop using the term "change management", because it goes hand in hand with certain assumptions that no longer apply to us. Instead, we speak of transformation. The following case study will give you a first insight.

1.5 Case study: The first three months of 'I like to move it'

The head of the controlling department of a media company is under great pressure. A difficult workshop is about to take place in the top management circle. Two million euros have to be found for next year's budget and that gives her a headache. She knows such meetings. When the going gets tough, most managers don't dare to counter the management, and for some, emotions run high. She decides to bring the Neuwaldegg advisory group on board to work with the management group.

As expected, the workshop is very lively. A wide variety of proposals are put forward: There are heated discussions between management, marketing, controlling and technology. The individuals bring a lot of expertise to the table and work in a highly professional manner. Even though they basically work well together—in the workshop some find the arguments offensive and very difficult. New product ideas are developed, other products are to be cancelled, and it becomes apparent that some proposals are really emotionally sensitive.

Our work as counsellors was to shift attention from the factual to the social dimension. We broke existing patterns of conversation and invited listening and reflection. This led to greater openness in the exchange of assessments.

After two intense days, it is clear to all: "No matter how hard we try, we will not find the two million euros. More of the same will not help us any more." The situation remains difficult, emotionally stressful and unsatisfactory because there is still no solution in sight. But the leaders are also relieved because there is finally clarity about the current status quo of the organization and straight talk has taken place. There is hope in this group that this "new way" of working together will be able to overcome the challenges of the future.

1.5.1 The initial spark

This is the starting point of the agile transformation, later called "I like to move it". From our point of view, the special thing about this initial spark is the "authenticity" of the moment: No looking away, clarity about the ambiguity, the open insecurity of the individuals and the mutual acceptance of unpleasant things—in a space where the individuals feel safe. And why this title? Because many members of the organization are of the opinion (a vote was taken) that this is exactly what it is all about: Moving together into the future also means that each individual moves. And the best way to do that is to be prepared to do it.

And the willingness is there from many sides and is also backed up by figures, data and facts! It becomes clear that print subscriptions have been decreasing for years and the turnover could only be cushioned by price increases. In addition, the age structure of print subscribers is 60 plus and the publisher has little access to younger target groups. The good news is that digital subscriptions are growing, but not to the extent to make up for the declines in print. The figures are still in the black, but that will change in two to three years, according to calculations.

Internationally, data from other media companies show similar developments. Everyone in the industry is under pressure, many things are unresolved. Therefore, the management team decides to go on a learning journey, visiting media houses and congresses all over Europe. They hope to learn from the radical transformations of others, and they find what they are looking for. Some Scandinavian newspaper houses had dramatic slumps a few years ago, were on the brink of the economic abyss, had to fundamentally reposition themselves and rethink everything. But their first steps after radical transformation seem promising.

The team's experiences were evaluated and resulted in the following insights for their own company:

- **New digital product:** The weighting of products will change in the future. Instead of daily newspapers, the focus will be on digital subscriptions. Print will not disappear completely from the market, but its role in the future is unclear, even if it currently brings in the most revenue and guarantees the survival of the company.

- **New business model:** It is no longer about free content, but high-quality journalism is in demand, which also has to be paid for. Readers want to be able to distinguish fake news from real news. This requires professional journalists. The advertising market is also changing. Visits no longer count; in the future, high-quality advertising will be placed in a targeted manner.
- **Customer at the centre and new, digital way of working:** The customer is at the centre by evaluating and processing their data. Journalists use this as a basis for decision-making when writing new articles. It is not only the journalists' gut feeling and expertise that decide which articles, headlines and word formations work for the readers. Journalists learn daily from the processed data which formats and contents are well received, read and understood.
- **Journalistic/social mission versus populism:** Digital decision-making bases that are geared to the female reader trigger fears among many that they will increasingly live in an information bubble where only pleasing information is available. There is also a fear of losing the democratic, enlightening mission with which the house has grown up, if only economics counts. A fork in the road has been reached that requires a conscious decision: Do we go in the direction of populism and the mass market or do we continue to feel bound to a social and journalistic mission? The latter means that issues that are important for democracy and enlightenment are still taken up by women journalists. Both paths work and are followed internationally. In this respect, there is an opportunity for the company to strengthen the original roots of journalism by preparing topics for minorities in such a way that they reach a wider audience.
- **Personalization:** The focus is on the individual. Everyone can decide personally what they want to read about, how and when, and with whom they want to make contact. This corresponds to the current expectations and communication behaviour of female customers.

After so many new insights, it is important for the leadership circle to discuss all of this broadly in order to find a common goal picture and a course of action. Much is comprehensible to the managers, but the assumptions about the approach are as different as they can be. Each speaks from his or her own area of thinking and immediately proposes initial measures: The editorial department, for example, wants a process to set up reports from the departments digitally. The advertising market wants to create a project for new advertising platforms. The reader market is of the opinion that all print subscribers should become digital subscribers as soon as possible. The innovation sector wants to invest in technology first. Many different perspectives that have no common denominator.

We are familiar with this process. Even though it is clear to everyone that a fundamental change is needed, managers do not yet manage to break away from everyday habits and logics. There is a danger of thinking too quickly in terms of solutions and reproducing the familiar. This is quite normal, and it would be almost strange if it were not so. But it takes patience, a change of working mode in the leadership circle and a viable vision of goals when making such a serious change.

1.5.2 Proven interventions

We like to use two approaches in phases like this: With the systemic loop we collect and observe information to develop hypotheses (see Section 4.2). This broadens the perspective and the leaders can look at what they love in a more differentiated way and also let go. With the Neuwaldegg transformation map (see Section 4.5), the leaders compare their assessment of organizational change competence and motivation. In doing so, we question how the individuals arrive at this assessment and which experiences contribute to it. In the course of the process, the images become sharper for the leadership circle and a common orientation emerges: It is all about transformation! The motto is: Focus on the new and keep an eye on the existing.

The new common ground is the understanding of what is to be done (transformation) and what is to be oriented towards (the purpose, which still needs to be formulated; see 3.3). To realize this kind of new customer-centricity, more agile forms of cooperation are needed. This generates an enormous amount of strength and cohesion in the leadership circle and makes it possible to quickly agree on the next steps together.

Mutual expectations in the leadership circle have risen due to the joint intensive process. But the reality in the transformation workshops is one thing—everyday life is something else! The discrepancy between "the new direction and the new us" and "the current reality" quickly becomes noticeable for the leaders. The temptation to devalue is very high: "Didn't he understand anything? In the workshop he wanted exactly the opposite!", "She'll never learn!", "It's just the way it's always been!" Disappointment spreads and the belief in the transformation sinks quickly.

1.5.3 Three weeks of crisis

Soon the transformation team was in crisis mode every three weeks. Expectations of the leaders are rising. They watch each other at every turn. Sometimes the managing directors decide more in the direction of print and do not promote the digital strategy. Sometimes individuals simply cancel entire meetings. After a joint decision, a department head implements something completely different and again and again, up sticks down. Instead of crisis, we as consultants focus on reflection and sample descriptions, and we always keep these four aspects in mind:

1. Understanding does not mean being able to implement.
2. Learning and unlearning takes time.
3. Requiring stamina and frustration tolerance.
4. Positive things are quickly lost, we have to keep looking at what has already been created and developed.

Here, the importance of social innovation in this process of change becomes clear. The leadership circle is in the eye of the transformation hurricane: It is the centre of power, the repository of history and knowledge, home to well-acquired patterns of cooperation and this is where transformation is supposed to come from? Impossible! No one trusts them to do it, not even themselves at first. And yet, they can pull themselves out of the swamp. It is their task to move forward in this process and to carry out the fundamental pattern changes! It's about new products and forms of communication and collaboration that integrate agile principles. It is about a second order change (see Section 4.5)—for the organization, the leadership circle and also for individuals. We will show you how things have progressed and what we have planned in Section 4.4.1.

2 Crisis-proof through resilience and agility

It was supposed to be a normal meeting day. The team of an international service provider meets every fortnight to pursue and consistently implement the growth strategy that has been introduced. A lot has been invested in the last few months, the team has doubled in size and the last new member has only been with the company for a week. Today they are celebrating their debut. Everyone is still brave at the debut, but at the latest at check-in it becomes clear that nothing will go according to plan today.

Because there is one dominant theme: Corona and the accompanying cancellations by the clients. The team members are uncertain and have countless questions: Is this even a crisis? Do we need scenarios? What is our responsibility towards our clients? How do we deal with it when we ourselves are affected by the disease? What about the orders and the economy? And there is also an unspoken question: What does this mean for the newcomers? What can they rely on? Are they even threatened with dismissal?

A hectic atmosphere spreads. The facilitation team tries to cluster the different questions, looks for responsibilities and possible first steps and answers. It feels gloomy and tough. The meeting itself is not particularly productive, every step is difficult, the view and perspectives seem narrowed. Suddenly someone says: "What if we look at this situation in a completely different way? Namely: We assume that we will all manage it together. What if we do what we do with our clients? Because that's what we're really good at." At that moment, you could have heard a pin drop. This sentence had the effect of a release, the energy and mood began to rise.

Perhaps you have already guessed? This team was us in Neuwaldegg. The crisis has really hit us too. In the very year in which we celebrate our 40th anniversary as the Neuwaldegg Advisory Group, we had to announce short-time work for some employees after this meeting. But this "wake-up call" from one of our members in this meeting has made us capable of acting again and as a result several new products have been created. Projects were pushed forward in spite of the contact freeze. Probably this approach would not achieve this effect with every team. For us, it was the best step at the time and a decisive moment. First, we interrupted a chaotic pattern by referring to our core competencies. Second, it was determined that we would manage the crisis together through short-time work. And third, it made it possible to focus our attention on what we had already worked on, and we could now use that for ourselves. This applies to much of what we describe in this book, but first and foremost to the organizational resilience model that we had already been working on for more than a year. It also helped us to cope well with the time of crisis and to remain able to act in the process.

And this is precisely what organizational resilience research is meant to inspire. It shows what organizations do that have come through various crises well, be it wars, financial crises, accidents or market collapses. We would like to look at this in the next chapter and use the findings of resilience research for organizations. You will be amazed at one or two things, because you may be familiar with many of the things that describe resilience from the discussion about agility. We understand agility as all the efforts an organization makes to cope with increased complexity, that is, to remain capable of acting in its environment or, as we say, to remain capable of playing. Agility serves to cope with complexity, and one can measure all methods and proposals by how they contribute to this. Resilience describes the ability of an organization to cope with crises. A resilient organization is robust and crisis-proof.

Agility and resilience, therefore, relate to different contexts—agility to complexity and resilience to crisis management—and thus fulfil different requirements. Of course, these contexts cannot be separated by type, but rather merge into each other, and skills that are useful in one context can also be useful in the other. Nevertheless, the two contexts are not identical. For us, resilience is the more general approach and we see agility as a component of resilience. Therefore, we have chosen a model that helps us to analyze the resilience capacity of organizations It also helps us to capture the rather unspecifically described agile organization in more detail. The proposed resilience model offers a broader and more holistic view of the challenges faced by organizations. Thus, the concept of resilience helps you to make organizations crisis-proof and to classify agility well.

We will take you on the following journey: We start with organizational resilience and will use the Tension Square to identify different focal points for management. For each focus, we will provide you with a grid to help you position your organization and derive suggestions for your practice. We continue with a guide to crisis prevention by training and practising different skills. We then delve into the topic of agility by highlighting the historical development of agile methods for you. These are important in an agile transformation, but by no means sufficient to make an organization agile. That is why we describe agile organizational forms using the Holacracy model. This shows in a compact way what organizations have to work on when they change over to agility. In the penultimate part of this chapter, we show how much the models of agility and resilience can benefit from the systemic perspective. The chapter concludes with a client example, a traditional industrial company, where many things were applied, but the process was nevertheless difficult and even had to be abandoned for the time being. Nevertheless, this example helps to understand the principle because it shows how work can be done and what the pitfalls are.

2.1 Resilience: Develop sustainability and become more resilient to crises

At first glance, you probably don't associate the term "resilience" with organizations. Most people think first of the psychological resilience of individuals: How do individuals deal with difficult situations? How does one recover after a blow of fate? What can be done to protect oneself? Psychology, education and health science have been doing a lot of research on this in recent decades and are always suggesting helpful interventions for individuals.

Originally, the term "resilience" comes from English and means resilience, resistance and elasticity: "When people develop psychologically healthy despite serious stresses or adverse life circumstances, we speak of resilience. This does not mean an innate characteristic, but a variable and context-dependent process. Various long-term studies around the world have identified protective factors that help support resilience to stress" (Fröhlich-Gildhoff & Rönnau-Böse, 2019, p. 9).

The Kauai Study on Resilience

One of the best-known long-term studies is the Kauai Study by the American Emmy Werner: She and a research team followed the entire 1955 birth cohort of the Hawaiian Island of Kauai. Almost 689 people were observed over 40 years, interviewed and data collected on their lifestyle and health. One-third of this sample lived in a high-risk group characterized by poverty, illness or family disharmony. The findings were astonishing: 34 per cent of the subjects from the risk group developed well and were resilient, while this was not the case for the other two-thirds. In addition, protective factors were found to help resilient individuals: Emotional caregiver, stable family cohesion, high social competence and positive self-efficacy expectation (Fröhlich-Gildhoff & Rönnau-Böse, 2019, p. 16).

Resilience research at the organizational level explores companies that survive and grow despite the most adverse circumstances such as wars, financial crises, resource failure, environmental disasters and accidents. In 2017, the research team around British researcher David Denyer, professor of "Leadership and Organizational Change" at Cranfield University, conducted a meta-study with the aim of finding the common thread of resilient organization capabilities and competencies. What is special about this study is that the data basis is based on 40 years of research in a wide range of organizational resilience disciplines: 181 scientific studies, a large number of publications/books and several case studies lead to helpful insights, concepts and food for thought for organizations (Denyer, 2017).

Organizational resilience defines the ability of an organization to anticipate, be prepared for, respond to and adapt to small changes and sudden disruptions—in order to survive, grow through them and even flourish (Denyer, 2017, p. 5). So what distinguishes a resilient organization from one that does not have this capacity:

- A resilient organization can combine several contradictory ways of acting, always with the purpose of surviving and growing and developing.
- It not only reacts, but can also adapt and change in the long term, for example, by adapting processes, developing new products or changing strategies.
- She always has two types of change in mind: The gradual ones that occur step by step and the sudden ones that occur spontaneously.
- The organization is continuously preparing to respond to this, so it is alert to it and finds a common practice for it.

The questions that arise when considering this: How can you determine whether and to what extent your organization is resilient? And where can you start to make it more resilient? Which steps serve to prevent crises and should be implemented during so-called normal operations? Answers to these questions can be found in Denyer's Tension Square, which we will describe in the next step.

2.1.1 The Tension Square: Protective factors in organizations

The Tension Square works like a map, except that instead of the north-south axis and west-east axis, the poles resistant or flexible and defensive or progressive are used. This results in four fields that describe different capabilities and practices of organizations: Preventive control, performance optimization, mindful management and adaptive innovation (see Figure 2.1). Each field thus has its own focus: Control, performance, mindfulness or innovation.

Perhaps you have already gained a first impression and examples of the four types have occurred to you. Therefore, we would like to invite you at this point to make a spontaneous assessment: Which focus—or combination of different focuses—is well developed in your organization, team or field, and which field is currently rather underexposed? Example: What we, the Neuwaldegg Advisory

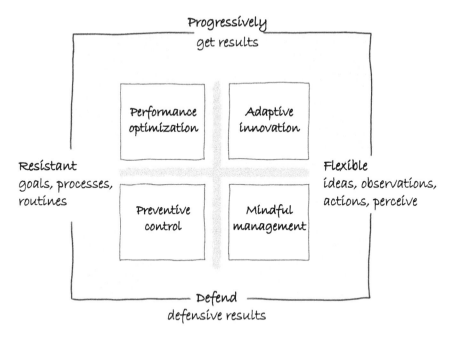

Fig. 2.1. Tension Square according to Denyer (2017)

Group, are good at is adaptive innovation and we are also no strangers to performance optimization. Where we may learn is above all in preventive control. But don't worry, we won't stay on this general level, because you will be able to check your initial assessment right away with concrete questions.

But what does this classification mean for resilient organizations? What is surprising about this is that they pursue several focuses and not just one: They use contradictory methods that are both stabilizing and flexibilizing. And they also behave in opposite ways, acting defensively, defending on the one hand, and progressively, forward-looking on the other. Resilient organizations use all these contradictions to their advantage and are not to be found in one focus alone. They do well in all four fields. They are masters in uniting these paradoxes, in managing these differences. This is what makes you so crisis-proof, because it enables you to cope well with complexity (Denyer, 2017, p. 10).

As with resilient individuals, the four dimensions describe protective factors of organizations that ensure survival and growth and thereby promote sustainable development. This approach helps to build a stable substructure in organizations that supports organizations in crises and at the same time creates a good framework for agile competences to develop sustainably.

Preventive control

Preventive control integrates defensive behaviour and combines it with stabilizing methods. This makes sense because organizations are expected to be reliable. They establish framework conditions to meet these expectations by setting opening hours, drawing up contracts, offering products on an ongoing basis and paying suppliers on time. For example, if you as a customer buy a car today, you expect the car manufacturer to deliver it on time, make sure it is safe, complies with current legal requirements and that it will still be running the day after tomorrow. To ensure all this, organizations have taken many precautions: Control mechanisms, securing data, certifications, transparently measuring deviations, calculating future developments and problems (Denyer, 2017, p. 11).

A good example of this are organizations with serial production. Order and plannability are emphasized, the focus of management is on quality management and the systematic avoidance of errors. What is loved is what can be standardized. Clear processes and structures are used for control, division of labour and a clear hierarchy are often the result. However, this alone does not make an organization resilient.

A key aspect for such organizations is building redundancy and financial resources: Resilient organizations have a financial cushion and do not have to limit their resources when danger is imminent. They do exactly the opposite by providing resources. A 2006 study by Gittel, Cameron, Lim and Rivas shows that organizations that had to lay off staff and had little financial reserves after 9/11 in the US had both difficulties in relationships with customers and suppliers and difficulty in becoming profitable again. In contrast, companies like Southwest Airlines, which had prepared for crises, did not have to lay off staff and quickly became profitable again. Preparing for crises has not only become more important since the Corona crisis. The interconnectedness of companies in recent decades has created increasingly fragile interdependencies: Dependencies on suppliers, critical node formations and over-optimization in many areas that no longer allow for cushions. This has created bottlenecks that have proven to be life-threatening in the literal sense of the word. A positive, long-tested example comes from the airline industry: A female co-pilot in an aircraft is unproductive most of the time and could easily be rationalized away from a cost perspective. Co-pilots are redundant and only fly for safety reasons. And that's a good thing, because in the one case where the female pilot fails, he is indispensable.

Managers who can be located in this quadrant take care to build protective layers according to the principle of an onion, which thereby always protects the other layers and is not dependent on one layer alone. This is done through sensible standard distribution procedures and processes, through training and frameworks that continuously integrate change. They protect critical assets and resources, such as people, products, property, information. Key performance indicators are used for control and are continuously communicated so that measures can be derived from them.

As a preventive measure for the crisis, a data-fact cockpit creates security, which is then to serve as a basis for decision-making: Turnover figures, liquidity, costs, resources, open invoices, and so on. They also practise scenarios in the sense of best, worst and real cases and derive strategic thrusts on their basis again and again. This competence also helps in times of crisis to have quick options for action available.

Positioning: Positive and negative manifestations

For each of these quadrants, you can ask yourself how strong this dimension is in your team, department or the whole organization. The comparison in Table 2.1 will help you to make an initial assessment and will immediately show potential areas for action.

Table 2.1. Positive or negative manifestation of preventive control based on Denyer (2017)

Positive manifestations of preventive control	Negative manifestations of preventive control
Known problems are solved with already proven procedures.	System and acting persons behave impractically and rigidly and act only according to a set of rules.
Standardized processes unfold their full effectiveness through fine-tuning.	Word-for-word implementation of practices that have been written down is considered normal.
Repetitions of planning and deviations have a stabilizing effect.	Inefficient and complex processes and systems are established and lead to analysis paralysis.
Disruptions are countered by rapid planning.	Pre-planned responses to disruptions are unclear or impractical.
Budgets, resources and the financial situation are transparent and easy to visualize; there is a cockpit of figures that is continuously reviewed and used for steering purposes.	The financial position of the organization is linked to individuals or roles. Budgets, financial situation and financial resources are complicated and difficult to see through. Figures, data and facts are kept under lock and key.

Try to think of these juxtapositions in terms of concrete events and see them as a tension, a continuum instead of an "either-or". Think about what aspects you are already good at in order to strengthen them. Then find out what you can get better at by identifying the weak points. Always consider the context of your organization! For example, this dimension is more complex to assess for an industrial company than for a team consisting of five people.

Mindful management

This quadrant is mainly about prevention, or more precisely the practices of prevention. This combines flexible methods with defensive behaviour. It is about defending results. The members in such an organization have a good eye for potential risks and do everything necessary to prevent them. Good examples are oil and gas suppliers, aircraft manufacturers and companies, aircraft carriers, intensive care units or even nuclear power plants. They are permanently dependent on preventing risks. Weick and Sutcliffe call these "High Reliability Organizations" (HRO) and have written a classic on this topic that is still worth reading today (Weick & Sutcliffe, 2016). HROs operate in highly complex and dynamic environments and could fail at any time in their daily work, but almost never do. These systems show peculiarities in teamwork and in the cognitive processes of the members. They contribute incessantly to the prevention and reduction of incidents. Essential practices of these systems and their members are: Focus on mistakes, aversion to simplification and manufacturing diversity, sensitivity to operational processes, striving for resilience, respect for expertise (Denyer, 2017, p. 11).

In order to implement these practices and improve resilience, it is helpful for employees to integrate the following aspects (Sutcliffe & Vogus, 2003; Masten & Reed, 2002):

- Psychological capital, which consists of four synergistic factors: Self-efficacy, optimism, hope and compliance.
- Experienced autonomy in one's own individual actions and control over behaviour in the main tasks. This develops a sense of capability and competence.
- Competence awareness leads individuals to respond better to unfamiliar or challenging situations and to persevere despite failures and challenges.

A good example of this is the surgical team of a well-known trauma hospital. For major operations, this team consists of about eight members and has a hierarchical structure headed by a surgeon. However, the hierarchy is partially suspended in the critical phases of an operation because each member of the team is allowed and expected to communicate his or her perception. And after every operation there is a manoeuvre critique, which only makes sense if the team speaks openly. Only in this way can each individual and the team as a whole improve. To foster this climate of communication, the team meets four to six times a year for team events outside of work (cf. also Section 3.8).

Mindful management practices for crisis situations, establishes procedural guidelines and constantly asks itself questions such as: Are there enough different perspectives in the team? What about psychological safety? Do all members dare to think and say everything out loud without being harmed? How prudently do they act and is everything in view? What patterns and unwritten rules are currently in place? What is reinforced and what has less effect?

For leaders, this quadrant means promoting two sides of the same coin above all (Weick & Sutcliffe, 2016; Weingardt, 2004; Ebner, 2019; Seligman, 2014):

1. **Establish a spirit of contradiction in the organization:** A vigilant, curious attention that is open to undesirable variants, misconceptions, wrong courses and surprising events and also takes weak signals seriously. A good example of this is ground squirrels, which collectively direct their attention with all their senses in different directions so that they can collectively pick up on dangers and react to them. Leaders encourage this behaviour by establishing a constructive approach to mistakes and appropriate routines. Through expectation management, they clarify what constitutes "good news": No news is bad news, good news is reports about surprises, mistakes and successes. They deal sensitively with setbacks and are also aware of the emotional challenges behind them.

2. **Create a strength-based leadership practice:** You design a framework that strengthens and supports employees. We use the PERMA model of positive psychology. It describes five "ingredients" that promote life satisfaction: Positive Emotions, Commitment, Relationship, Meaning and Accomplishment (see Section 3.6.3). Leaders promote positive emotions, engage their staff according to their strengths, foster relationships with each other, continually establish meaning and autonomy in the work and demonstrate successes, which in turn make self-efficacy tangible.

A ward manager told us: "The issue of errors was always a problem in our ward. We did fix the errors, but always came up with them way too late and it usually involved looking for culprits. So I took on this issue and told my team that this would be our focus for the coming year. Since then, we have introduced different meetings. At our weekly meeting, everyone gives an update: What succeeded this week, what I am grateful to whom for, and what was at least one mistake that I observed or fixed or that I noticed. We collect the mistakes in a document. Once a month we have a lessons-learned session of three hours. There we go through the sheet, add one or two important events and evaluate them. The focus is on learning. If someone doesn't enter anything, we ask. Together we always look for ways to sharpen our perception even more. Since we've been doing this, a lot has changed in us! On the positive side. The colleagues are enthusiastic about it, are in better contact with each other and very much appreciate the fact that we are constantly improving and learning together! And we make far fewer mistakes, which has even been noticed by the doctors, who have now adopted the same approach."

Positioning: Positive and negative manifestations

We know few examples like that of the ward manager. We often experience major weaknesses and challenges in this quadrant with our clients. Here, too, it helps to look at both sides of the coin and find out which strengths need to be strengthened and which potentials and new patterns can be worked on.

Again, the more concretely you can describe situations, the more helpful they are for your location assessment. Which aspects of this are particularly supportive or obstructive in your organization? Which practices have you already established, or which would you like to have? Write down your thoughts on this and check them with your colleagues. Or ask your clients: What do they think? Where do they see strengths and potential?

Performance optimization

We like to associate performance optimization with competitive sports: The athletes are competing with each other and, like in a bicycle race, it's about going a few seconds faster or getting a few centimetres more in the pole vault. It is similar with organizations when it comes to performance optimization.

The automotive industry embodies this type more than almost any other. The principle is to make the impossible possible. We still manage every complexity! With us, every customer can even get his or her individualized car, which we mass-produce. From the affordable entry-level model to the luxury limousine, from the compact city car to the off-road vehicle, we have the solution. Challenges are sought, deviations are mastered, the "performance culture", making the nearly impossible possible, is at the top of the list. Competition is encouraged and setting and achieving goals is considered the ultimate. Here, what can be improved is measured and optimized. "If you can't measure it, you

Table 2.2. Positive or negative characteristics of mindful management based on Denyer (2017)

Positive manifestations of mindfulness management	Negative manifestations of mindful management
There is mistrust that something could go wrong.	People are too sure of how something will go.
Quickly perceive, understand and address opportunities and problems.	Overlooking signs of problems; people who point out problems are ignored and mistakes are not reported.
Mistakes are constantly being discussed and serve teams to learn together.	Mistakes are experienced as disturbing because they disrupt the harmony in the team and there is no form for dealing with them.
Organizational members in difficult situations exercise judgement while being discreet, have an idea of how to proceed and remain capable of action.	Individuals do not take responsibility in solving problems and delegate decisions to others.
Employees are allowed to act when problems and errors occur.	Individuals are quickly blamed for mistakes or misapplication of processes.
Managers know about the strengths of their employees and trust them to make good decisions in their field of action. They are there for them when they need advisory support.	Managers have little confidence in the expertise of their staff and think they have to decide everything themselves.
The role of expertise is conscious: They decide when necessary and let go when others have more expertise. They are humble with their expertise.	Hierarchy has a stronger effect than expertise and is controlled and steered by leaders. Leadership is a status and not expertise. The power and effect of expertise on others is not conscious to the acting persons.

can't manage it" is a common saying. This approach has indeed led to very efficient and cost-effective products and services. However, it was also postulated as the only correct management approach for a long time without questioning the assumptions behind it.

There is a reason for the performance optimization approach: Companies are under pressure from globalization and cost optimization. It is essential for them to optimize their performance in order to remain viable in the market under these conditions. They do this by developing methods and practices that stabilize, while at the same time acting in a way that stretches them to new goals. In concrete work, this means that they focus on consistency by improving their own products, making sure that the products and offers meet the needs of the customers and that they are satisfied with them. At the same time, however, it is also about wanting to achieve new goals, to expand the business and to discover new needs. In summary, it is about the operational improvements of one's own products and services in the interest of the customer (Denyer, 2017, p. 15).

An example of resilience that shows a different approach to efficiency in the automotive industry is Toyota's manufacturing strategy. Unlike other car manufacturers, the production sites are not planned for selected products (according to the motto one factory for one model) and high quantities in order to achieve low costs, but the factories overlap with their products. Each factory can also produce models—or parts thereof—from other factories. The production capacities overlap and are thus redundant. This enabled Toyota to be able to deliver again shortly after the 2011 nuclear disaster in Fukushima, which affected several plants.

In the event of a crisis, you have to assume that the performance of your organization will drop in the first moment. Therefore, it is important for the management to know the core competencies of their own organization well in order to be able to refer to them in an emergency. Similar to what we did as the Neuwaldegg Advisory Group: We knew what we were really good at, were able to quickly bring out the strengths of individuals and thus allocate resources efficiently and effectively. In addition, leadership has the following tasks when it comes to optimizing performance: Work on and sharpen the formalized structures for authority and decision-making, focus on planning and coordination of procedures and processes, distribute resources sensibly, structure roles and tasks and establish clarification processes for this.

Positioning: Positive and negative manifestations

This dimension is well established in many companies. Because resilient organizations also have characteristics that good competitive athletes have: They are consistent and disciplined, in a positive sense, but not as an end in itself. Greatest efficiency is not the highest goal, as shown by the example of Toyota, but it correlates with preventive control that integrates layers of protection for crises.

In our work on the agilization of organizations, we experience an interesting confusion here. Some companies think they are becoming more agile (or resilient) by further improving their efficiency, and they are doing the exact opposite. Again, drawing out the opposites shown in Table 2.3 helps to situate your company.

Table 2.3. Positive or negative manifestation of performance optimization based on Denyer (2017)

Positive manifestations from performance optimization	Negative manifestations from performance optimization
Getting better at what is already being done well.	Few ideas on how things can be improved.
Known solutions are quickly implemented.	Too much certainty about one's own path and success. Views from non-experts are excluded.
Clarity on direction, goals, roles and responsibilities	Individual identity and own motives are in conflict with the company's goals.
Strong leaders to whom people can relate.	Lack of leadership at all levels. Lack of decentralized/distributed "ownership" and responsibility.
Different decision-making processes are used for different issues.	Decisions are always made in the same way or it is unclear how decisions come about, or decisions arise in a group dynamic process.
Processes and roles are continuously and transparently adapted based on the challenges of customers and the environment.	Processes and roles are unclear or are not subject to ongoing development. Roles and processes are developed and adapted by "experts" who do not work directly with clients and their challenges.

As you can see, the bar for a resilient organization is quite high, even in a field that has supposedly been well practised in recent years. The automotive industry, for example, was one of the best in this field for many decades. And yet it, too, experienced significant setbacks because, among other things, it overstretched its focus and was unable to catch up with the processes and roles. The next few years will be exciting in this respect, as the automotive industry will still be faced with many tasks.

Adaptive innovation

This is a field you will probably associate with agile organizations. This is about changing before the costs of not changing become too great by establishing flexible practices that are strongly forward looking. This requires learning new things by changing underlying values and assumptions, creative problem solving, innovation and learning to gain competitive advantage. A fundamental premise for innovation here is that the future is not an extrapolation of the past, but needs new and creative approaches. There are different paths, different starting points and different trajectories that make innovation possible. This requires experimentation, new discoveries and inventions from different places in the organization and communities. Many organizations would describe this as agile (Denyer, 2017, p. 16).

Organizations that are really good at this are the digital, global giants like Google, Apple or Amazon. Within a very short time, Amazon had established a regional focus in some regions during the Corona crisis with AmazonFresh: Consumers could shop in their own neighbourhoods and thus support businesses from the region. A completely different example comes from the construction industry: For a long time, the traditional construction industry was of the opinion that this sector would not change dramatically. Mortar, bricks, steel and wood will always exist and the way of building will not change fundamentally. The American startup company Icon has asked itself other questions: How can it be that many people around the world cannot afford housing? Or in crisis areas like New Orleans often have to wait years for their house? What can we do to make housing sustainable? Icon sees it as a human right to have an affordable roof over one's head. And lo and behold, in 2019, the company released a 32-sqm house for about 8,000 euros that they can print within 24 hours using a 3D printer. In this way, crisis-ridden people quickly get the chance to live in dignity and safety again. A good example of how the future can be thought of in a completely different, new way and also how much an industry can be shaken up.

Organizations that already pay good attention to this dimension before crises have an advantage over those that have not practised this. This was also noticeable in the Corona crisis: Those that could flexibly and creatively adopt digital ways had more advantages and needed less effort than others. Practising these competences only in a crisis would be a great challenge for organizations.

Leadership and management in this dimension have the task of identifying adaptive challenges, disrupting conventional solution thinking and building new routines. It helps to think and act systemically, to look for patterns and connections, to examine triggers and dynamics. The focus should always shift between the individual parts of the system and the system as a whole. Above all, complacency and excessive ego have little place in this leadership context, which often also means saying goodbye to traditional understandings of leadership. The task of leadership is to create constructive controversy, to promote discomfort, to work in loop logic and to establish a meaningful way of dealing with all this. This is not so easy! It is a matter of creating an atmosphere that tolerates dissent and different perspectives on problems and translates them into action.

Positioning: Positive and negative manifestations of adaptive innovation

The credo of management in the last decades was mainly preventive control and performance optimization. Adaptive innovation is new to many, especially in its concrete implementation. Here, management has to create a context in which employees can creatively follow different paths so that innovations can emerge: In processes, in projects, in cooperation. This approach is also about the permanent development of people and teams. The areas of tension allow you to find out where you stand in adaptive innovation (cf. Table 2.4).

In this chapter, you will find a lot of suggestions for this field of learning: How to deal productively with tension, what is needed in teams and from leadership and how such a transformation can succeed. It is important that it is a step-by-step development and that you find out for yourself which topics you should tackle in terms of the transformation of your organization.

Table 2.4. Positive or negative characteristics of adaptive innovation based on Denyer (2017)

Positive manifestations of adaptive innovation	Negative manifestations of adaptive innovation
Tensions are used productively, interrupt existing patterns and generate new options.	"Fixed" mindset: Rejecting adjustments and changes
Creative thinking and problem solving by individuals taking risks from different perspectives and in a safe environment.	Few diverse teams and perspectives. Disagreeing voices are not heard. Members are too scared to try something new.
Collective strategic action with many interactions, coalition building, negotiations and compromises.	Silos in the organization: Employees refer to "the others" or "us". Resources and ideas are not shared.
System-wide changes across borders: Multidimensional and fundamental changes.	Quick solutions, local adaptations and reinventing the wheel again and again. Change is resource-intensive and rarely profound.
Leadership sees itself as facilitation and has good process thinking, also in a social context.	Leadership is hierarchical and sees itself as a pivot for new ideas.
Taking up and letting go of ideas is easy for members of the organization.	Projects and innovations are carried out according to plan, come what may.

Using the Tension Square as a diagnostic tool

With the site analysis via the four dimensions, you quickly get an accurate picture of the strengths and weaknesses of your organization or team. It is important that you have all four fields in mind, because resilient organizations are not the best at applying one field, but they serve all four dimensions in an adequate way. At the same time, you have to find out for yourself what the significance and the extent of each quadrant is for your organization. It makes a difference whether you work in a nuclear power plant or in a consulting firm: Mistakes have a different immediate impact in each case. That is why the Tension Square is translated individually for each organization to the respective context. At the same time, caution is advised: Don't say goodbye too quickly to some thoughts that they could make you more crisis-proof! We use the Tension Square as a power tool in agile transformations to regularly look at the whole organization and generate specific options for action. We describe a small example later in this chapter. The Tension Square also offers helpful orientation in the event of a crisis, as we described at the beginning with ourselves: In order not to lose sight of the whole and the future. In the next part, we will describe how you can "train" your organization concretely so that it becomes more crisis-proof!

2.1.2 Becoming more resilient with High Reliability Organizations

Resilience of an organization can be prepared and practised. It provides a framework that can also be described as a training programme for organizations to become more crisis-resistant. For this we use the suggestions of Weick and Sutcliff, whom we have already briefly introduced in mindful management. The two have specialized in researching precisely those organizations that have the crisis permanently in front of their eyes and align themselves accordingly and yet almost never fail. They have established the term "High Reliability Organizations". These organizations are the ideal role model for preparing for potential crises because they are particularly good at something: They operate permanently in the uncertain and have the unexpected permanently in mind. In order to be able to organize this well, they have developed five skills that these High Reliability Organizations, hereafter referred to as HROs, constantly practise in normal operations in order to be able to play it out well in a crisis. We briefly explain each of these capabilities and highlight practices that you can use to harness this capability in your organization. You can find more ways to do this, especially in the toolbox in Chapter 5.

Use errors productively and consistently and focus attention on errors

HROs take advantage of mistakes because they know three things. First, any mistake can lead to a crisis in the short and long term. They see these as early warning signals. Second, they recognize the learning potential in them, thereby building up negative knowledge and continuously adapting their systems to it. And third, they are fully aware that we humans like to block out negativity. Therefore, HROs have established doubt as a basic mental attitude when it comes to focusing on mistakes. This attitude is reflected in the ability of a "spirit of contradiction", which we have already described in the dialogue field of mindful management: It is about confronting people with different points of view, stimulating discussion and criticism, seeking and discussing controversies, and looking for and addressing anomalies. The opposite of this would be an "approval spirit". In addition, members of such organizations know that mistakes occur because of the processes and the way of working and rarely just because individuals fail. Therefore, they do not look for culprits, but consider what needs to be done or adjusted so that these mistakes no longer happen: Making shift handovers more accurate, incorporating rest periods or simplifying application programmes (Weick & Sutcliffe, 2016, p. 47f).

A tragic example of this lack of competence is the aircraft manufacturer of the company Boeing. In 2018/19, two planes crashed and hundreds of people died because this organization and management had neglected almost all the skills of High Reliability Organizations. Their focus was on competition, efficiency and cost savings. Careful work process and dealing with mistakes fell by the wayside. The main thing was to do it quickly. For example, during an inspection, a tool was found left behind in the tank of an aircraft. When this came out, a manager in charge reacted quite indignantly: "Someone didn't do his job!" This attitude quickly makes clear what seems to be lacking in this management: It was not understood that it is not due to individuals, but to the way the processes in the company are organized (Dominik, 2020, p. 23).

When mishaps or major mistakes happen, they can be attributed to at least three causes. They were not anticipated at all; the deviation was not registered in time or the persons did not deal with the unexpected event sufficiently and could not develop a form for dealing with it. To counteract these causes, the attitude of mindful doubt helps. In order for doubt to be used constructively and cooperation to be strengthened, the following practices help (Weick & Sutcliffe, 2016, p. 55):

- Specify and express expectations so that deviations stand out quickly and provide a frame of reference.

- Raise awareness of vulnerability and ask about risk so that the environment is sensitized to vulnerability to mistakes and surprises and wants to learn from them.
- Look for bad news and communicate it. Make it clear that only good news or no news is "bad news".
- Do not conclude mistakes too early and look for connections.
- See near misses or "just fine" as failures and actively deal with them.
- Dealing with mistakes as a strategy. If someone says: "This is my strategy; this is what is important to me", this translates into "These are the mistakes I don't want to make! This is where I need reliable performance!" (Weick & Sutcliffe, 2016, p. 55).

Aversion to simplification and the production of variety

"When people work in a diverse complex environment, they also need diverse complex sensors with which to sense the complexity in their environment. Simple expectations produce simple perceptions that fail to capture most of what is going on" (Weick & Sutcliffe, 2016, p. 61). This means that organizational members can continually create complexity, allow it to happen and hold it in order to make decisions at a certain point. In doing so, they make use of contradictions, work with a "both/and" attitude, integrate social and content diversity and also have an approach to how they shape such processes. In teams, one can ask the following questions: Do we have a team that is socially and substantively diverse? How do we develop our mindful sensorium and or what do we need for this? Who takes on the different roles in our team so that many possibilities and perspectives emerge? Is everything allowed to be thought and said across hierarchies in our team and in our wider environment and how do we encourage and protect this? How do we ensure that decisions are not "simply" made without reflecting on them, and what decision-making procedures do we use and in what context?

Let us return to the example of Boeing, which illustrates how such mindful sensorium can erode: Boeing is a proud and successful company that has been under pressure from international competition for decades. For example, customers no longer wanted to pay for expensive pilot training for new operating systems. That was one of the reasons why originally training-intensive renewals were only designated as minor updates. The whole organization was geared towards this. This was no longer allowed to be questioned because it did not fit the strategy. Experts were no longer heard and had to subordinate themselves hierarchically. The changes were also presented to the supervisory authorities as a minor adjustment. Necessary further developments and dangers were talked down in the organization, too few different premises became relevant for control. All these steps and simplifications contributed to the fact that more and more undesirable developments were able to creep in. Boeing incurred billions in losses as a result of this approach, and it is not yet entirely clear how they can turn things around (Dominik, 2020, p. 23).

Simplifications and the loss of diversity can be sustainably harmful for organizations and even become a question of survival. Why we give this example here: Such simplifications happen to every organization and every person. Social systems and our brains love simplifications. Often we don't even notice it, and social pressure leads us to allow little else. That is why it is important to practise concrete practices that consciously counteract the simplifications. Organize your opposition! They help to create diversity in our daily actions and at the same time prevent us from simplifying people (Weick & Sutcliffe, 2016, p. 67f):

- Working title: Choosing names carefully and giving them as provisional or working titles gives the impression that the process or project is not yet finished and not everything has been considered. It also helps to question and shelve some words and descriptions if they convey something "wrong". Questions for this could be: Which working titles and terms in our team convey too much security and are not chosen openly enough? What are we currently developing and what names do these developments have? Which words should we unlearn because they signal something wrong? For example, a client of ours developed leadership guidelines together with all managers and staff. When individual words were discussed at the end, which were then "set in stone", it quickly became clear: These leadership guidelines get a 1.0 appended to them and will be evaluated again in a year's time. They are meant to be a framework and invite further development.
- Enable public thinking and doubting: Communicating scepticism in public helps not to simplify things. In meetings or presentations, different perspectives support by, for example, the Advocatus diavoli giving constructive-critical feedback and the Angelus giving positive, strengthening feedback. Questions to ask: In which contexts can we be more critical and tend to be harmonious too quickly? Which rules help us to doubt more often?
- Continuously adapt opinions: In order to manage this, there needs to be an awareness of one's own evaluations and a form of continuously reconsidering and revising them—especially when situations change. It is important to be aware of this change and to communicate it, for example, in a check-in. Questions to ask: How do we institutionalize an ongoing updating of opinions? Which meeting formats can be used for this? How can a meaningful rhythm of reflection also look at the individual level?

- See disruption as an opportunity: Conflicts and disruptions are interruptions with the chance to learn and derive something new. Therefore, look for those and be surprised when too much goes smoothly. Questions to ask: When do we/I experience interruptions and conflicts? How do others experience this? How do I behave and how do others behave? How can these interruptions be used meaningfully and what simple practices support this? How are interruptions recorded and what do we understand by them?
- Open perspectives: Look for ambivalences and try to keep them open as long as possible. When faced with either-or solutions, ask yourself what the "both, and" can be. The Tetra lemma also helps here as a decision-making aid: One, the other, both, neither or something completely different. The Neuwaldegg loop also opens up perspectives through processual work (Sparrer & von Kibéd, 2009).
- Edit black-and-white views: Find rituals that reveal black-and-white thinking patterns and address them. It can be helpful to use the method of subgrouping (see Section 3.8.2) to make these differences discussable.

Develop sensitivity with regard to operational processes

HROs know how processes and procedures interact and are used to adapting them on an ongoing basis in their daily work. Just because a process has been defined in this way does not mean it has to be continued in this way forever. This means they always have the big picture in mind, can break this down to their own context and way of working, and know about the interfaces and key people (Weick & Sutcliffe, 2016, p. 73f).

This sensitivity needs support so that deviations and interruptions can be recognized, taken up and used for learning and adaptation. This requires a good sense of the here and now, which is promoted by the following framework conditions in joint practice:

- Clarity about the *big picture* and *individual contributions* to it
- *Exchange with others* on the current situation
- Keen eye for operational processes, also beyond *one's own territory*
- *Clarity* about who can make *decisions* and is available in case of *problems*
- *Feedback* on things that are not going well

An additional practice is to keep everyone's *basic curiosity about operational work* high in order to look beyond one's own nose and explore one's own limits: What are upstream and downstream steps, who else is affected, what are the effects and how can I adapt changes? Perceiving is one thing, communicating this perception is another. Therefore, use your voice when you notice something. Speak up and, as a matter of principle, do not assume that others have already seen or know. Human perspectives are different, the world often changes too quickly. Address your tensions and make them available to the company so that everyone learns and the shared ability to face the unexpected increases. Make suggestions on how things could be better or different from your perspective.

Striving for resilience

HROs have resilience in focus and also know what it is for, namely the strong stretching of one's own competences and resources in the emergency situation. "Resilience is a mixture of experience, ongoing action and intuitive recombination, often based on a minimal structure already in place" (Weick & Sutcliffe, 2016, p. 90). Adaptability and improvisation are, therefore, particularly important in a crisis. As was visible in the Corona crisis, the preconditions were different: Organizations that had already addressed the issue of home office and had an infrastructure for it were able to switch over easily. Organizations for which home office was unthinkable found it extremely difficult to adapt to the new situation.

Weik and Sutcliff recommend *working continuously on one's own "sense-making"*: Thinking and acting at the same time and constantly updating one's own thoughts. This form makes sense especially when people cannot grasp what the future holds. This means that individuals must *constantly adapt* themselves and their contexts and *at the same time work on their adaptability*. The best way to do this is to think about what can help reduce the impact of a disruption and what skills, resources, reserves or adapted processes it would take. A *lean mindset that is not too strict* also helps to support resilience. However, if one's own systems are set up too efficiently, there are no options for action when interruptions and disruptions occur!

An important basic attitude here is an *ambivalent attitude* towards oneself. One's own experiences should always be put to the test: On the one hand, one's own experience helps to deal with new situations—but it also makes one blind. On the other hand, every situation is new. The fire chief describes this attitude in the interview below. Adopting it is possibly the hardest of all virtues of an expert: "Your goal is to act at the same time as if the unexpected situation were exactly like and completely different from any other situation you have ever had to deal with" (Weick & Sutcliffe, 2016, pp. 91f, 101).

Respect for expertise

With this, HROs pursue two thrusts. Firstly, they know about the importance of expertise, which is why those who know the ropes also make decisions and pass on this decision-making competence if someone else has better expertise. They are also the best ones in the respective situation to derive insights and patterns because they are better able than others to observe and assess the respective context. By the way: Leadership is also an expertise, whereby the challenge is to also allow the wandering of decisions and to support the experts in the first place (Weick & Sutcliffe, 2016, p. 105f).

Secondly, the experts are aware of their power and impact and use it humbly. An interview with a fire *chief* illustrates this attitude particularly well (Weick & Sutcliffe, 2016, p. 109): "*Fire chief*: The next *fire* I'm called to, I won't know anything about. *Karl Weick*: That can't be true. What do you mean by that? *Fire chief*: When I arrive on the scene with this mental attitude, I get more different perspectives communicated to me by other people, I increase the uncertainty even more and I get more people to observe closely themselves and also to communicate what they have observed. None of us have ever had to deal with this fire." This prevents people in the immediate environment from abdicating their responsibility to those who supposedly know best, and at the same time it refines relevant information. And this attitude integrates yet another facet: The knowledge of not knowing.

To practise this skill and apply it in your daily activities, review the following:

- Ask for help and emphasize this as a strength.
- Let experts decide in unexpected situations.
- Let the fantasies play and imagine hypothetical scenarios for the unexpected.
- Be humble about your own expertise and be suspicious when others overvalue their expertise.

2.1.3 Agility helps to become more resilient

As you can see, we can learn a lot from HROs that are permanently facing the crisis. The way these organizations tick contributes to the fact that they manage crises well and remain capable of acting afterwards. They succeed above all through one competence: They can deal with high complexity, and they have practised this. Agility also supports the handling of complexity. But it has a different perspective, which is to deal with the current complexities in the market and in the world. This requires an agile ability to play and that is where both approaches meet: Both help to deal with complexity, even if the emphasis is different. This is also the reason why we don't want to force an artificial separation here, but rather make sure that moving organizations focus on training their agile capabilities and become more resilient in the process.

This is also shown by the example of the media house we described in Section 1.5. It had to change because the needs of readers were permanently changing due to digitalization. It embarked on the path of digital transformation in order to be successful in the future. In the middle of this transformation, it was hit by the Corona crisis. Suddenly, the question arose: How resilient are they positioned? Some teams had only been transitioning for a few weeks. The new IT platform was only a few months old. Some teams and leadership were still struggling with the new roles. What applies and how robust are the programmes, processes, structures, staff and culture?

From the perspective of transformation, the crisis came at the worst possible time: Are we being set back or are we even doing it as before? Interestingly, these questions were never asked, on the contrary! The general tenor was: Thank God we started the transformation long ago. Some even said that the process so far was just the dry run for the crisis. Even external stakeholders who had commented critically on the development now began to support the process.

We have also had this experience with other clients; steps to transform towards an agile organization have proven successful in the crisis. Clients who had dared to make this change have maintained and expanded it. Examples include agile teams, different meeting formats or a new form of leadership. Our conclusion is therefore: Agility helps to become more resilient. If the transformation was started in normal time, one can build on it and use those elements that have already been tried and tested. In our experience, this applies to all nine levers of transformation that we will describe in Chapter 3.

But such changes are very difficult. Hardly anyone does this voluntarily, as it goes to the very foundations of the organization. In our view, the Tension Square is helpful here because it opens up the context more broadly and shows management concrete fields of action in which they are already good, where they need to sharpen up and what needs to be learned anew. For example, for many years the media house was not particularly strong in optimizing performance, really good at quickly picking up on adaptations and had a very traditional understanding of leadership and control. Processes and role clarity were underexposed, which is why this was also addressed in the transformation process. A concrete example of how to work with this can be found in Section 2.1.4.

Working on your own resilience is especially useful when the organization is not in crisis mode. In a crisis, it is difficult to develop new patterns and behaviours. It can easily happen that useful behaviours are developed in a crisis, which quickly disappear afterwards because they are not incorporated into the organizational routine. The greatest opportunity to learn resilience comes at the end—in the final phase of the crisis, when normality slowly returns. It is a good opportunity to learn from the crisis mode, start the transformation and thus better prepare the organization for coming turbulence.

The Corona crisis was a major event of unprecedented dimensions for our generations since the Second World War, the full impact of which will only be apparent later. One trend will remain with us—the digitalization of organizations. Through it, the complexity for organizations continues to grow even after the crisis. If we dare to make a forecast today, in mid-2020, it is that the contexts of crisis and complexity will converge, that is, converge and continue to overlap. So we suspect that coping with crises of all kinds and complexity will be part of the daily business of organizations in the future. A return to longer periods of stability seems quite unlikely to us, given the complexity and interconnectedness of the economy. Organizations, as we have seen, can deal with this great uncertainty and they can learn to do better and better, even in the service of society. This is our hope.

2.1.4 Application example: Tension Square

Here is an example to deepen the understanding: The management of an advertising company has us accompany them after a phase with some crises, so that new digital advertising formats and communities can be served in the future. The focus is on learning new competences, how more customer centricity and new innovation processes can be lived. The overarching goal for the future is continuous development and independent adaptation to new challenges. The company must be put on a new footing in two central processes. Teams from different areas are put together to work on topics such as customer focus and the development of new products. After a brief assessment of the current situation, the focus is now on action and implementation. The same framework conditions apply to everyone:

- The teams are made up of various experts in order to be able to integrate as many perspectives from the different areas as possible. They share specific roles with different responsibilities in the team.
- Each team works in a self-organized way according to jointly defined agile principles.
- Once a month, team representatives meet and present their current results to the Product Owners. They make directional decisions based on agreed decision-making processes and rules so that the teams can continue to work quickly.
- All teams are supported by experienced counsellors. In addition, a new IT infrastructure is available so that the teams and their members can easily network and work together.

Development of Team A (customer focus): Team A quickly gets going and soon celebrates its first successes. The team members quickly find their way around the IT infrastructure and continuously adapt it to their needs. This supports them especially in overlapping work. They share their interim results between meetings, both those that work and those that do not. What is striking is that almost everyone can contribute their opinions and these are discussed constructively. Priorities are quickly decided, the respective roles fill their responsibilities and new mini-teams are always formed. The agile principles seem to strongly raise the potential of the group and attractive prototypes emerge. The consultant's task is above all to provide different methods and to deepen the reflections with the team so that the progress and also the learnings are conscious. The team is highly motivated and 100 per cent convinced of the approach.

Development Team B (innovation processes): In this team things look different. The process is slow and most are frustrated because the methods are not having the expected effect. Again and again, the team members analyze new data and look for examples from other organizations. There is a feeling of not knowing enough. At the same time, there is little experimentation and new ideas are hard to come by. At group meetings there is whining and black painting, few care about the results of the last meetings. Role responsibilities are shifted back and forth, no one likes to take on responsibilities. The whole thing gets worse when Team A tells about their own experiences. The framework conditions seem to paralyze Team B.

A closer analysis shows that the conditions of Team B are different. The team members communicate a lot with each other, but hardly use the new IT system. Everything is agreed verbally, no one documents in such a way that the documents can be found again. At meetings, a few talk a lot, most listen. It becomes apparent that the team members have hardly any experience with teamwork. They are used to working as lone warriors. In their previous everyday life, they did not have to design and optimize work processes and administrative tasks themselves. It was not important that others could understand their work.

The Tension Square shows the strengths and weaknesses of this team. We see that the dimensions "preventive control" and "mindful management" are well developed, but there is little experience and skills in "Performance Optimization" and "Adaptive Innovation". This is where we can start and initiate changes that turn individual skills in silos into collective actions. The decision is made to include new team members with IT skills who demonstrate how the IT tools can be used and show how openly one can deal with mistakes and ignorance without losing face. And lo and behold: The others quickly learn and many things suddenly work better!

It is important that the management of the advertising agency takes a back seat in this phase and sees itself as a coach or facilitator and has provided the necessary resources—new team members—without making much of an appearance itself. By the practical example of the actions and reactions of the new employees, the team can see what exactly is expected and how they can acquire these skills themselves. The leadership's task is to observe how this development succeeds. This restraint was not easy for the leadership at the beginning, but now, as things stand, they hope to be able to withdraw the new team members again soon, when the process has stabilized in Team B.

Development is well underway at the agency, which is now more resilient than before the process began. The company has begun to constantly optimize its performance in two central areas and is starting to share innovations in everyday life without neglecting its existing strengths in preventive control and mindful management. Now it is time to keep at it and "play" all four dimensions. We wish the company every success in this endeavour.

2.2 Agile methods and how they came about[2]

It may surprise you, and yet: Agile methods are not a recent invention. Only the increasingly urgent need has intensified and meanwhile brought them into absolute focus. A look at the history of agile methods is therefore worthwhile, not only to broaden the understanding of the topic, but also to be able to draw from a larger repertoire depending on the situation. Although agility is essentially known from software development, it was by no means invented there. Rather, its roots can be found in the context of quality assurance of production processes. The approaches Scrum, Design Thinking and Lean Startup are described in more detail below, as these methods are used again and again in organizations and also in transformations and support a different form of working.

2.2.1 Historical view of agile methods

The deming circle

As early as the 1930s, a four-step process consisting of the steps "Plan-Do-Check-Act" (PDCA cycle) was developed and the idea of going through these four phases continuously and always anew in order to learn from what is current

---

2   This section was written together with Gregor Tobeitz.

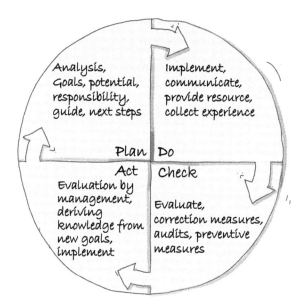

Fig. 2.2. Deming circle-PDCA cycle

and to improve processes. This was taken up after the Second World War by R. Deming (see Imai, 1992) and used at Toyota to develop the famous Toyota Production System-the main source of today's lean method. The Deming cycle and the associated PDCA cycle (see Fig. 2.2) are still the basis of all quality management systems today as a description of a continuous improvement process (CIP).

The Rugby Approach

In the 1980s, Harvard professors Hirotaka Takeuchi and Ilujiro Nonaka studied organizations that could bring successful innovations to market much faster than their competitors. They found that these companies—Fuji-Xerox, Honda, Canon and others—assembled hand-picked, multidisciplinary teams on a project-by-project basis and were able to use them to generate, disseminate internally and implement new knowledge much faster. They compared this process to a rugby team that does not move the ball (symbolizing knowledge, ideas, values and emotions) forward according to predefined paths, but where rapid adjustments and numerous interactions between team members determine the path of the ball.

In 1986, Takeuchi and Nonaka published an article in the *Harvard Business Review* describing the characteristics of the Rugby Approach:

1. *Built-in instability:* The management only provides strategic direction, otherwise the team is largely autonomous.
2. *Self-organized:* The team itself decides on goals and further development. It is interdisciplinary, so that different ways of thinking and behaviour patterns are combined.
3. *Overlapping development phases:* Instead of following a traditional "relay race" method of product development, where one group of functional specialists hands over their completed phase to the next functional phase, the entire team moves forward cohesively, step by step, passing the ball to each other-until the product is ready. The development steps in the different functional units thus overlap.
4. *Multilearning:* Learning processes take place on different levels as well as in different functions at the same time.

Scrum and the Agile Manifesto

In 1993, software engineer Jeff Sutherland was given the ambitious task of developing a new product for the software company Easel Corporation. Sutherland knew the various methods such as the PDCA cycle and the Rugby Approach. Together with his colleague Ken Schwaber, he developed what is now known as the Scrum method, which was first presented to the public in 1995.

Towards the end of the millennium, there were already quite a few innovative people looking for new methods for software development. The information age was just exploding. Startups and traditional organizations alike were looking for better ways to adapt to the unknown and turbulent environment.

In 2001, 17 software developers who called themselves "organizational anarchists" met in Snowbird, Utah, to share their ideas. Among the participants was Jeff Sutherland. This meeting went down in history with a document called the "Agile Manifesto".

Four values and 12 principles were laid down in the manifesto. The four values of the Agile Manifesto are presented as pairs, whereby the focus should be placed more on the first-named value than on the value in second place (even-over principle):

1. Individuals and interactions take precedence over processes and tools.
2. Functioning software takes precedence over comprehensive documentation.

3. Cooperation with the client takes precedence over contract negotiations.
4. Reacting to change takes precedence over following a plan.

The 12 principles laid down in the Agile Manifesto include basic attitudes such as: "Our top priority is customer satisfaction through early and continuous delivery of valuable software". Or: "Build projects with motivated people. Give them the environment and support they need and trust them to get the job done."

As you can see, this manifesto is primarily about a value attitude and less about tools. To this day, the Agile Manifesto is the foundation for agility. This alone shows that agility is a value system and not a pure mechanic or methodology.

2.2.2 The Scrum framework

Scrum quickly turned out to be a method with a lot of potential and was further developed. Shortly after the turn of the millennium, the aforementioned Ken Schwaber and his colleague Mike Beedle published the book *Agile Software Development with Scrum*, in which the Scrum framework and the development process were presented in detail for the first time. They presented a very lean process that is subject to only a few rules: The Scrum framework consists of five underlying values, four events, three artefacts and three roles (Beedle & Schwaber, 2001).

The "sprints" with their four events

The core of the process is formed by so-called "sprints", which are used iteratively to drive development forward. Each sprint has a fixed time frame (timebox) in which an intermediate result or increment is produced that can subsequently be evaluated and tested. Sprints are of a fixed length, always have the same sequence of events and a defined result. The process consists of four events: Sprint Planning, Daily Scrum, Sprint Review and Retrospective.

1. Sprint Planning: This is where decisions are made about what is to be developed in the new sprint and how.
2. In Daily Scrum, the team synchronizes and coordinates its activities on a daily basis.
3. During the Sprint Review, the "increment" or the interim result is presented to the users and assessed.
4. The last meeting of a sprint is the Retrospective, where the Development Team reflects on, evaluates and continuously improves its collaboration.

Three tools

Every product to be developed needs defined requirements that are listed in so-called artefacts or process documents. These requirements are recorded in the **product backlog**, but are not completely defined from the outset. The product backlog is rather a living document that evolves with the product, that is refined and supplemented. It adapts to all changes: Budget, personnel, strategy, changed customer wishes, but also legislation or market movements influence the content of the product backlog. It is the central document of the development project and the only repository for all customer requirements.

A **sprint backlog is** created for each sprint as documentation of the sprint. It is usually visualized on a task board with the respective status of the individual tasks, as shown in Fig. 2.3.

Finally, the **increment** embodies the sum of all intermediate results developed in sprints so far, including the requirements implemented in the current sprint, which must meet the *Definition of Done*. The Definition of Done describes criteria under which a task (backlog item) can be assessed as finished. It forms the basis for the common understanding of the Scrum team and ensures transparency and clarity. Like the product, the Definition of Done also develops iteratively and incorporates the experience from the past sprints in a development. During the retrospective, the Development Team can reflect on the Definition of Done on the basis of the last product review, evaluate it and adjust it if necessary. Figure 2.4 shows a schematic representation of a sprint with its artefacts.

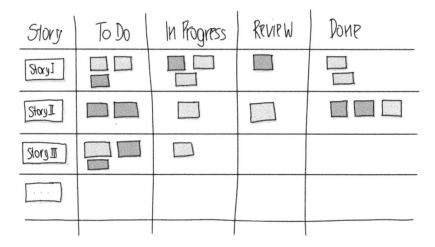

Fig. 2.3. Sprint backlog

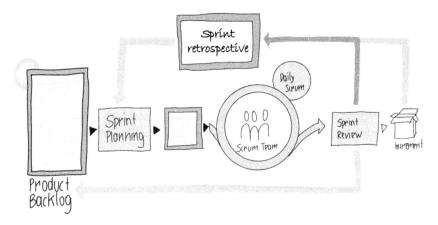

Fig. 2.4. Scrum framework based on https://www.scrum.org/

The three roles

The Scrum framework gets by with only three roles: Product Owner, Scrum Master and Development Team. They are not organized hierarchically in any way.

The **Product Owner** is responsible for the what of the development and represents the vision of a product, which she communicates inside and outside the agile project. As the name of the role implies, she is the owner of the product and also has budgetary authority within the project. Product Owner is the customer or the role she represents. Therefore, the Product Owner should also be equipped with appropriate competencies from the client. Above all, the holder of the role needs technical competence to be able to make decisions quickly and soundly. The role provides for tasks such as maintaining and making visible the product backlog. This role establishes the importance of the client paying attention to the quality of the outcome early on and throughout the process.

Product Owner and Development Team work on an equal footing and at eye level. The two roles jointly refine the items in the product backlog to such an extent that they can be implemented in a sprint. At the end of each sprint, the Product Owner takes the increment in the sprint review and checks the results or the implementation of the individual items against the respective Definition of Done. The Product Owner then revises the product backlog on the basis of the current increment and the general development progress.

The **Development Team** is responsible for the development process and ideally comprises between three and nine people. The team is composed across departments and has all the competences required for independent and self-organized planning, processing and implementation of the product vision or the items in the product backlog. The size of the team is crucial for the success of an agile project, as there is usually a lot of direct communication, coordination takes place quickly and decisions are made without having to make a great deal of organizational effort.

The Development Team is responsible for the concrete implementation of the backlog items or requirements in the product backlog. It delivers a functional increment to the Product Owner during the sprint review and is guided by the defined Definition of Done. The Development Team works in a completely self-organized and self-responsible manner.

Finally, the **Scrum Master** is an expert for the Scrum process and supports the team in complying with the Scrum rules and in further developing the cooperation. The role of the Scrum Master is a special form of leadership role that serves the team as an expert, coach, mediator, trainer or facilitator in the sense of servant leadership. The Scrum Master supports self-organization as well as obstacles and conflicts and is the interface to the rest of the organization. He prepares meetings and acts as a moderator, pays attention to the group dynamics and ensures that the agile values and principles are lived.

2.2.3 Design Thinking

Rebecca is 39 years old and works as an innovation coach in a German bank. She used to be in another area of the bank and volunteered for a new agile project. That's when she first came into contact with Design Thinking, because she received training for this project. Since then, she has tried out a lot internally: Supported other departments in innovation or customer-centricity processes. After two years, she decided to fill this role fully and is now an innovation coach. She loves working with people in workshops and driving change at the same time. At the moment, the organization is facing big challenges like digitalization, new business models and completely new processes. Therefore, internal requests are becoming more and more complex and conflict-ridden. For Rebecca, it is clear: She needs to broaden her content and deepen her knowledge of organizational development and agility in order to be able to provide good and professional support. What Rebecca would like for the first step is a book in which experts explain the background well and tell of their experiences with similar problems. There should also be some concrete instructions for action that she can try out right away.

What you are reading here is a persona, that is, a fictional person with a user case, which we created for our book to make it more tangible for our readers in the writing process. These two elements are central methods used in the Design Thinking process. It is important that this persona is as real as possible, so that it is pulled here again and again. What happens with it: As a result, the reader (and customer) is always at the centre of events, and the whole process is always oriented towards her (Lewrick et al., 2018, p. 38f).

Focus on people and customers

The most important ingredients in the Design Thinking process are: People, customers and the market. This process thrives on using fun methods to encourage members to try out new things, to go different ways and at the same time to stick to a looping process that carries permanent learning. The purpose of this approach is to arrive at innovation and solutions through iterations. This was also the intention of the design and innovation agency IDEO, which launched Design Thinking to achieve precisely this.

In the meantime, different forms and processes have become established that have many similarities at their core. In principle, a distinction can be made between micro and macro cycles. Let's first start with the micro-cycle, which Rebecca primarily works with and which is the best known. This cycle deals with the problem in the following steps, as shown in Fig. 2.5:

1. **Understanding:** This is about the customer needs and their challenges. In addition, the overall context of the problem must be grasped.
2. **Observe:** Deepen the customer perspective in the form of observation or the use of data analysis. Important: Evaluate this material well!
3. **Define point of view:** Interpret and weight findings.
4. **Find ideas:** Use methods that promote creativity; become more creative with each iteration.
5. **Develop prototypes:** Make ideas tangible without them having to be perfect.
6. **Testing:** Best done with the client.
7. **Reflect:** Before a new cycle, find out together what went well and what can be improved (like retrospective in Scrum).

The macro-cycle, on the other hand, takes up the individual micro-cycles and brings them into a meaningful logic through certain foci, so that, starting from the vision, a solution is also achieved. You can find an illustration of this process in Fig. 2.6.

The strength of Design Thinking is definitely that working with the innovation methods gives the co-creators a lot of pleasure. Due to the structured approach,

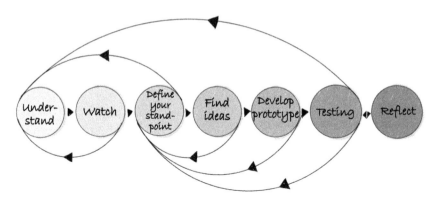

Fig. 2.5. Microcycle of Design Thinking based on Lewrick et al. (2018, p. 38)

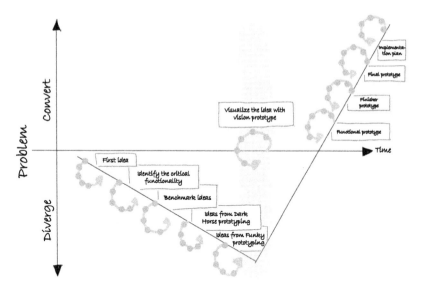

Fig. 2.6. Macrocycle of Design Thinking based on Lewrick et al. (2018, p. 45)

which is very flexible and intuitive in the individual elements, this method is also suitable for beginners who want to approach a problem differently.

2.2.4 Lean Startup

The special thing about Lean Startup methods is the conscious handling of uncertainty and trying things out instead of thinking them up: Instead of trying to get a grip on uncertainty through detailed planning, it is used, the focus is turned inwards on one's own assumptions (hypotheses) and these are constantly tested.

The story of Zappos, the first company to start selling shoes online, is that its founder Nick Swinmurn wanted to find out if there were any female customers willing to buy shoes online. Instead of doing a customer survey, Swinmurn photographed the warehouse of a neighbouring shoe retailer, posted the photos online, then bought the shoes ordered from him there and even shipped them himself. Now he knew that his hypothesis—female customers buy shoes online— was correct and could take the next step (Hsieh, 2010, p. 58f).

Lean Startup is a set of methods that were originally intended for software development and are now used for product and business development. The approach promises to achieve success faster and in a more targeted manner, as unnecessary paths are avoided (lean) and the mentality of startup entrepreneurs is used. The following principles apply:

- Experimentation takes precedence over differentiated planning; that is, quickly testing one's own hypotheses, making mistakes early on, constantly learning and radically changing tack if they fail (pivoting).
- Customer feedback takes precedence over intuition; this means seeking customer feedback early and regularly;
- Iterative design takes precedence over traditional design development; that is, work out the Minimum Viable Product (MVP; the smallest conceivable product), that is, start small and enrich the product or concept with feedback and constantly develop it further.
- The principles result in the cycle build-measure-learn, as the following Fig. 2.7 shows.

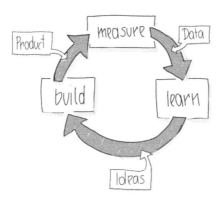

Fig. 2.7. The Lean Startup cycle: build-measure-learn

The cycle is run through several times and planning is subjected to this logic. Basically, the more often and the faster the cycles are run through, the better. The art of managing it well lies in selecting the right criteria for observing customer reaction and the willingness to question one's own assumptions and, if necessary, to radically re-plan, that is, to "pivot". Pivoting is something startup entrepreneurs find cool and are proud of. It is not a mistake to have made a wrong assumption. The mistake would be not to have tested assumptions properly.

For example, if you measure customer interest based on clicks on the homepage (X customers have looked at this shoe model) and not the actual willingness to buy (number of orders), you get a distorted picture. When pivoting, it is important to check fundamental assumptions: For example, at Zappos, whether someone really buys shoes that he/she has never seen or been able to try on. Or as in the development of electric wheelchairs mentioned in thesis 2 (see Section 1.3.2): The assumption of the Development Team was that electric wheelchairs could only be brought to the market through the distribution channel of insurance companies, which were supposed to cover part of the costs. When they made it clear that they were not interested in this, it was necessary to radically rethink, that is, to develop a different product for a different customer group (athletic wheelchair users) and to market it through a different distribution channel.

Lean Startup methods were widely disseminated through the bestseller by Eric Ries (Ries, 2019) and the boom triggered by successful startup companies from Silicon Valley (Airbnb, Paypal, Zappos).

2.2.5 The further development of agility

In the last chapter, we presented the most important stages in the history of agility, but not all of them. But as you can see, the model of agility is not that new. For sure, however, its development is far from complete. What all agile formats have in common is a strict process design with the loop logic and the iterative approach as well as a clear role definition that determines who is responsible for what.

These methods have been developed for projects, that is, tasks with a limited duration. They work there, but they should not be applied to whole organizations. This is a different issue with a different complexity. This is what we want to address here with Holacracy. Holacracy is currently the most comprehensive concept for agile organizations. We introduced this concept in the Neuwaldegg consulting group in 2012 after difficult discussions (Boos & Fink, 2015; Boos & Fink, 2017). Since then, it has been used in our organization and we are learning a lot in its application and further development. Even if you are not thinking of implementing Holacracy, understanding this model will help you understand what to work on if you want to develop a moving organization. You will be able to see that it makes little sense to only turn individual "screws" of your organization if you really want to make it agile.

2.3 Agile organizational forms: How Holacracy can be used

Brian Robertson was an American programmer and loved his profession—but at the same time he was unhappy in his IT company: He experienced that the good and innovative products and employees did not prevail. Most people seemed to be primarily concerned with protecting their own area and with power. Disappointed, he decided to found his own IT company. And lo and behold, the same problems arose in the company that he knew from his old company. Frustrated and curious at the same time, Brian went in search of solutions. In his search, he came across the model of sociocracy, which he studied in more detail (see Section 2.3.7). And then one day he had a bold idea: He wanted to invent his own organizational system. A system that has the whole in mind and in which the game is played in a completely different way! In which power is not parked with individuals, but is sensibly divided among the respective experts. A system that treats adult people as adults who shape and decide for themselves, and not as children who have to be taken by the hand by leaders. A system that is aligned to the purpose and adapts, develops and controls, that could organize itself like a living city: There are rules that provide orientation, such as traffic lights, commandments and laws, and yet the residents themselves decide how they move.

This is how we heard the story around the birth of Holacracy. In the meantime, many things have evolved and a number of organizations around the world are experimenting with Holacracy. They are pursuing similar goals: It is about more agile forms of cooperation, innovation, more flexible structures, more purpose orientation and self-organization. The underlying core question for almost all of them is: How can I structure my organization and fundamentally reorganize it so that the entire system is more adaptable and can react adequately to customers? We also asked ourselves this question in 2014. And our choice was Holacracy.

With his model, Brian Robertson provides a consistent and detailed model with structures and processes, which is now constantly being developed further by the organization itself and an international community. However, this was not the only reason for our decision: Firstly, we are always interested in trying things out ourselves, we can't do otherwise. We want to know how this form of self-organization works in practice. Secondly, we were under additional pressure. Young talented counsellors were no longer interested in our old "junior-senior learning model" and the feeling of having little power and influence for a long time. In this respect, the aim of introducing the new system was to be able to retain and attract the women counsellors of the future (see Boos et al., 2017). And thirdly, Holacracy is an agile organizational form that focuses on important elements of systems theory: Roles, decisions and purpose as its focus. Enough material for us to find out more about ourselves and applied systems theory!

2.3.1 Holacracy—what is it?

If you observe holacratically organized companies from the outside, you will notice the following: Every organization is different, does different things and the way of getting along is totally different. In fact, just like any other. However, if you get the chance to take a closer look at a few of these organizations, you will recognize red threads: The process of certain meetings is the same. It is not managers who make decisions here, but the people who are responsible for the current task. If problems or "tensions" arise, they are dealt with in a very specific way by the people involved.

A blueprint with explicit rules of the game

Holacratically organized companies follow a certain blueprint. This describes certain principles for the structure of teams (here called circles), for the conduct of meetings, the way roles are to be described, and rules of the game for decisions. This creates an organizational form that is constantly evolving itself. Everything else, the contents, products, manners, roles and much more, emerges from walking together. This blueprint finds its form in the Holacracy Constitution. In this constitution, the rules of the game are laid down in a binding way for all to see, how power and influence can be distributed. That is why owners sign the constitution: As a sign of agreement and binding compliance. In a Holacratic organization you can change almost anything, only the rules of the game are fixed: Holacracy aims to clarify unclear expectations. In other words, you are always working to create more clarity by making explicit what was implicitly expected. This is a challenge that needs rules and commitment and must hold even in stressful situations, hence the need for this contract signing (Robertson, 2016).

At its core, Holacratic organizations are about the following:

- **Define roles** and make transparent what decisions are expected of them, instead of parking decisions with a few leaders. One person has many roles and these should change again and again.
- **Distributing power and authority** across roles through a transparent decision-making process, rather than accepting informal power structures and implicit expectations of leaders.
- Great importance is attached to (governance) **meetings** and they are divided into different types: Meetings that are about power and influence are called "governance meetings" and have their own rules. "Tactical meetings, on the other hand, are about content and are much more efficient than holding long meetings with unclear agendas.
- **Continuous learning and adaptation** as an organization to which everyone contributes, instead of long change processes initiated by a few every few years.
- Aligning with a **common purpose,** which is always the point of reference in daily activities and to which actions are aligned, instead of strategies and target images that are pursued over years, regardless of whether the environment has changed.

2.3.2 Basis and structure of a Holacratic organization

In the beginning is the purpose

Holacratic organizations need an explicit purpose for what the organization exists and what they want to bring into the world. This purpose is the centre, the fire and the engine of the organization. Each member of the organization implements the purpose every day through their roles: In projects, with clients, in meetings and in normal work activities.

Energize rolls

Every Holacratic organization defines roles. Roles are a set of expectations directed at a specific position, and are thus independent of the people who perform the role: For example, the porter, the marketing assistant the product developer. The roles are described in a specific form and assigned to a circle (team).

Each role has an explicit purpose and responsibilities. Also, if necessary, rights (domains) are defined that describe what only this role can decide (see Fig. 2.8). Each role is assumed by at least one person, although people usually assume several roles. Taking on a role is also called taking on a "role lead".

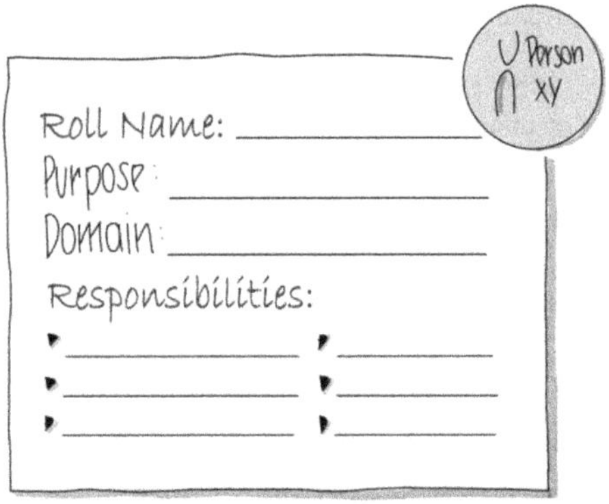

Fig. 2.8. Holacratic role description

Describe roles

- Purpose: This refers to the fire of the role. What does this role want to bring to life in this circle? Why does this role exist?
- Accountabilities: This specifies the tasks and activities expected of this role.
- Rights (domains): They determine what can only be decided by this role and by no one else. You can also understand the domain as a "property right". It would be strange, for example, if your neighbour grabbed the keys to your car in the morning and simply drove away, wouldn't it? It would be different if she asked you and you made an agreement. Who in your organization has the domain for the ongoing updating of the website, the price setting in the offer, the acceptance of rush orders, the new remuneration system? If responsibility only has to be decided in an acute case, or if—this is the "classic"—it moves up the hierarchy, it becomes stressful and slow. But the important thing is: Domains should be handled with care, otherwise many allotments will be produced. The main focus is on the purpose as well as the responsibilities and ongoing tasks.

Holacracy distinguishes between predefined roles and those that the respective organization develops for itself. The predefined roles are somewhat reminiscent of those in the Scrum framework: Circle Lead, Facilitator and Secretary. They are roles that the circles (see below) need in order to function well. They have their own rules. In contrast to the functions in classical organizations (Head of Department Quality Manager), roles tend to be cut smaller and changed more quickly. This means that roles are constantly evolving, which is why it is particularly important that they are transparent for all members of the organization. In this way, everyone can constantly check what is expected of the respective role and what is not.

Energize circles

If the processing of a purpose by a role becomes too complex, it can be converted into a circle that contains several roles. If the tasks and responsibilities are more complex from the beginning, a circle is formed. Like a role, a circle has its own purpose, which is aligned with the respective superordinate purpose, and contains explicit responsibilities and activities that are continuously developed. These are also transparent for all. This creates a circle and purpose hierarchy instead of a classic hierarchy (see Fig. 2.9). These forms of hierarchy are not to be confused with a democracy or "everyone is equal" attitude. In Holacracy, authority is distributed: Individual roles or even processes can have more authority than others. The way this can be dealt with is regulated!

In addition to roles, the following aspects are added to purpose, tasks and rights (domains) in the case of circles (see also Fig. 2.10):

1. **Each circle has four fixed roles that** have specific tasks: Circle Lead, Secretary, Facilitator and Circle Rep.
2. **The Strategizing format** clarifies the focus of the circle by setting heuristics in the form of "even over" rules (where should the circle develop towards, what are the priorities?) instead of a strategy meeting that sets the focus for the next three years.
3. **There is a meeting structure that** each circle uses regularly for itself: Governance meetings and tactical meetings.

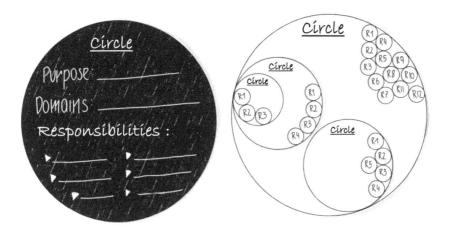

Fig. 2.9. Circle structure in Holacracy

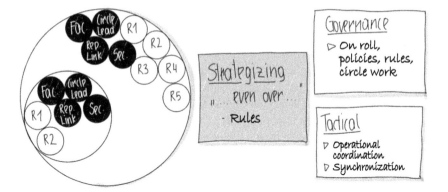

Fig. 2.10. Holacracy: Circle structure, fixed roles and important rules

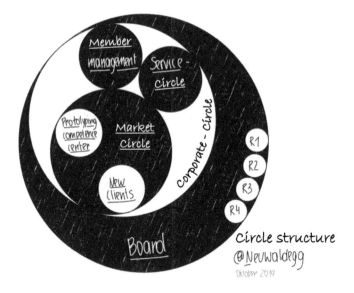

Fig. 2.11. Neuwaldegg district structure 2019

When an organization starts with Holacracy and has signed the constitution, a Super Circle is set up. The Super Circle often contains the owners who set up the first basic structure and determine the purpose. They appoint the Circle Lead of the next circle and from then on the rules of the Holacracy Constitution apply. The Super Circle has no more tasks. Our Super Circle, called the Board, includes roles such as capital providers, purpose stewards and roles that think about the future ownership of the Neuwaldegg Advisory Group. Our next circle is the Corporate Circle. In this circle, the organization starts to live in all its different facets: An HR circle, a market circle, product circles, and service circles (see Fig. 2.11).

Fixed roles: Circle Lead, Facilitator, Secretary, Circle Rep

Each circle has four specific roles, each of these roles fulfils a specific purpose!

The **Circle Lead** is determined by the Circle Lead of the parent circle and is responsible for thinking along with the interests of the parent circle and at the same time keeping the purpose of the own circle. The Circle Lead role fulfils this by filling other roles necessary for this circle with people, giving feedback to the role leads and clarifying the focus of the circle (strategizing). The Circle Lead role holds and documents the expectations and responsibilities of the circle. Everything that is not described here, other activities and decisions, are taken over by other roles. It is important to note that this role is not a leader and has no more authority than those described in the constitution.

The **facilitator's** task is to moderate the tactical and governance meeting formats according to the Holacratic ground rules and to support the circle and the people to process their tensions productively. There is a process flow to follow for this. The role of facilitator is not to make everyone in the meeting feel comfortable, but to make sure that the individual role leads take a step forward with their respective tensions. For this, it is necessary to know the rules well and to be able to provide options so that the role leads can adequately contribute their ideas, suggestions and tensions. Conversely, this means that role leads do not need to know exactly what their tensions are. Facilitators create the framework and are supporters in processing the tensions of the role leads. This role is chosen by the circle members!

The **Secretary** role is responsible for documenting all decisions digitally and transparently within the meeting formats. It supports the Facilitator role in terms of adhering to rule-compliant formulations and decisions, interprets all jointly processed rules (if these are not understood) and knows the constitution in detail. When to call meetings is decided by this role. The role of Secretary is also elected by the circle members. Important: This role is not to be confused with that of an assistant or secretary, as it involves a deep engagement with the Constitution.

Circle Rep: This role is also elected by the circle and represents the interests of its own circle in the superordinate circle. This means that if there are requirements and issues, this role brings them to the higher-level circle and processes them.

At Neuwaldegg, members have three to thirteen roles. Since some roles have very few and only selective tasks, this is possible! For example, all counsellors have the role of counsellor in the market circle. In addition, they can take on other roles that are responsible for organizing team days or strengthening the research community or coordinating network partners. The main difference to classical organizations is: In these, you are accepted for one position and over time you acquire quite a few other topics and responsibilities that are not explicitly described. In Holacracy, all these roles are explicitly differentiated, processed together and placed in the context of the common purpose.

2.3.3 Operational work in Holacracy

Working holacratically also means doing things differently and in a new way in our daily work. People who are members take on the following rights and duties as role leads:

1. **The principle of litigating tensions:** When people talk about tensions, many think of conflicts or tensions. However, something else is meant here. Perhaps you know this: In our daily work, we continuously recognize things that "should" be different so that we or others can work well. We constantly sense what we can change. It is precisely this sensing of tensions that is the motor for continuous learning! A tension describes the difference and the field of tension between the "here and now" and the future (Fig. 2.12). Therefore, it is the task of every role to collect and bring in tensions. There are different ways in which these can be processed: I approach other roles and clarify my tension, I use certain meetings to do so or I propose a new "rule or form" in the governance meeting on how to deal with it in the future (more on this below).

2. **Fulfil role purpose and responsibilities:** When you take on a role lead in Holacracy, it is your job to energize the purpose and responsibilities and drive them forward step by step. You do this by planning and implementing "next actions" or projects for each of your roles. You are responsible for how you prioritize your tasks. The guiding principle is your role and circle purpose: What supports it best in the current circumstances? This also means that budgets are allocated by role leads themselves—according to a certain process and within the scope of the circle budget.

3. **Organize yourself:** As role leads, you organize your time yourself and keep track of your tasks, challenges, projects and next actions. It is important that you manage all tasks in a digital system, prioritize them and work through them. In doing so, you work transparently so that every member of the

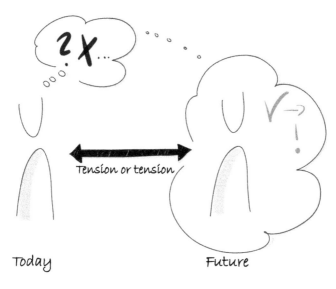

Fig. 2.12. Tension: Tension between today and the future

company can have an insight at any time if there is a need for it. This practice is strongly based on the method "GTD—Getting Things Done" by David Allen (2019). The basic idea of GTD is to establish an effective and relaxed way of working so that the fast pace of the agile organization can be easily managed by employees.

4. **Autonomy and authority:** You take ownership of your roles and can do everything to energize your role and also have the authority to decide in it. This is what is meant by the term "role lead." The principle of being able to move and learn quickly applies. Brian Robertson uses the expression "be a Ferrari" for this. The only restrictions are: Not to violate the rules of the constitution, not to decide in the domains of other roles. Figuratively, a domain means that you cannot dig up another role's garden without asking for their permission.

Tactical meeting

The tactical meeting serves to synchronize the daily operational business. At the same time, it helps to establish routines in regular formats so that the circle can always align itself with the common purpose and everyone feels and notices how it is energized. In every circle, it is about processing tensions: Getting one step closer to the possible future. This is achieved by

Fig. 2.13. Tactical meeting: Clarifying the next action

bringing in these tensions and clarifying in the meeting: "What do you need?" This is not to say that such questions and requirements cannot also be clarified outside meetings with the respective roles. Tensions can generate the following outputs(see Fig. 2.13):

- Ask for a **next action:** In order to move forward well, I need a next action from another role, or I am not yet clear about the concrete next step. The focus is always: How can the circle best fulfil the purpose and mission? In this format I can clarify what the next step might be and who is responsible for it. Info: A next action is a physical single step towards the future.
- Question about a concrete result or **project:** For a larger question, for which more is needed than just a next step, I can clarify the framework of the project here, sharpen it and assign who is responsible for it.
- Ask for information or **help:** I need support or information so that I can continue to work, to energize my purpose and my tasks. This meeting is the right place to ask and ask for support.
- **Sharing information:** I have the assumption that others need this information so that I can best serve my purpose and also that of the circle. I can share everything I need to do this in the tactical meeting.
- Try to establish **expectations**: I have expectations of other roles or of our cooperation. In the tactical meeting, I can clarify what I am concerned about. However, this is not dealt with and decided in the tactical meeting. This can only be clarified in the governance meeting.

What is special about the tactical meeting is the precisely structured process for which the role of facilitator is responsible and over which this role also has sovereignty. A real difference to other meetings is that discussions are kept short, the tension-bringers are focused and the pace is fast. The exact process as well as tips and tricks can be found in our toolbox in Section 5.2.33.

Governance meeting: Designing rules of the game and explicit expectations

The special feature of Holacracy is that operational play itself and the design of explicit rules of play are deliberately separated (see Fig. 2.14). Different needs and requirements are continuously made explicit and adapted. Thus, the company is constantly learning and changing. At the same time, the defined decision-making structure ensures that power and authority are distributed in the organization and that mutual expectations are permanently clarified. The members of the organization thus continuously work on their "how". This clarity and stringency in the handling and distribution of power issues is the unique selling point of Holacracy.

All this happens mainly in the governance meeting: There circles, roles, domains, responsibilities and policies are processed, reviewed and found to be valid or not. The governance meeting process ensures that the proposals for the purpose of the circle and the roles make sense and are not enforced by "perceived" powerful people. Conversely, this also means that decisions and responsibilities are not concentrated among leaders.

Policies

Policies regulate what needs to be additionally clarified between circles and roles. Here is Brian Robertson's example mentioned above: If you have a car,

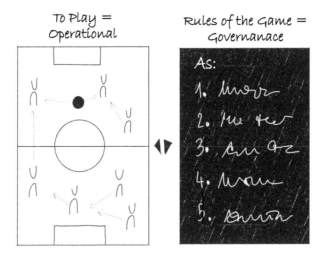

Fig. 2.14. Holacracy: Separating operational play itself from the design of explicit rules of play

this is your domain. Your neighbour should not just get in in the morning and drive away. At the same time, you can use a policy to regulate what who can do and how. For example, you could stipulate: "On every Monday and Wednesday, anyone from neighbouring house No. 5 who is over 18 may use the car if they bring it back with a full tank."

As with many things, policies also serve to gain more clarity. They extend or limit the powers or authority of a role or a circle. Therefore, they regulate everything that explicitly or implicitly belongs to the circle and must be observed. The starting point of a policy is always: What does the role/circle control? If it is clear who this is, the following can be clarified with it:

1. A **restriction of an authority of** one or more roles of a circle. An example of this is the handling of passwords: "Each role that creates a company account with a third-party provider must use a secure password of ten characters including special characters".
2. **Authorization of an authority** from one or more roles of a circle. For example, it can be specified how much money can be spent without asking: "Small amounts up to 20 euros can be spent by all roles without the resource process." Or: "No role except the PR role may release press releases."
3. Create access to a **domain of a role** or the circle. For example, a policy can open access to a domain of the role website (only the role website is allowed to decide what goes on the homepage and how): "The roles XY are allowed to adjust the dates of the event on their own".
4. **Define** a specific **process of** how something is done in this circle: "Roles setting up projects for new products apply this Scrum process during the project period …".

What policies and Holacracy do not do is organize people. The focus is always on organizing roles. Therefore, many things that need to be regulated at the person level, such as expectations regarding attendance time, dress code or travel regulations, need to be clarified upon entry or, since Constitution 5.0, can[3] also be regulated via "work agreements".

Governance meeting

This meeting is an unusual format and seems strange and edgy to many at first. Why? Imagine a colleague from controlling is working on the responsibilities of your role in marketing because she thinks you should do something new in the

---

3   See www.holacracy.org (date of retrieval: 14.06.2020).

future and you can't stop her. This is exactly what can happen to you in a governance meeting. Others edit your role even though they don't fill it themselves. You might think they are spitting in your soup.

But it is about the role and not about the person. Please change the perspective: Other role leads in your circle have a tension because they cannot continue to work well if they do not get information in time. Since this accountability is not described in your role, it cannot be expected of your role. Only when this expectation has been litigated in the circle and is deemed reasonable does it become an expectable part of your role. Only then can others approach you and ask for it. Before that, you do not have to give space to this need. In this respect, everyone is working to ensure that your role also makes an optimal contribution in terms of the whole.

This is just one example. It takes some time to internalize and understand the purpose of this process and the individual steps. At the same time, the rules and questions in the process are very well thought out. That is also what makes governance meetings so interesting. One thing in advance: This is about clarifying fuzziness that is made explicit. That can be quite exhausting. And at the same time, this is one of the great pattern changes when it comes to authority and power distribution. Here we are learning together how governance can look different, with everyone being responsible for the circle and uninterrupted development.

Governance process

In the governance process, circles, roles, expected responsibilities and tasks, domains, policies and elections of the facilitator, secretary and circle rep roles are carried out (see Figure 2.15). Within the framework of a guided process, the proposals are spanned and, with the help of all, deepened, clarified and better understood. For this purpose, clear process steps are given (see Tools). In order to come to a decision that will apply to this circle or role in the future, an objection is made, on which each circle member expresses his or her opinion. Objections are checked for validity using the inclusive decision-making process. In addition, role elections are conducted as part of the governance meeting. The exact process description can be found in the tools.

2.3.4 Membership and the individual in holocratic organizations

Not everything can be clarified through Holacratic rules and roles. Holacracy regulates roles, not people! That is why a commitment at the person level is needed with employees when they join or during their membership—which is nothing new. This includes contracts that regulate, for example, attendance times

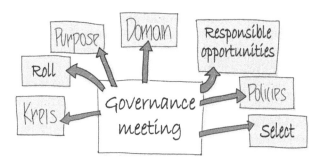

Fig. 2.15. What is clarified in governance meetings

and clarify that the respective person adheres to the Holacratic constitution, or "work agreements" that can be agreed between two or more people. What is new about this approach is the clear differentiation between role and person: I cannot tell a role when they should be where—only the person themselves can decide that! Or whether they want to live in Berlin or Vienna—also a personal decision! Or whether they can be present in person at certain meetings of the organization or not. A clear agreement is needed here!

2.3.5 Transparency through digital support

Holacracy is a form of codified self-organization: Explicit rules and guardrails that create the basis for self-organization to unfold among role bearers. Like in football, there are basic rules that players do not have to worry about so that they can play their game. This creates the freedom to concentrate on the real thing: Establishing a basic rhythm for organizations that creates stability. No one has to think about what kind of game it is: Football, handball, volleyball, a mixture of all of these, or something else entirely. So everyone can focus on the purpose of their own roles and implement them as it suits them.

These principles and rules are recorded in a digital system and can thus be viewed by all at any time. They are transparent for all, creating clarity and clarification. All decisions on governance, projects and also roles are recorded. This has several advantages:

- I can always check what expectations I can have for certain roles.
- I bring in my own tensions more easily and can process them because I can easily retrieve my expectations digitally: What is not yet clarified of what I anticipate, and what is already?
- Or I don't know which role/person has which responsibilities.

- Or I dealt with what the others can actually expect from me in my roles.
- I would like to know what projects this circle or a particular role has.

In addition, this way of working promotes two things: "Fairness" and "several brains contribute with a view to the whole". By being transparent about the rules, the way the game is played and the current expectations, everyone has the opportunity to intervene and contribute to the jointly designed rules of the game, as long as they are within the Holacratic constitution. No one person can change these rules of the game on their own by virtue of their authority or position; the same procedure applies to everyone.

This form of clarification, of making things transparent and of explicit rules are, in our view, one of the most serious differences to traditional organizations. In most organizations, much is implicit and individuals, mostly leaders, decide what is most likely to make sense and be good for the whole. Therefore, this form of working is a real change for many and a permanent learning and unlearning. A member of a self-organized company in Berlin once said: "At first, the carpet is pulled out from under your feet. Everything that is unclear pops up. Before, I didn't notice these blurs at all. Practising that is really challenging at the beginning!"

2.3.6 Challenges and learnings

This form of structuring and organizing is a very intensive and radical path for many organizations. Holacracy is a special form of agile organization. This path does not make sense for every organization. The key question should be: What are our requirements and which system is suitable for this? We can say from our own experience that practising this agile form of organization is an enormous learning field for companies. Learning can also be quite painful, and yet we would not want to miss much of what we have experienced in the introduction of Holacratic structures. We learn a lot of what we do new and different today through this form of cooperation: Strongly structured meetings, different decision-making procedures in different situations, and we live our roles, constantly redesigning them and thus always experiencing something new. We experience this practice as a good source for moving organizations and their transformation processes.

Nevertheless, we do not want to keep quiet about the challenges we experience. Again and again, we also raise different questions, reconsider what of all this makes sense and what does not. In the following, we present some critical points or challenges that we experience and to which we do not yet have clear answers.

Commitment at the personal level

Time and again, self-organized companies describe how difficult it is when people do not really agree and cannot cope with this responsibility or change. The system is highly sensitive when members do not play along or even work against it. We ourselves had such experiences at some points and it became really tough. The employee of a holocratically organized startup in Berlin said: "If someone doesn't play along, then that person poisons the whole system. Dynamics arise that have exactly the opposite effect and have a destructive effect on people, teams and customer relationships. We cannot and will not afford that!" The only thing that helps is a negotiation process at the person level, which quickly brings up the question of membership—and this question is always existential. In our view, this is a real challenge because the system is so sensitive to such disruptive factors.

This is why the introductory phase often requires not only support, but above all perseverance. Also in the sense of the "broken glass" theory: Always keep at it, correct undesirable developments and "repair broken windows right away" so that the whole area and the project do not erode. The theory originated with Wilson and Kelling (1982), who described a correlation between the deterioration of a neighbourhood in American cities and an increase in crime. They found that the crime rate in these neighbourhoods increased rapidly as soon as windows and house facades were left unrepaired.

At the same time, we believe that not every system has to fit every person, just as the Holacracy system does not fit every organization and context. The American online retailer Zappos, for example, offered a year's salary for leaving to all employees who could not get into the system after the introduction phase of Holacracy. As a result, some really did leave.

Expert knowledge Holacracy

For many, the language of Holacracy is very legalistic and therefore it quickly feels like specialized knowledge. The many trainings and certifications offered on it underline this. This can give the impression that those in the know are also those in power. This is what happened with us at first. Some people were very familiar with the subject matter, others were not. This quickly made it clear: There needs to be a system and a way of dealing with it that empowers everyone to use the system well—and that started at the system and person level! Therefore, formats are constantly being developed that enable newcomers to arrive well and at the same time be motivated to train in it on their own.

Then we also have discussions in which some think that if something takes so long to learn, it is too complicated and dysfunctional. It needs more of an intuitive start like a smartphone: A quick guide that works for everyone and is more comprehensible. But this is a disruptive approach that requires a real paradigm shift, especially on the issue of power and authority, so it cannot be that simple. It is about behaviour change and about practices in organizations that have been consolidated for more than 150 years. The demands of the new organizing can only be learned as we go. In this respect, we are only at the beginning. Maybe there will be faster apps in the future, but for now they are not available.

Make everything explicit

This process corresponds exactly to the opposite of what has been part of the competence of organizations up to now: Action is taken from implicit knowledge, which also manifests itself in the culture of the organization. The culture and the implicit will remain with every organization. What changes is the demand to make everything relevant explicit in order to be able to deal with it better. In the long run, this fundamental change can possibly overburden organizations and their members—this permanent open working, always being playable, taking up tensions and bringing them into play.

Holacracy's ground rules are not changeable

The ground rules, the constitution of Holacracy, cannot be changed by individual organizations. They can only adopt them or not. The constitution is thus like a constitution that cannot be changed by a citizen, a company, a party or a government. You decide to follow these rules (and their amendments, because there is already the fifth version of the constitution). For us, after seven years, this decision was a correct one. This also has to do with our vocation: We would feel invited as organizational consultants to "tinker" with the system because that is what we like to do as consultants. In addition, from our point of view, we also need enough time to practice in order to be able to decide what fits and what doesn't and what can be developed further. For this, too, "not questioning" is strengthening. From a pragmatic perspective, it is "ready to take" and already relies on a worldwide community that continues to develop it. Everything else will emerge as we go. But we are also aware that there are other ways and forms that make sense. There are enough examples of this.

Inhuman, cold system

Again and again, we are asked why organizations should do this to themselves when it is such a challenging system that causes so much pain when implemented.

Well, to be honest, we don't know of any organizational form that doesn't cause pain. The purpose of organizational forms, in our view, is not to create painlessness—painlessness is not living. An organizational form should support the survival and growth of the organization and its employees—and growth can also be associated with pain. In this respect, the relevant question is: What is the right organizational form for us in this phase of our development?

At the same time, some of the agile organizational forms and methods have emerged precisely from this dissatisfaction. People in traditional companies have realized for themselves that they cannot adequately contribute and that the meaning of work is increasingly lost, that is, that the question of the meaning of the job, burn-out symptoms or power games are rampant. In this respect, one can say that agile organizational forms, and in this case Holacracy, produce other situations, which in turn produce other emotions and questions.

One advantage of these agile organizational forms is that the corresponding emotions pop up more quickly and have a higher chance of becoming workable. However, this requires formats that the respective organizations develop themselves. In this respect, Holacracy does not offer any clear solutions, but calls on organizations to design this tribe space themselves, in which people are given space and relationships and developments are shaped (see Section 5.2.37).

The current discourse in the communities is precisely about this point. Holacracy and self-organization solve many old problems of classic organizations and at the same time produce new ones that sometimes make the system seem "cold and inhuman". That is why a lot of attention is being paid to the topic of "Role & Soul" and ways are being tested on how an integration of needs can succeed well. One answer of Holacracy is already anchored in a further development, Constitution 5.0: Work agreements between members. In addition, there are now numerous examples of how different companies are dealing with this in a meaningful way. We are also constantly developing apps to shape our tribe space and create space on the relationship and person level (see Section 3.8).

2.3.7 Other self-organized models and approaches

Of course, there are many other approaches and models that promote self-organization and agility. We would like to briefly mention three that we find interesting and inspiring and that we believe are relevant for moving organizations.

The collegially managed company

In their book, Bernd Oesterreich and Claudia Schröder provide ideas and approaches for how agile organizations can be designed. The following picture is

Table 2.5. Checklist: Comparison of Holacracy and traditional organizations

Holacracy	Traditional organizations
Higher Purpose	instead of Profit maximization as an end in itself
Organization in circles	instead of Hierarchy
Acting out of multiple roles	instead of Person and function in one
Roll rotation	instead of Relationships in the foreground
Further development of the organization through real tensions	instead of Organizational change on the drawing board
"Sense and respond"	instead of "Predict and control"
Separation of the rules of the game and the playing field (Tactical & Governance)	instead of Constant mixing
Integrative decision-making process	instead of Consensus
Self-leadership and distributed authority	instead of Heroic Leaders or Hierarchy
"Safe enough to try"	instead of Planning ahead for the long term
Transparency	instead of Silos and bunkered know-how

central: "Collegial leadership is the leadership work distributed dynamically and decentrally among many colleagues instead of centralized leadership by a few exclusive executives" (Oesterreich & Schröder, 2016, p. VII). They themselves have changed their organization to self-organization.

Practices and models have emerged from this that take up different approaches and have also proven to be useful tools for other organizations. Unlike Holacracy, this approach is divided into four phases: Preparation, Conception, Operational Self-Organization and Organizational Self-Organization. These phases test what is appropriate for the organization and how. Central questions are: Leadership and decision-making, process organization, personnel work and the way of communicating. For all of these questions, there are suggestions on how to work with them, such as the leadership monitor, which makes the most important decisions, or the economy process, which takes the place of the budget.

The Spotify model

As the name suggests, this approach was developed at Spotify. From our point of view, this approach is exciting because Scrum logic is at its core and Spotify has asked itself how this can be applied at an organizational level. A new structure was chosen, which is made up of the following aspects:

- **Squads:** Squads are the basis and work similarly to Scrum teams. The nature of a squad should be similar to that of a startup: They are self-organized, consist of multidisciplinary people and develop products or competences. Each squad has a long-term mission. Most of the time, squads work in a shared office building, as this strengthens collaboration.
- **Product Owner:** Each squad has a Product Owner. This person is not a team leader, but works with other Product Owners on a common roadmap and is responsible for the product backlog and priorities in his or her own squad. How a squad implements the requirements is up to them.
- **Agile Coach:** Each squad is accompanied by an Agile Coach. This person promotes collaboration, points out obstacles and conducts retrospectives and sprint planning meetings.
- **Tribe:** A tribe develops related services or products and consists of several squads. Each tribe has a tribe leader who is responsible for creating the optimal framework. A Tribe consists of about 100 people so that they can still relate to each other. There are regular meetings where the squads share insights into their work.
- **Scrums:** This meeting format is for squads that work interdependently and is used to share and give each other updates. Each team is represented by at least one member.
- **Chapters and Guilts:** As the teams are multidisciplinary, chapters are formed within the tribes so that the experts of a profession can exchange and develop. Beyond the tribes, guilts are formed to exchange ideas on interesting topics or areas of expertise. Both chapters and guilts are accompanied by coaches.

Sociocracy 3.0

James Priest and Bernhard Bockelbrink have further developed sociocracy as an open source model with different agile principles and methods. Sociocracy is an organizational form that is based on consensus, that is, in which a decision can be prevented by a strong objection from a circle member. This gives the individual more authority. Many basic rules of sociocracy have been adopted by Holacracy. In contrast to the basic form of sociocracy, only parts of it can be used in the 3.0 form, depending on what suits the individual case. According to the consultants, this approach is suitable for all sizes of organizations.[4] The seven central principles to which all organizational members commit themselves are important:

---

4   See also: https://sociocracy30.org/

- **Effectiveness:** Spend time only on the things that bring you closer to your goal.
- **Consent:** Seek, clarify and raise objections to decisions and actions.
- **Empiricism:** Test assumptions through experimentation and constant verification.
- **Continuously improve:** Change incrementally to enable continuous empirical learning.
- **Equality:** Involve people in making and developing decisions when they are affected.
- **Transparency:** All information is accessible to all employees of an organization unless there is a reason for confidentiality.
- **Accountability:** Act when necessary, implement when agreed and take responsibility for the running of the organization.

In addition, 50 patterns are described that are procedural guides and can be used for different tasks and company areas, such as decision-making procedures or meetings. The organization itself decides which patterns are helpful and can adapt them individually (even if no circle structure is used). On the homepage, there are numerous aids and instructions that can be used free of charge (see also Rüther 2017).

2.4 The agile on the systems theory approach

Systems theory currently offers the most comprehensive concept for understanding agility and its associated requirements. Presenting this in a compact way is a challenging undertaking. We would like to explain our understanding here and go into detail about those people and model that have shaped our thinking. Systemicists have been concerned since the 1940s with the question of how systems can survive in a constantly changing world. Early on, the focus was on topics that were completely new at the time: Information, control, adaptability, control loops and feedback.

2.4.1 A brief review

For example, long before agility became a buzzword, the systemicist Talcott Parsons created the AGIL schema (Parsons, 2012). He was able to show what capabilities social systems need to develop in order to survive in a dynamic world. AGIL means: Adaptation (adjustment or the ability of a system to react appropriately to changing external conditions), goal attainment (the ability to formulate and pursue goals), integration (inclusion or the competence to be able to connect different parts of a system) and latency (maintenance, i.e. the ability to sustain existing patterns and structures). Parsons developed a concept that is very similar to resilience (see Section 2.1).

Later, the German sociologist Niklas Luhmann (1976) took up Parsons' work and developed a theory for the functioning of social systems. His thoughts focus on the question of how systems deal with complexity and what controls them. He contributed significantly to the understanding of social systems no longer as open systems that are in active exchange with the environment, but to conceive of them as closed systems at their core. When it comes to their own control, systems are stubborn and can only be influenced with difficulty even by the powerful in the system. This must be understood if, for example, decision-making processes are to be changed. This is why attempts at targeted changes that affect the identity of systems are so difficult.

2.4.2 An exceptional team effort

The fact that we can draw on systems theory today is due to the amazing teamwork of a motley group of women scientists who met in 1946–1953 in the so-called Macy Conferences. Under the patronage of the Macy Foundation, women anthropologists, linguists, electrical engineers, neurobiologists, psychoanalysts and mathematicians met. Outstanding scientists such as Norbert Wiener, Margaret Mead, Gregory Bateson, Kurt Lewin, Heinz von Förster and many others developed a general theory of regulation, control and feedback in ten conferences on the basis of the new understanding of information, analogue/digital and feedback. This was to apply to living beings as well as machines, to economic, biological and psychological processes and was called cybernetics. They thus laid the foundation for modern systems theory , which will be characterized here on the basis of six principles that are relevant to our topic.

1. Non-trivial machines

It is thanks to the Viennese emigrant Heinz von Förster, then secretary of the last conferences despite very poor English, that minutes of these lively discussions still exist today. From him comes the important distinction between trivial and non-trivial systems. The beverage dispenser is a trivial system because every time a coin is inserted and a button is pressed, the result is the same, the ejection of a can. Non-trivial systems, such as animals, humans, in other words all social systems, can react differently to the same input. There is no clear cause-effect relationship.

Social systems have an inner state, feelings and memory, which means that the same input, such as chocolate (or annual bonus), can lead to a completely different output. Social systems are not trivial machines and should be treated differently.

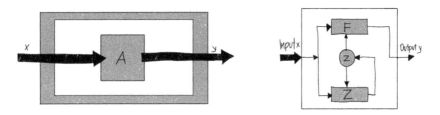

Fig. 2.16. Trivial and non-trivial machine (Förster & Pörksen, 2008, p. 57f)

2. Construction of reality

Social systems are unique, not only because of their different histories, but also because they form their own picture of their environment. They construct their own view of the world. Every system, every living being builds its explanations about the world out there, about itself and the others. The image of reality is not a photograph, but is made, that is, constructed—hence the term "constructivism" (Watzlawick, 2006). Our concepts and knowledge influence our cognition, "… for whatever we do, we can only compare our perception of the apple with other perceptions, never with the apple itself as it would be before we perceive it" (von Glasersfeld, 2006, p. 25). Seen in this light, leadership, education or change work are attempts to influence constructions of reality.

3. System-environment relationship

There is no system without its environment. System and environment are an "evolutionary unit" (Simon, 2018). A company needs its market, its competitors, its suppliers, its stakeholders. It takes care to maintain the system-environment distinction and to forge communication with relevant stakeholders. The system has to draw a line and keep in touch, just as, for example, at every family party it has to be determined who may attend and who may not (does the ex-wife or the daughter's new boyfriend belong?). The system-environment relationship must be understood as a unit; only when you understand the system in its relationship to its environment can you understand what makes it tick.

4. Controlling complexity

Differentiation from the environment is a system performance that every system has to perform continuously. If a system were to pick up every impulse, it would quickly become completely confused and die a death of complexity. For example, in social media you cannot follow every comment, every "news" item. If, on the other hand, a system completely caps itself off and does not take in any stimuli from the environment at all, it becomes autistic.

How systems manage this complexity gradient—the environment is always more complex than the system—fascinated Niklas Luhmann (Luhmann, 1984). He found it utterly astonishing that systems usually succeed in remaining connectable and yet do not suffer complexity death. He investigated the conditions for this and showed that systems are very open on an operational level (when exchanging information and goods), but closed on a control level, namely when they decide what to include and what not. At the control level, no system likes to be influenced. Here the system is closed and develops itself. This process is called autopoiesis ("creating itself") in reference to biology (Maturana, 1984) and makes it clear why changes, a relearning at a fundamental level is so difficult and why interventions from the outside so often fail.

5. Social systems consist of communication

Whatever happens in a social system, a shout, a smoke break, a payment, it has to pass through the "eye of the needle of communication". Social systems need communication. Only as long as they communicate do they exist. If they stop communicating, they die. In organizations, the relevant communication is the communication of decisions: Only as long as it makes decisions does the organization exist. If it no longer makes decisions, it is dead.

6. Evolution cannot be planned

From what has been said so far, it follows that social systems are constantly in motion with their environment and the evolution of social systems cannot be planned. Impulses (interventions) can be set to influence development, but the result of this influence is open.

Whatever is set as an intervention must be done as an act of communication. The intervention is successful when the way of communication changes the system. This is the goal of any organizational change.

2.4.3 A good theory

Kurt Lewin said that nothing is as practical as a good theory. Especially when things get complex, you need a good theory, because without a theory you are helpless in the face of complexity. Everything can have meaning, and nothing has to mean something. A good theory offers points of reference, handholds that you can hold on to in order to align your thinking and locate ideas. It helps to check assumptions, protects against being carried away by current events and fashions, and supports the right choice of terms.

Using the six premises, we have shown how systems theory helps to understand the complex world of agility. To conclude and summarize:

- Social systems, agile teams and organizations are not trivial machines. Therefore, only methodological knowledge is of little help. It is important to understand them, to explore them, to connect to their history, their culture, if you want to work with them and develop them.
- Our inner images and beliefs, our constructions of reality accompany us everywhere. In situations of upheaval, we have to leave the highways of our thinking and enter terrain not yet travelled.
- The system-environment relationship takes on a special significance due to the upgrading of the customer focus in the agile world. Agility means being able to play and communicate with a wide variety of stakeholders. Agility requires opening up to the outside world, virtually preaching the early and frequent involvement of customers, but without closure there is no continuity and development.
- Dealing with complexity is the starting point of all agility efforts. In the so-called VUCA world (Volatility, Uncertainty, Complexity, Ambiguity; see also thesis 2, Section 1.3.2), orientation aids, such as the Tension Square, are needed to find one's way around and remain capable of acting. We need concepts and a theory that is complex enough to grasp complexity and make it usable.
- Agile organizations take up the realization that evolution cannot be controlled, you can only use it, learn and take the next step.

2.5 Case study: Need for movement in the mobility industry[5]

If you want to reach pole position in the vehicle industry, you have to face three massive changes in the market at once: digitalization, e-mobility and the entry of new competitors from outside the industry (Tesla, Google). Like all companies in this industry, our client was trimmed like a perfect clockwork. Its production lines regularly spit out large numbers of the various models, each car a high-tech product. Nevertheless, it was clear to our client: We need a game changer that turns everything that exists upside down. We need a prototype with which we can practice and learn to cope with the new requirements in our core business of vehicle construction. The new vehicle must be electric, autonomous, networked

---

5   This section was written together with Gregor Tobeitz.

and available on demand. The traditional vehicle manufacturer should become an innovative mobility service provider as quickly as possible.

The goal is soon clear: To design and build an autonomous electric van. What had usually taken two to three years is now to be achieved within one year—from the first Post-it to the first drivable prototype. The target group for this transporter is a manageable number of special customers with individual wishes, such as for autonomous journeys on their own company premises or in ship harbours.

2.5.1 Phase 1: The first agile steps

As a classic carmaker, the company is still committed to the art of engineering. The new competitors in e-mobility, however, no longer approach car development like engineers, but much more like software developers: They build the first prototypes in a short time, stuff them full of new sensor technology, test them and go to market with them as quickly as possible, where they then continue to develop the product. Because of this approach, these competitors not only get to the market much faster, but they also collect a lot of data and experience in real-life operation during this time, which then immediately flows back into further development and thus further increases their lead over the classic carmakers.

In the first phase, we put together a cross-functional team of ten employees and managers. We train all participants in agile working methods and prepare them for the still very foreign agile world. However, we limit the training to the essentials and do not dwell on details. Technical jargon is not a prerequisite for being able to work agilely, and the real learning happens while walking anyway. The management makes it possible to provide a workplace for the team outside the factory premises.

Instead of the usual project plan, we introduce the team to the system of backlogs from the Scrum framework. The big difference and also advantage: Instead of working out a project plan for the next four months, the aim now is to gain clarity only about the next steps. Turning away from linear project logic to loop logic means that we immediately pick up the pace.

Next, we make sure that the team is ready to work, and for this many questions need to be clarified, among others: How well do the members know each other? Is everyone on 100 per cent secondment or only available part-time? What resources are available? Working through the long catalogue of questions one after the other would cost us a lot of time—so we use the Scrum technique for this as well, by picking out several prioritized points and working through them in parallel or overlapping in short, intensive "sprints".

First resistances

Self-directed work sounds irresistible to most. Only in practice do many realize that this also necessarily entails a willingness to take responsibility and that one's own decisions have to be represented and defended. The democratic style of working also takes some getting used to for many: "I don't feel like constantly questioning, discussing and arguing everything. Just tell me what needs to be done and I'll do it." However, our experience is that the longer the process takes, the more likely these people are to see the added value and feel comfortable. Not surprisingly, too: In an agile approach, the people involved constantly come up against the limits of the classic organization, not only the prevailing mindset, which is expressed in phrases like "that doesn't work for us" or "we've never done it that way before", but also numerous regulations, rules and organizational logics that cannot be easily disregarded. Intensive communication with the responsible bodies is just as necessary as clearly documented procedures and process steps to reduce the risk of liability and lawsuits. Regulations and laws can be questioned, but they cannot be ignored.

Scrum postulate: What the customer wants is what is done

For many, it was similarly unusual to involve the customer as early as possible. Scrum logic postulates very radically: Only what the customer wants and explicitly demands is done. Everything else—even if it makes the technician's heart beat faster—is left out. This unconditionality can cause an earthquake in companies that have been accustomed for decades to involving their customers in development only at a very late stage and then only through clearly defined channels. We, however, establish co-creation workshops in which customers are involved intensively and in partnership from the very beginning.

It would be naïve not to think about and take into account earthquakes and hurdles, and in any case, this is a decisive factor in whether such attempts at agility succeed or not. Questions such as "Are we ready to open up to the outside world, or does the fear of being shown our cards prevail? What can we gain from this, what do we risk?" must therefore be repeatedly addressed, discussed and consciously decided on a case-by-case basis in the organization. This is a learning process at the personal as well as the organizational level, and it does not happen in a linear fashion, but rather in loops.

Ongoing role clarification

Another key success factor of such agile working methods is the recurring clarification of one's own role. What is my role in this project anyway? What are the expectations of my role? Do they even fit together? What are my tasks, what is my decision-making area, what is my responsibility? A first clarification step in this project takes place in the course of a team-building measure, where one's own understanding of one's role is worked out and then placed next to the role models of the colleagues and compared, which sometimes leads to heated discussions.

An additional good opportunity for role awareness is provided by the reviews that take place at the end of each sprint. During these reviews, the results of the sprint are presented to the Product Owner. The team members create a management template with two proposals to choose from. But we briefed the Product Owner in advance not to accept these, to make the team aware of their role responsibilities. Each team member is an expert who has to decide for herself and present the result. A Product Owner only has a veto right in certain cases.

This intense preoccupation with the different roles is irritating for everyone. Team members ask themselves: How does my understanding of my role fit in with the others? Is there agreement on this in the team? It is very unfamiliar for most of them to keep looking at the working relationships and to name and deal with current tensions. As technicians, they are used to focusing on the content dimension, but not on the social dimension. Accordingly, the question is always asked critically: "Does it have to be like this?" But above all: "Does it have to be this often?"

The intense social interaction is unusual: After each review, we take 2.5 hours for a retrospective. Every day in the morning there are 20-minute "daily stand-ups" where the whole team meets to coordinate and synchronize. We also take a lot of time for sprint planning, a whole day. Often enough, we are asked whether this can't be shortened or the frequency reduced. Not deviating from that is a challenge.

2.5.2 Phase 2: Prototyping

At the end of phase 1, the team of developers actually creates a finished concept for building a new prototype. Not to the same degree of detail as is usually the case with the concept books in the company, where everything is already specified and defined down to the individual screw, but comprehensive and detailed enough to be able to start building a prototype. And above all: Twice to three times faster than was previously the norm in the group!

Already in the first phase, it was clear that the interaction with the sales department is critical for success in order to get in touch with the customer quickly and comprehensively. In phase 2, the project is expanded in the area of development: Several teams are added, but they are not yet familiar with the agile way of working. In total, we create 6 teams with up to 40 people to be able to build the prototype. These teams are larger than usual and need a special way of working and support. What we have to take into account: The most competent people from the line are not always assigned to this project—who likes to give away their best people? We therefore define the necessary competences as precisely as possible and also use personality tests.

This enormous expansion requires that we develop a completely agile organizational structure for a total of 250 employees as well as managers, which works outside the line organization. In addition to the backlogs and sprints from the Scrum framework, we use the circular logic from Holacracy and the loop approach from Lean Startup (see Section 2.2). All new members are familiarized with the new way of working in agile boot camps. In order to coordinate the six teams well with each other in development, we establish another circle with representatives of the six circles as a form of lateral leadership. Soon it is realized, we make qualitatively better decisions, we are better coordinated with each other and we become faster.

Phase 2 is also dominated by the postulate of customer participation. The teams decide on two specific clients with different requirements. To compensate for the lack of know-how, we look for a suitable partner and find a client from the logistics sector who is familiar with agile methods.

The problem of different speeds

In the first phase it was already apparent that the different pace of the teams was a problem. In phase 2, this phenomenon becomes even more drastic: The development team is faster than the others, which is partly due to the fact that this team is the only one that is permanently present, while the others are only assigned part-time to the project and therefore always have to switch between project and line. It is therefore crucial to gradually infect the other areas of the line organization with the new mindset and familiarize them with the changed way of working so that interfaces do not become problem areas.

2.5.3 Phase 3: New operating system

After only eight months of development, the first vehicle can finally complete an autonomous journey on the factory premises. So we usher in the next phase with the goal of transferring the project into a more stable organization that will operate and continue to build the product line beyond the individual vehicle. We establish a transformation backlog in which we deposit the requirements for the new agile organizational structure.

The task we are now facing is to form an agile organization from a project organization. In contrast to the classic organization, this organization should not have any classic departments. We want a cross-functional organization that is committed to continuous change. The underlying idea is: When tension arises, that is, when a need for change arises, this organizational structure must also be able to update itself. This is the big difference to a classic line organization.

Agile meets hierarchy

A small team of ten people can still fly well under the radar in a large, global corporation and operate relatively undisturbed. But if one team becomes several teams and these start to access the line as a newly emerging organizational unit because they now need it for their own advancement, things quickly get hairy. Then the distributed authority of the agile way of working meets the hierarchical authority in the line, that is, then the just emerging agile organizational unit is confronted with the organizational requirements of a large corporation, but they do not fit here. To counteract this, we repeatedly held town hall meetings with the line managers in the first phase and then even more so in the second phase, as well as open days so that they could see for themselves what was going on here. This proved to be helpful, but not enough.

It was extremely important that the product sponsor, a divisional board, kept a protective hand over the project. Even more so because there was no clear governance, no clear rules of the game on questions like: What does it mean to make decisions about resources when an agile team approaches us (line managers)? How are resources and budgets allocated? How are conflicting demands on the organization handled without always escalating everything to the sponsor?

Soon, however, the dangers of a classically hierarchical protective hand became apparent. For this powerful manager had simply instructed the leaders of his department: "Help them! Give them what they need! No discussion." But this did not convince his people. When this powerful sponsor then fell ill from one day to the next in phase 3, the protective hand was gone. And with it the willingness of the line to support the project.

This is the point we are at today. We don't know if and when the sponsor will return. We know what is needed for the next step, namely that the classic organization also understands and accepts the sense and benefits of agile units. Only then will there be a chance for a prosperous coexistence. This requires a high degree of transparency so that the line knows what is happening and why. And this in turn requires a high degree of communication and exchange and willingness on both sides to approach each other. Above all, however, it needs clear rules and agreements at the level of the company on how to deal with the sometimes contradictory logics of hierarchical organization and agile organization when it comes to the distribution of resources.

2.6 The key messages of this chapter

- Resilient organizations are well equipped for the future because they can deal well with crises and thus with complexity. This is why it will be all the more important in the future to be crisis-proof, as organizational resilience research shows. Four capabilities are needed for organizations to remain viable and grow: Innovative adaptation, performance optimization, mindful management and preventive control. It is important to establish a "both/and" attitude so that paradoxes can be used well.
- Agility is a necessary game-changing capability for organizations to deal with the challenges and acceleration of complexity in the future. Digitalization in particular is driving this change and demands a different way of playing. Therefore, it also makes sense to learn the new game form of agility, because it not only provides meaningful approaches to organizing, but also makes organizations more crisis-proof.
- Agility is not a set of methods, but rather the ability to play, which requires that you not only know the methods, but also the game and the mindset.
- Due to the already existing challenges on the market, many methods have developed that have supported affected project and product managers in dealing with the complex requirements: for example, Scrum, Lean Startup and Design Thinking have proven their worth. These approaches have triggered a real hype and are now widespread. The process logics and interventions help to make good progress in agile projects, which is why they are almost always included in agile transformations.
- Holacracy and Co. do for organizational structures what Scrum and Design Thinking do at product and project level. An agile form of organization that meets the complex demands of the markets, is flexible, constantly learns and adapts itself. This is where self-organization comes into play, which turns traditional organizational logic upside down. Moving organizations have a lot to learn from these approaches, because one thing becomes clear here as well: It is about clearly defined process flows, in terms of content as well as social and temporal aspects, which need some new competences and skills on many levels.
- Systems theory has basically always been "agile". We systemicists have always worked circularly in loops. We emphasize that it is about differentiation. That

is also the reason why many things do not seem new to those who work with systemic approaches. Nevertheless, due to digitalization and accelerated communication, much is changing and needs to be re-learned and re-specified. This is exactly why it is important to start from a good basis: To deepen the basic systemic assumptions, to understand what makes organizations tick, to learn the principles of transformations and how to steer them, and to be able to professionally apply proven working methods and models such as the Neuwaldegg loop.

3 The nine levers of agile transformation

For most organizations today, the mandate is to move to agility. This is a highly challenging undertaking: The basic understanding of first-order change that has characterized it so far—that is, the belief that organizations need to be trimmed for efficiency through structural change—is no longer sufficient. It is being replaced by the paradigm of agility, which—as we have already emphasized elsewhere in this book—necessitates a much deeper second-order change: The caterpillar becomes a butterfly and not merely a caterpillar that can crawl faster.

In order for this transformation of the organization into a moving organization to have a real chance, it is necessary to start at many levels. And that is exactly what this chapter is about: The nine levers in an agile transformation, which show what the central aspects are in the change itself. They are the essence of what we have experienced and recognized in many years of transformation support:

- **Lever 1: Decisions in organizations**
  In the first section we deal with the systemic view of the organization as a whole. Since organizations are made up of decisions, decisions are on the one hand the central lever, and on the other hand they can be concretized through certain premises that point to all other levers. We present the organizational development triangle, which shows you how the dimensions interact.

- **Lever 2: Culture, organization and transformation**
  In the second part of this chapter, we start with the culture of organizations, which is always a particular challenge when it comes to change, because culture consists of the soft facts, and these are the hardest when it comes to change.

- **Lever 3: Purpose—common good and transformation**
  Then we focus on Purpose, the decision-making programme that establishes the relationship between the organization, the ecosystem and society. Here we describe our experiences based on the great book by Fink and Moeller "Purpose Driven Organizations" (2018) and add further experiences in transformation processes.

- **Lever 4: Role-taking, role-making and role diversity**
  As already described in the theses in Chapter 1, individuals are becoming more and more important in all organizations. This lever deals primarily with the differentiation of role and person and how to work well with the role concept in moving organizations.

- **Lever 5: Organization as a resonance space for growth and development**
  We use the concept of DDO (Kegan & Lahey, 2016; see also thesis 4 in Section 1.3.4) to describe a development-oriented organization. Individual development and learning is at the centre of collective action so that the organization develops as a whole.

- **Lever 6: Ten skills that individuals need**
  Organizations expect everyone to perform. Here we describe requirements that individuals face in order to participate powerfully in Moving Organizations.

- **Lever 7: Leadership, power and the transition**
  Agile organizations and leadership need power, but in a different form than it is used today. What this means and how a shift can be made is shown in this section.

- **Lever 8: Agile teams**
  Teams are a central hub of any moving organization. They help to cope with complexity. How teams can become agile and what is needed to develop their capacity to play is explained in this section.

- **Lever 9: Social innovation**
  A moving organization needs social innovation. What this means and how digitalization can be used for this purpose will be described in this last of the nine levers.

If you have read this chapter, you know and understand the important levers of transformation that we repeatedly integrate in our consultancy processes so that progress in the sense of a moving organization is successful. Depending on how your organization is currently positioned, you decide which levers you want to use to change your organization.

3.1 Lever 1: Decisions in organizations

Organizations as we know them today are just 200 years old. They are relatively young social systems, and they are different from families or society (Witzel, 2012, p. 20). The most important innovation in the "invention" of organizations was that membership in them is limited in time and subject to conditions. In organizations, unlike families or society, one can join, leave or be excluded. This enables organizations to ensure that their goals are pursued and that the focus is on task completion.

    When organizations exist for longer or exceed a certain size, they develop a hierarchical order. We can thus define organizations as social systems (Kühl, 2011) that

- limit their membership in time and attach conditions,
- pursue purposes, and
- Forming hierarchies.

Organizations consist of decisions. If no more are made, the organization dies. Only as long as it decides does the organization exist. Decisions are therefore the central actions of every organization. This means all decisions, those of the porter, the order processor and the board of directors. Every organization lives from the fact that decisions are constantly being made.

For organizational change, this means: If you want to have an impact on organizations, you have to influence the way decisions are made. Only by changing the way decisions are made can you tell if you have been successful. This is especially true for agile organizations. Their goal is to make the process of their decisions more fluid in order to be more playable. Therefore, the view into the world of decisions in organizations is of central importance.

3.1.1 What are decisions?

Decisions are determinations; they transform the indeterminate into the determinate. What was unclear before is now clarified: The doorman lets the stranger into the company, an applicant is hired, the customer order is produced. Each time, a decision is made. What was unclear before is now clear. Each decision triggers new questions, new decisions. This is the special systemic view of organizations: Organizations consist of decisions and not of people, machines or products.

In this sense, every organization makes thousands and thousands of decisions every day and consists of a stream of ongoing decisions, which one can ask how it is controlled so that chaos does not arise. For this to happen, decisions must be connectable. Decisions that have already been made serve as a reference point for further decisions, they orient but do not determine what will be decided next. Luhmann calls this loose coupling (Luhmann, 2000, p. 374).

Organizations would never be so successful; however, if they left it completely open in every decision how the connection to decisions already made is made. Decision premises help in this mixed situation of decisions (Luhmann, 2000, p. 224). Decision premises correspond to the three characteristics of organizations mentioned above (purposes, hierarchy and membership) and are complemented by a fourth premise, culture. Decision premises act like meta-decisions (decisions about decisions).

The triangle of organizational development inspired by Luhmann provides a helpful framework for thinking (cf. Boos & Mitterer, 2019, p. 54ff; Fink &

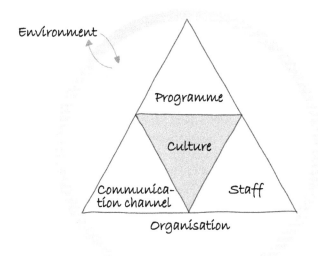

Fig. 3.1. Neuwaldegg triangle of organizational development

Moeller, 2018, p. 79): Fig. 3.1 shows how the dimensions interact and which levers of agile transformation are necessary in which dimension.

Basically, an organization always develops along its decisions, that is, if an organization is to change, one should influence its decisions, or more precisely, the way these decisions come about. To do this, one has four types, systemically called decision premises, that can be influenced: Programmes, communication channels, people and culture. If an organization is to be changed, one or more decision premises can be addressed. For a change to a moving organization, however, the change should cover all four premises.

3.1.2 The four decision-making premises and their levers

Programmes include goals and market strategies. A new organizational structure and process organization influences the **communication paths that** people take and determines how information flows in the organization. Managers and staff set priorities as **personnel** and contribute their skills and competences to the organization. And the premise of **culture** describes the how, the togetherness. Viewed as a whole, these dimensions are interrelated and influence each other: If, for example, the goal is to work in a team-oriented and more agile way, the question

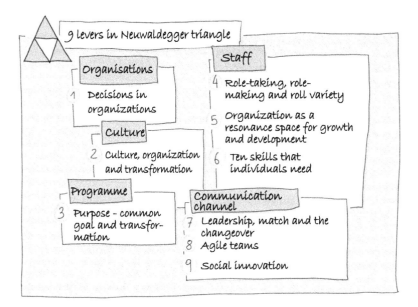

Fig. 3.2. Neuwaldegg triangle and the nine levers of agile transformation

arises as to what managers and employees can do or must bring to the table and which processes and structures support precisely this. If, in turn, an IT infrastructure is introduced, the question arises as to how this affects the goals and which goals are supported by it and, at the same time, what this means at the staff level.

The triangle now offers us valuable help, as we can show which levers we start with the interventions and which other dimensions should be taken into account in order to achieve the goal. Whoever works with organizations and wants to influence them must refer to at least one of the four decision-making premises.

Programmes serve to ensure that factually correct decisions are made. This involves tasks and goals, business plans, target agreements, working time regulations, limits for investment approvals or parts lists. Decision-making programmes help an organization to determine whether a decision was right or wrong. Luhmann calls these programmes decision programmes (Luhmann, 2000, p. 225), which sometimes causes confusion. We have therefore decided to use the short version programmes, but we mean the same thing. Two types of programmes can be distinguished: Conditional programmes and purpose programmes (ibid., p. 261).

Conditional programmes are "if-then rules" and input-oriented. They specify what must be done when a certain condition occurs. Example: When the temperature drops below 23 degrees, the heating is switched on.

Purpose programmes distinguish between objectives and means. They define which objectives/purposes are to be achieved: The choice of means to achieve the objectives is left free. Example: Annual target is the production of tens of thousands of pieces, how this is achieved is left to production.

Agile organizations need both, but especially purpose-oriented programmes like Purpose, as we describe in Section 3.3. However, it is not practically possible for all decisions to relate only to a purpose and for this to be used as a kind of "control criterion" (Luhmann). This would make the whole process highly complex. Therefore, complementary programmes are necessary, such as the distribution of tasks and competences or the definition of process steps, in order to achieve the purposes.

Communication channels describe how decisions are made. For this purpose, positions and departments are defined, decision-making competencies are specified, organizational charts are drawn up and processes are established. This results in responsibilities and the definition of competencies. In short, this is what business administration calls organizational structure and process organization.

Organizations do not have to be very large for the linking of the carefully described bodies to become a problem. Coordination is needed and this is where hierarchy comes in. Hierarchy creates relationships of superiority and subordination in which decision-making power is distributed unequally. The task of hierarchy is to coordinate.

In traditional organizations, which are geared towards division of labour and efficiency, hierarchy is the central principle. Not so in the moving organization. They are not hierarchy-free, but hierarchy is used differently, as we will show. A key lever is teams and the new way they work together and make decisions (see Section 3.8).

Personnel is the decision-making premise that takes into account personal styles and preferences and links personnel decisions (appointments, promotions, dismissals) to membership conditions and decision-making programmes. Even in very well-structured organizations such as public authorities, one experiences that different people in the same position with the same task decide differently.

People make a difference in organizations. The decision to hire a staff member determines many subsequent decisions. In agile organizations, it is even more significant who the organization recruits and how these people can and will contribute to the organization. Levers 4, 5 and 6 address this important premise in detail.

Culture is the fourth decision premise and describes everything that has developed over time in an organization but has never been decided. It is the customs that apply here and that one should know. You stick to it because otherwise there would be consequences, but no one has ever decided it that way. Because culture is a particular challenge in any transformation, we talk about this topic in detail in Lever 2.

The decision-making premises of an organization are interrelated. For example, no one can permanently oppose a company's strategy without calling its membership into question. None of the decision-making premises are set in stone; they are constantly being re-decided and adapted according to what works for the organization. "Organisations are like a constantly flowing river of decisions that continually adjusts its riverbed as the terrain allows or requires" (Fink & Moeller, 2018, p. 49). Also, none of the decision-making premises is more powerful or fundamentally superior to the others. Agile organizations in particular decide on a case-by-case basis.

3.1.3 Good decisions, bad decisions

So there is no getting around decisions in organizations. Good decisions are those that can be followed up, that is, that lead to further decisions. Bad decisions fizzle out and have no consequences. What helps us to make good decisions?

Decisions are determinations that differ with regard to

- their result,
- their occurrence, and
- their consequences.

In terms of outcome, decisions can be measured by how good the decision was and how much it is accepted. Decisions can, therefore, be assessed in terms of their quality and their acceptance. The quality of a decision depends on the knowledge and skills of the people involved. This is where expert knowledge is needed. That is why people like to seek the advice of experts.

The acceptance of a decision, on the other hand, depends on the decision-making procedure chosen. Whether the boss' individual decision or the team decision makes sense, whether voting is secret or open—the procedure must be accepted so that the decision is supported.

The third aspect describes the consequences of a decision: What does the decision do to those affected? Decisions are interventions in the social system and affect the further performance and willingness to cooperate of those involved. In order to strengthen this, decisions and the procedure used must be understood and accepted, otherwise you have a decision but the team is completely shaken up, as in the case of a replacement for a manager that hardly anyone in the team wanted, which is why many employees left the area.

All three aspects of a decision are of central importance for the moving organization. Teams play a major role, so individual decisions are often replaced by group decisions and the majority principle is resorted to, according to the motto "one person, one vote". This has serious disadvantages when it comes to key decisions, as recent research has shown. The most important one is: It produces winners and losers (Visotschnig, 2018). The dynamic of "winner here, loser there" is something that a moving organization must avoid at all costs, as it can no longer be agile as a result. No match is won with a winner and perceived losers in the team! (For alternative methods, see the tools in Sections 5.2.1, 5.2.2 and 5.2.3.)

3.1.4 Our recommendations for the "decisions in organizations" lever

Moving organizations will be measured by how they make decisions. They can only do this by broadening decision-making, that is, distributing authority, having multiple participants and making important decisions in a way that is accepted. This can only be done by using accepted decision-making procedures.

The choice of the decision-making process ensures the acceptance of the outcome. Deciding this is the task of the respective leader or the organization, which has long since ceased to have to choose only between the individual decision (role decides) and the group decision (the majority decides), but has a wider choice, as shown, for example, by sociocracy and Holacracy (see Section 2.3).

Another decision-making method is systemic consensus (Visotschnig et al., 2009). This turns the tables: Instead of asking for approval for a proposal, the degree of rejection is surveyed (see tool in Section 5.2.2).

An example: In the course of the transformation of a company, the top management has been strengthened as it has taken over tasks of the management. Now it was necessary to decide on a name. The eight members made this decision through systemic consensus. Each member had ten votes of resistance and could distribute them as they wished among the five available suggestions. Then it was decided as a rule: Should two members distribute all their resistance votes to one proposal, this would be understood as a veto and the proposal must be eliminated. The old name "Management Board" was one of the proposals, as the status quo is always decided in this procedure; it received 42 resistance points. There were concerns about the name management board because of the English terms. However, it had the lowest resistance value of seven points and was taken. Through this result and the process, everyone was strengthened and really proud of it.

Not all decisions have to be made by the team. As a rule of thumb, link as many factual decisions as possible to roles. Fundamental decisions and decisions with symbolic value (such as the name of the management board) are better left to teams.

The way of deciding is essential for a moving organization and should be carefully considered. We, therefore, recommend setting up a system in which

- it is clear how decisions are made (hierarchical decisions are better than none),
- the decision-making process is disclosed and accepted,
- decisions are dealt with transparently,
- each recognizes how to be effective, that is, greatest possible role clarity,
- dissenting opinions are sought and used,
- the decision-making process is discussed and constantly improved.

3.2 Lever 2: Culture, organization and transformation

For this chapter, please imagine that you are a Viennese. If you were strolling through Vienna in the early 2000s, you would have usually kept your eyes on the ground. You would not want to step in dog excrement—or as it is called in Vienna, Hundstrümmerl. With more than 55,000 registered dogs that wanted to be exercised regularly, this was quite likely because the dog owners did not think of cleaning up their pets' mess. What a city like Zurich had already achieved, namely to be free of dog excrement, seemed impossible in Vienna. Since the 1980s, several initiatives by the city had failed. A motorbike with a hoover, higher fines, even flags in the excrement had remained ineffective. Even the specially commissioned municipal council had thrown in the towel in exasperation, saying that Viennese women were incorrigible.

When you walk through the alleys of Vienna today, you think a miracle has happened. The streets and paths are clean. Dog owners voluntarily dispose of their dogs' excrement with bags (Sackln). 100,000 bags per day end up in the 25,000 public rubbish bins provided for this purpose. How could this succeed?

In 2005, Vienna launched the "Gackerl ins Sackerl" campaign. A number of well-coordinated measures were introduced simultaneously and accompanied by media. About 3,000 bag dispensers were set up all over the city, where the bags could be taken out free of charge around the clock. The dog owners had to dispose of the filled bags, otherwise they were threatened with a fine. For this purpose, park sheriffs were sent out onto the streets. Everywhere there were small signs "Das Gackerl ins Sackl" with a funny beagle and a notice about the fine of 36 euros. Large posters showed exemplary dog owners. Approximately 120 dog zones were set up where dogs could run free, "belonging" to them. For a few weeks, "Gackerl ins Sackl" was the topic in Vienna.

Even today, this costs the city around 7 million euros. Almost 35 million bags have to be disposed of and about 400 fines are imposed every year. The city has changed. You hardly see dog owners who don't pick up the excrement. The citizens are behaving differently. People talk to dog owners if they notice something. Part of Vienna's culture has changed.

This is all the more remarkable because culture is difficult to change in a targeted way. Cultures are constantly changing, only targeted attempts at change rarely succeed. This is what makes culture so special in the context of change projects. Every culture influences the behaviour and decisions of those involved. Culture itself can only be influenced directly by decisions to a limited extent, as the city of Vienna proves: When ordinances were passed and fines imposed in the 1980s to become dog excrement-free, citizens' behaviour did not change. Only the emotional campaign ensured the breakthrough. Culture is tricky, unwieldy and difficult to change, or as Luhmann says, "an undecidable decision-making premise".

A clock has no culture

Just think of the authorities, which were suddenly to become citizen-friendly, the venerable post office as a monopolist, which had to become customer-oriented in a short time, the patriarchally run company, which was prescribed a zero-error culture. Many initiatives are started, a lot of money is spent and a lot of projects go to waste. Culture change cannot be brought about by flipping a switch.

Those who understand organizations as machines will not understand culture. A clock has no culture. Those who equate organizations with machines will understand culture as a shortcoming. Culture becomes a catch-all for everything that cannot be controlled by rules and instructions. This explains the boom in culture topics today: Initiatives that were still called strategy 15 years ago (quality strategy, zero-defect strategy, employee strategy, etc.) are now called culture: Innovation culture, feedback culture, risk culture.

3.2.1 What is culture?

Culture is a sum of observed habits that have taken root in a city, a family or an organization. Each of these systems has its own culture. To all the people in the system, in that culture, it seems quite normal to behave that way. You often only notice the culture when you come into another culture and encounter new habits, "the smell of the place". In England, everyone always gets to the back of the queue, but no one stops at a red pedestrian light unless a vehicle is coming. So which rules apply in England and which do not?

Culture, however, is not the same as rules. Culture is the instruction manual on how to interpret rules. Culture functions as a guide for correct behaviour. In this way, culture helps to guide behaviour.

Social systems need culture because there are alternatives. We could stop at a red light or we could cross the street. We could be on time for a meeting or not. Other than a clock, we have choices all the time. Where there are no alternatives, you don't need culture; therefore, a clock doesn't need culture. In other words, culture lives from the tension between should and can, from the freedom to either follow rules or ignore them. The way this freedom is dealt with is what we call culture.

For something to become part of the culture, it needs repetition. Just because someone gets to the back of the queue here and there, no behaviour becomes culture-shaping. Only through observed repetition, through cultivation and through rituals does culture emerge.

Why do social systems need culture?

Culture brings about integration, creates redundancy, organizes selection and processes complexity. The **integration effect is** noticeable in the "we-feeling". Like an invisible skin, it wraps itself around the team, the family, the city. We and the others. We here are different from the others. Integration comes about through observation and comparison. Often old, funny stories are told in which rule-breaking and how it was dealt with are made clear ("… there the boss just grabbed the delivery van …"). This helps to understand the rules and distinctions that apply here.

Every culture has its rituals and creates **redundancy** and thus reliability. If you are at home in this culture, you can rely on the fact that this is how things are done here without much effort of control. In some places, even if you are late, you are still let in at the theatre (not in Vienna!). In some board teams, you have to inform your colleagues before the meeting in order to get the decision through in the meeting. In this way, culture coordinates actions without having to write it down.

Culture has a **selective** effect on decisions and membership. For example, when pensioners are invited to company Christmas parties even though they are no longer with the company. On the other hand, not every new member has the same importance in the team, and statements on certain topics should not yet be made by new team members. In an existing culture, newcomers first have to familiarize themselves and gain acceptance. In this way, culture protects against free-riding.

Culture helps to process **complexity**. The environment is always more complex than the team, the organization. There is always more going on outside than inside. Somehow it has to be "decided" what the system will take into account. You can see this well in rule-based organizations, like government or hospitals, which have so many rules that you have to learn when to follow which ones and when not to. Culture does this through its rules of precedence.

The effect of a strong culture could be observed very nicely in some organizations during the crisis. They had a strong sense of 'we'. People tackled, ordered, communicated and acted without having to be asked to do so. Applicable rules, such as those about attendance or order quantities, were interpreted differently. Somehow everyone knew what to do. It turned out that organizations that had cultivated their culture were able to play it to the full. Those who had a resilient culture were better able to deal with complexity.

Disadvantages of culture

But culture also has two disadvantages: One is its non-controllability. You cannot change culture through decision-making, or to put it another way: If an attempt is made to change culture through decision-making alone, nothing changes. Companies that decide to adopt a new leadership model do not change leadership behaviour. If you want to change culture, you have to play outside the box, that is, use other decision-making premises to influence culture (Luhmann, 1976). Culture works, but it is difficult to influence in a targeted way. This is also and especially true in crises.

The second disadvantage of culture is the complexity of the concept. Culture is not a management concept, a set of rules, a resolution (Baecker, 2003). Culture is a second-order activity of observers, "a redescription of the descriptions that orient daily life" (Luhmann, 2002, p. 311). Understanding culture well becomes necessary if you want not only to maintain it, but to change it. In short, if you want to transform a culture, you should engage in theory, otherwise you can easily succumb to the temptations of simplification.

The advantages and disadvantages of culture are evident in digitalization, especially in virtual communication. The culture of a meeting with physical presence cannot be transferred one-to-one to a virtual meeting. But the quality of a virtual meeting is strongly influenced by the existing culture: Is everyone there the whole time? How attentive and prepared is everyone? How openly do people speak? Leadership and good facilitation play an even greater role here. We will go into further suggestions on how to deal with culture and communication in a virtual world in the section on social innovation (see Section 3.9).

Organizational culture—seen systemically

In practice, the theory and image of the iceberg by Ed Schein (2017; cf. Fig. 3.3) are very common and connectable.

Schein distinguishes three levels in a culture:

- **Artefacts** (artificially created)
  - technology, art
  - strategies, processes, structures
  - dress code, form of address
- **Values**
  - predetermined, not questionable
  - learned, verifiable in reality
- **Basic assumptions** about
  - Relationship of organization to environments
  - time, space, reality

Fig. 3.3. Iceberg model according to Ed Schein (2017)

- human nature
- social acts
- social relations

The iceberg model has one advantage besides comprehensibility: It shows that the formal side of an organization floats on a much larger set of informal assumptions and that one has to go deeper into the deep end to influence them. Unfortunately, in comprehensibility there is also the seduction to linear action: Just rearrange the artefacts or define the values and communicate them to everyone and the culture will change. This is not what Ed Schein had in mind, but many culture change processes have fallen for this fallacy.

An organization usually has several cultures. Systemically, we understand culture as a decision-making premise which

- in organizations such as the weather arose of its own accord and cannot be imagined without,
- is not the result of a formal decision, but influences decisions,
- cannot be directly influenced by decisions,
- addresses expectations and serves as an instruction manual in this culture,
- as a premise is usually not questioned,
- becomes part of a culture through imitation and repetition,
- used to be called an informal organization.

3.2.2 Changing organizational culture

In our consulting work, we receive requests time and again to change the culture of an organization in a targeted way. The background to these requests are often weighty changes in the environment: New competitors, strong globalization, introduction of a new technology, a different generation of employees. Previous strategy changes, a reorganization or management measures have not brought the desired results. As a result, in order to survive, the organization must also change its culture. Managers are now faced with the paradox of having to specifically change something that cannot be specifically changed. How can this be done?

Based on our experience, we recommend that before embarking on a targeted culture transformation, you should ask yourself the following questions:

1. What are the concrete concerns and questions behind this wish?
2. Is it culture change or culture maintenance?
3. Is it a cultural transformation, or is it merely a matter of cosmetic makeover, that is, of developing a show side (see below)?
4. What relevance does this issue have for the outside world?

Culture for the showcase

Every social system has a showcase: It is shown what it wants to be seen and what it wants to communicate about, thus protecting itself from topics it wants to avoid, for example, the current conflicts and scandals in the organization (Kühl, 2018).

Some of the so-called cultural processes are, therefore, meant to show a certain "show culture". One wants to be associated with certain values and messages. Therefore, at a career fair for new employees, for example, the innovativeness and team culture of an organization are often put on display. After all, that's what we humans do too: The nose piercing is supposed to suggest rebelliousness, the membership in the football club is supposed to suggest local ties or the conspicuously creative clothing is supposed to suggest being an artist.

In the same way, some of the so-called cultural projects serve as a showcase. The aim is to show the environment that work is being done on a certain topic, for example, on the culture of innovation, in order to demonstrate innovative strength. Mission statements are created because one would like to be seen that way and not otherwise. It feels good for many organizational members for some time to have such images. At the same time, just because a theme is on the front page, experienced employees will not get the idea that much should change internally. These expectations are mainly directed outwards and not towards the own system.

It is useful to distinguish three sides of an organization: The formal side (the decision-making premises), the informal side (the culture) and the appearance side (Kühl, 2018).

- **Formal level:**
  - the decision premises decided
  - the official rulebook
  - rules, procedures, organization chart
- **Informal level:**
  - undecided decision premises
  - the informal organization
  - the organizational culture
- **Show level:**
  - Outside of a social system
  - the facade

Of course, these three sides overlap. When we speak of culture hereafter, we mean the informal side, the inside. Instead of talking about values, we also recommend talking about expectations and naming what concrete behaviour is expected. These expectations become effective when they are supported by formal decisions, that is, when they can be attached to the outside of the triangle. Culture does not change through appeals alone.

3.2.3 Culture maintenance or culture change

It is important to distinguish whether a culture needs to be nurtured or transformed. The term "culture" comes from the Latin term *cultura* (= care, treatment). In organizations, cultivating culture is part of the day-to-day work of leadership: How do people treat each other? What is rewarded? What are the consequences of deviant behaviour? How open is communication? What gets collective attention? This is part of the everyday work of leadership. Cultivating culture is a leadership task and part of the "basic equipment" of a Moving Organization.

Culture maintenance is to be distinguished from the targeted transformation of an organizational culture. With culture transformation, we are in difficult terrain. It is important to proceed carefully here, because in culture transformation the "soft facts" become "hard facts" (Kotter, 2011). What appears to be soft becomes quite bulky as soon as it is to change. Cultural transformation is one of the most difficult and lengthy change projects and is particularly demanding in times of crisis. A crisis is an exceptional situation in which many rules of everyday life are suspended. How this happens and which rules then apply after all is "regulated" by the culture. Surely you have observed how your organization has been able to fall back on tried-and-tested cultural patterns, especially in phases of greatest stress. Formal decision-making premises, programmes—such as the product portfolio or the market strategy—or communication channels—such as the structural and procedural organization—even people are easier to change in a crisis than culture. Therefore, you should think carefully about whether and when you want to transform the culture and then proceed carefully.

What exactly is the Question?

Culture is en vogue again right now: Zero-defect culture, innovation culture, employee culture. Many topics are equipped with the concept of culture. Where people spoke of strategy years ago, they now use the term "culture". Presumably this renaming has to do with the fact that management has developed a different understanding of influence, a concession that one does not reach the goal in a direct way. Culture implies something different from strategy, presumably it also needs other actors.

However, we warn against cultural euphoria. When the term "culture" is applied to an issue, it usually becomes more vague and unwieldy. Instead of inflating an issue with the concept of culture, we suggest naming it as concretely as possible. Instead of talking about a lack of zero-defect culture, it is better to name the problems in shift handover. Usually, it is only a small section, it is some elements of the current situation that are dysfunctional, not the whole culture (Weick & Sutcliffe, 2016, p. 147).

Therein lies one of the great challenges of a cultural transformation, the precise description and definition of the desired behaviour. Both are complex and require know-how and diligence. When people talk about a culture of error and mistrust in a production company because they can't get a grip on certain quality problems, they won't get any closer to finding a solution through more culture. The art is to describe the issue in such a way that no blame is attributed, and then to name the desired behaviour in concrete terms.

This has been achieved with the dogs in Vienna. It is about reorientation and a kind of training programme that requires motivation to implement. Follow Schein's (1999, p. 189) advice and never start with the question: "How can I change our culture?". Instead, ask yourself the question: "What is the problem to be solved?

3.2.4 Culture and agility: Two sides of the same coin

Agile organizations use their culture. They have realized that they need to work on their culture.

Opportunities of cultural transformation

A helpful starting point is to make the desired image of culture explicit, to define cultural preferences in it and to develop practices that can be applied to concrete problems. The second step is to continuously reflect on the lived culture, that is, to observe it and regularly make it an issue.

Describing cultural preferences means describing desired behaviour in such a way that differences and deviations are recognized in everyday life. With this "frame of reference" (Weick & Sutcliff, 2016, p. 124), it becomes possible to interpret behaviour and communication rules. Especially in agile organizations, we have had good experiences with this kind of elaboration of cultural preferences, because it is an important competence for organizational members to be able to observe and name differences. It helps to describe current patterns and beliefs and to question their impact. These can then be used, for example, following Fink and Moeller (2018, p. 152ff), to formulate preferences. For example, by giving trust priority over power, or in other words, trust is more important to us than power.

After formulating the cultural preference, we recommend breaking it down into concrete actions, for example, before making a personnel decision, check whether the persons in question have the necessary professional qualifications as well as the trust of their colleagues.

For the second step and for the maintenance of cultural preferences, these need to be regularly monitored and discussed. In the example above, the question would be: "Did our staffing decisions really take into account the existing trust in the female candidates?" Or, "What have we done in the last year that has strengthened trust among ourselves?" Attention is paid to *how* people treat each other.

Challenges of cultural transformation

We have not had good experiences when the transformation to an agile organization is to be started with a culture project. Culture follows the decisions about programmes, communication channels and people, or rather accompanies them. Because *how the* programmes, communication channels and people are worked on should correspond to the desired culture. By the process of how transformation is worked on, one can often tell whether a culture change will succeed or not. This is shown by the following, unfortunately unsuccessful example.

The quality manager of a German industrial company contacted us: Lots of evaluations show that they have a massive problem with their error culture—small and large. Only recently, at one site, a project was planned for a long time and started with the implementation. This turned out to be a big mistake, because part of the production stood still for almost four weeks. It soon became clear that the women engineers knew that it would not work out as planned and had even voiced this, only the managers did not want to hear it. It had been known for a long time that employees in other factories were working imprecisely, even not tightening screws or forgetting tools in the product. Now the board was fed up with this error culture and wanted to change it fundamentally. The quality manager was given the task of starting an initiative that dealt with both the "hard facts" and the "soft facts" and named the issue of error culture. In addition, there were many agile initiatives going on in the organization and the manager felt that the issue of error culture was well suited to working according to these new agile principles.

After interviewing some stakeholders, we started with the core team. The diagnosis was made and the Neuwaldegg triangle was used to determine the directions. Concrete requirements for the organization in dealing with quality and errors were defined. Experts were gathered from all over the world to develop prototypes based on the requirements. The core team was very pleased with the results of the prototypes. Even the board and key stakeholders were there at the launch to support this initiative. Now it was a matter of developing it further and bringing it into the organization.

And suddenly things got bumpy. The decision-making body for the prototypes was a classic body with more than 25 participants that did not work according to agile principles and in which political action was common. The teams and their prototypes were literally dismantled and felt like they were being shown up. They experienced the opposite of a constructive error culture. The board wanted to see results quickly: Preferably training for people, because it was all about soft skills. Changes to routines, work processes and decision-making programmes were always put on hold and talked down. Somehow the core team kept getting the feeling that this initiative was slipping through their fingers. Until someone in the core team said, "I want an event with flags and good slogans. And best of all, a speaker and all the executives will go home happy. Can you set this up for us?" We also did not manage to get a common date with the boards for more than half a year. No sooner had an appointment been found than it was postponed again.

It was not long before the initiative was shut down. The quality manager realized that the change in error culture together with agile working did not fit the company. Even though not everything was in vain, we would still do things differently today, especially not link both topics, work more intensively with the decision-making body on our own self-image and drop out of the project after the second postponement of the board's deadline.

3.2.5 Our recommendations for the "culture, organization and transformation" lever

If you are planning to change your culture, we recommend that you check your plan against this checklist:

1. Do you have a clean diagnosis and can you describe exactly what the problem is?
2. Does your theme, the "Case for Action", have an external reference, that is, does anyone outside the organization (e.g. customers, suppliers, neighbours) notice when something changes and by what?
3. Is top management behind this initiative and aware that they should not demand quick results?

4. Can you avoid the term "cultural transformation" and instead name a specific topic?
5. Are there change agents (managers, experts) in the organization who know the organization well and fully support this project?

If you have been able to say yes at least four times, in our experience you can start the project. If not, you first have to do the necessary preparatory work. But if you want to get started, then we recommend:

- Form a core team with the above-mentioned change agents and work intensively with it, whereby qualified external advisors can be of great help here.
- Develop a concrete idea with the core team and with top management about what you expect and what the desired behaviour is.
- Work with the core team and management on theory, on understanding what constitutes culture, so that you can resist hasty answers.
- Avoid appeals and use targeted interventions that link to decidable decision premises (see triangle) so that the desired behaviour (e.g. always tighten screws) becomes routine.

At the beginning we asked you to imagine that you were a Viennese for the duration of this chapter. Now you have read the chapter and it could be your task to transform the culture of an organization. You have been brought in above all because of your Viennese qualities, because with all the professional know-how that you now bring with you, you will be able to bring a lot of patience and a good portion of Viennese charm to the table so that the project is successful. Good luck!

3.3 Lever 3: Purpose—the common good and transformation

Organizations are an important player in our society. They influence it: Our relationship with nature and also how we shape our daily lives. Their influence is undisputed. Time and again, however, the feeling arises that organizations are primarily concerned with their own advantage and are only concerned with becoming ever more efficient. What may seem right from an optimization perspective may not always make sense from a societal perspective. Organizations are embedded in a larger societal context on which they have an impact and which they need. These interactions are becoming more and more relevant in the increased uncertainty and also due to crises. Many examples, including scandals, show that today more than ever it is necessary for organizations to rethink their own role, responsibilities and contributions to society. They are challenged to take a stand and ask themselves what they want to contribute to.

In our view, this is what the Purpose can do. Purpose can be understood as a process in which the organization reflects on its role in society, in its eco-system. It is more powerful when it integrates the aspect of the common good (Meynhardt, 2020) and describes what organizations can and want to contribute to society. Figuratively speaking, it is like building a new apartment building. It can be planned in such a way that it only serves the needs of the residents and the neighbouring residents only have the legally provided possibilities to object. However, the housing complex can also be designed in such a way that it integrates well into the neighbourhood and how it can benefit the neighbourhood is considered. This means aligning the purpose with the common good. However, this is not the only response Purpose can provide.

Purpose can do much more. Used as a steering element in an organization, it provides orientation in complex and uncertain times. Purpose gives meaning to actions and acts as a magnet in crises: All decisions can be aligned with it. Orienting oneself to the Purpose is, of course, a decision that an organization has to make. We call these Purpose-Driven Organizations and describe them below. They have an advantage: They fulfil something essential that efficiency-driven organizations often lack, namely the longing of people to see themselves as relevant members, to know the meaning of their own contributions to the whole and also to be able to personally stand behind the decisions of the organization. A Purpose takes up all these aspects and thus creates a different kind of confrontation: Instead of personal distancing, people ask themselves whether they can be proud of the organization. Instead of separation, connectedness emerges, instead of increased efficiency, resonance emerges. And suddenly the focus is no longer on separating work and private life, but experiences of connectedness emerge. And this in turn pays off in terms of our basic psychological needs (see Section 3.5.1; Rosa, 2019).

There are enough organizations geared towards efficiency and effectiveness: International law firms, management consultancies, IT and telecommunications companies, but also non-profit organizations such as hospitals are examples of this. Some glide across the sea like soulless ships and they do not know what they are underway for. These organizations often have a permanently high turnover of staff who no longer see any point for themselves in working in these factories.

Organizations that are facing huge changes, such as media companies, financial service providers, railway companies and mobility providers, also have orientation problems. They are well established in their market, but markets are breaking away and digitalization threatens their business model. They have to solve many fundamental questions quickly, seek orientation in this complex situation and have to radically rethink. Carrying on as before is then not an option.

In both cases, it helps to clarify the questions: "What do we exist for as an organization, what contribution do we want to make to the community and what do we want to achieve?", "What is the real purpose of what we do?", "What is our purpose?"

In an exceptional situation, in a crisis, when everything around collapses, a purpose provides valuable services. If an organization knows what it exists for, it can prioritize and decide. An example: A global distributor of speciality chemical products was able to remain operational in the Corona times despite disrupted supply chains, idle factories and closed borders, because it had its Purpose: We are a stable and reliable partner for our suppliers, customers and society and are happy to put ourselves out there to help them succeed. Thus, even if it was not always possible to deliver, the information chain was maintained and maximum transparency was promoted for all those involved. The staff knew what to do and the partners had some security in the crisis.

There is always a reason why an organization was founded, that is, the purpose is always there, it is just not always expressed and used. In order to use a purpose, it has to be explicitly put into words.

"Purpose" is the technical term for the contribution an organization wants to make to society and the impact it wants to have. If the contribution is excellent technology that is to be used for as long as possible (impact), the purpose can be formulated as "technology for life", as in the example of Bosch. Or the Berlin company Soulbottle, which formulated: "We make it easier for people to behave sustainably with drinking bottles that are 100 per cent plastic-free, climate-neutral and fairly produced in Germany. Because all people want to consume without unnecessarily burdening the planet and have access to clean drinking water."

Organizations that actively use the Purpose know the reason for their existence and thus become more resilient (see Chapter 2). They describe their contribution to the community and use the Purpose for their decisions. We refer to such organizations as Purpose-Driven Organizations (Fink & Moeller, 2018). They use purpose to guide their decisions in the same way that other companies use their market strategy to set priorities. They use the insight that people prefer to work in Purpose-Driven Organizations because, as studies show, they are more successful than others. They grow faster, have more engaged employees and more intense customer loyalty (Meynhardt, 2020).

In Purpose-Driven Organizations, purpose is a central decision-making programme that is integrated into corporate governance, provides orientation and describes an organization's contribution to shaping the world. Purpose is the tool of choice when it comes to alignment and the long-term social legitimacy (common good) of organization (Gomez, 2019).

3.3.1 The Purpose-Driven Organization

Let's take a look into the world of a very well-established media company (which you are already somewhat familiar with from previous chapters): We see successes, slumps and upheavals, old and current products, increasing digitalization and the "Case for Action". The company is facing a market change. All the facts and figures show that the company needs a new business model quickly, which has to fundamentally reposition itself due to digitalization. When the company was founded, there was still a clear understanding that its own strength lay in its special regional connection. No one knew the region as well as they did, and for this they developed products and services that until recently were easy to sell. Their founding idea had been buried until the market crisis announced itself. Now it was time to revitalize the purpose and bring it into a current context. So "back to the roots", because if we know what we exist for, we can master any crisis!

Purpose captures the meaning and purpose of organizations and fulfils two functions (Fink & Moeller, 2018, p. 24f):

- **The emotional dimension:** People search for meaning and want to understand their existence and their actions in the world. Meaning in positive psychology is an important factor in motivation and life satisfaction. People who know what they are working for flourish. The psychologist Viktor Frankl, who survived the concentration camp, impressively described the importance of finding meaning (Frankl, 1977). Organizations that can explain what they contribute to society thus create motivation and retention for their employees.
- **The factual-contentual dimension:** Purpose is a programme of purpose and serves to steer organizations. It provides orientation for fundamental questions (sense of direction) and describes the "why", that is, why this organization exists. Every organization has a reason why it was created and why it exists, but often this reason is buried and must be uncovered and named, as is the case with our company.

Organizations that put purpose at the centre of their actions are called Purpose-Driven Organizations (PDO). They are an effective counter-model to organizations that see themselves as optimization machines. These are interested in maximum efficiency, in improving the input-output ratio in order to continuously increase

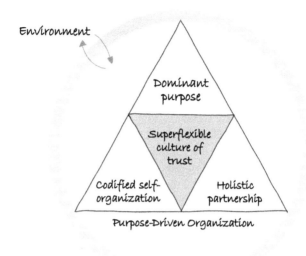

Fig. 3.4. Purpose-Driven Organization according to Fink and Moeller (2018)

their performance. Their strategy, business processes, hierarchical organization, understanding of power, leadership and culture all serve to increase efficiency.

A Purpose-Driven Organization is guided by another principle, the Purpose. This does not mean that efficiency no longer plays a role, it has just lost its dominance, because another principle that helps to clarify fundamental issues has become more important. A Purpose-Driven Organization can be described in terms of five disciplines. We follow Fink and Moeller (2018, p. 77f), who have elaborated these in a differentiated way and describe here the difference to efficiency-oriented organizations.

First discipline: Dominant purpose

Efficiency is being replaced by purpose. Purpose is a decision-making programme, just like strategies, the product range or working time regulations. The purpose of decision programmes is to be able to determine whether individual decisions are being made correctly. Has the new production line increased efficiency? Does the purchase of a supplier support the strategy? PDO uses Purpose as the dominant principle to guide decisions. Decisions are reviewed to see if they support the Purpose. Do you recruit people who are purpose-fit, who help develop the purpose? Does our market strategy help to realize the Purpose? The principle of a decision is then no longer just profitability, but its relevance to purpose and the review of one's own actions against the purpose.

Second discipline: Codified self-organization

This discipline regulates the communication channels, that is, the processes, organizational structures and meeting architecture. The hierarchical structure with the concentration of power in a few functions is replaced by distributed authorities, free spaces and rules. The term "codified self-organisation" is used to describe the interplay between existing free spaces (self-organization) and the necessary rules and processes. This discipline is of great importance for the daily use of Purpose in everyday organizational life. Much can be done here to live the Purpose concretely. Teams play a major role in the Moving Organization (see Sections 3.8 and 5.2.31).

Third discipline: Holistic partnership

The third discipline includes people, their skills, competences and also recruiting processes and human resource development. In traditional organizations, a lot of things are for career development. In a PDO, people have many opportunities and are upgraded. It does not become easier for them, but more challenging. For a PDO, individuals are essential with their qualifications, their attitudes and their willingness to learn. This is why the purpose fit, the alignment with the organization's purpose, is so important. The term "holistic partnership" expresses the relationship to the "whole"—to the purpose—and the way of dealing with each other in partnership, not based on power. We have described in various chapters of this book how this difficult transition from a traditional leadership to a partnership-based attitude can succeed (cf. Sections 3.5, 3.6 and 3.7).

Fourth discipline: Super-flexible culture of trust

Culture is the fourth discipline. As explained in Section 3.2, culture in efficiency-oriented organizations is a residual variable, a kind of overproduction that has to be accepted. It is quite different in PDO: How people deal with each other, how rules are used and also circumvented, are a central theme. Culture is cultivated, the impact of decisions of the other four disciplines on culture, especially on trust, is taken into account. Without a culture of freedom from fear and trust, no PDO or moving organization can exist. The cultivation of trust has a purpose: It serves the super-flexible realization of Purpose. Superflexibility is the "simultaneous provision for resilience and agile development" (Fink & Moeller, 2018, p. 150). For this, we need teams as a social system in which work and learning can take place (see Section 3.8).

Fifth discipline: Co-evolution in the ecosystem

The fifth discipline deliberately emphasizes the networking of organizations with their environments. In traditional organizations, this discipline does not occur, or it serves as a showcase to present itself well to the outside world, according to the motto: Pro bono we work with NGOs in selected projects, but this has no significance for our core business. PDOs are different: They start with this discipline by looking at their purpose, their position and their contribution to society, also called public value (Moore, 2013). By elaborating and harnessing purpose, PDOs define themselves as contributors to society, concerned not only about their own well-being but also about the evolution of their ecosystem. Through "co-evolution in the ecosystem", mutual influence is emphasized, exploring and developing new solutions together.

3.3.2 Five phases: The purpose in the transformation process

The book *Purpose Driven Organisations* (Fink & Moeller, 2018) comprehensively describes how a purpose is developed and how different methods can be used depending on the starting situation. In this book, we will show how the purpose can be used as an intervention in a transformation process.

To this end, we return to our media house. It sees the crisis coming: We know from other countries what happens when nothing is done. The board decides, after prolonged insistence by the leadership team, to start a transformation process. A transformation team with external advice is put together and begins its work. After three months, a purpose statement is formulated in an initial team. After that, the rest of the organization is involved: All 700 employees are invited to groups of 120–200 participants in large events. The mood at the beginning is sceptical, the uncertainty of the employees in the room is palpable. Their feelings were similar to those of the board or the managers at the beginning. But to get this far, the process had to go through five phases, which we will describe step by step.

Phase 1: Deep Dive and Explore—Understanding, Immersion and Strategic Corridor

The first thing is to make sure that everyone understands the "Case for Action" well: What are the motivations for our transformation process? What happens if

Purpose in agile transformation

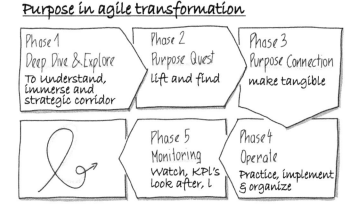

Fig. 3.5. Purpose process in an agile transformation

nothing happens? How are which developments in the market related to our current situation? Figures, data and facts are presented that illustrate the economic challenges, show the problem areas and depict scenarios. Trends are described that, if continued, will lead to a survival crisis.

But that is not enough. We need a broader view and a broader understanding: What else is happening in our immediate and wider environment? How is digitalization affecting us? How strongly are we networked and who are our important stakeholders? What makes our customers tick, what are their perspectives?

In this phase, it is important to gather a lot of information and not to draw conclusions too early, that is, to remain open as long as possible for what may come. We say "hold the tension!". The leadership team and the transformation team have gone on learning journeys, connected with networks and attended countless congresses in order to evaluate everything at the end and create a strategic corridor.

The strategic corridor is like a cash audit: What seems relevant on the basis of the current information? Which stakes do we want and need to knock down? Which fields need to be transformed? How radically do we want to proceed with savings and investments? Which basic principles should guide us in the future? Which concerns do we want to realize?

At this point at the latest, all participants realize that orientation and a common starting point are important. When it is clear what the organization has in front of it, the need for orientation, identity and inner fire that gives drive arises.

Phase 2: Purpose quest—Lifting and finding the purpose

Now that the strategic corridor is clear, it is possible to start with a purpose quest, the technical term for the search for purpose. There are many methods for this, which are described in detail in the book by Fink and Moeller (2018). It is important that everyone starts from the same basis and understands why it is being started now. The purpose group should be carefully put together. A good mix of management, executive board, young and older employees, members representing the future, representatives of the different areas, is important.

When you start a Purpose Quest, make sure it is facilitated. It is incredibly difficult to be both a participant and a facilitator. Be prepared for emotional highs and lows. Usually, just before you can put the purpose statement into words, things get particularly bad. Now it's time to take a deep breath and endure, it pays off! Because after the low come the really productive thoughts.

We have learned to work with a purpose statement that corresponds to a rough draft and only has to fit 80 per cent. It may well be that this is also adapted after some time. "Safe enough to try" takes the pressure off the participants that everything has to be perfect. It helps if the statement doesn't go down like oil. Something that is well prepared but still unfinished (rule of thumb two-thirds to one-third) opens up and invites participation. Conversely, this means that something that is fully formulated can only be approved or contradicted. We don't want either of these with the Purpose! The Purpose is meant to invite engagement, we want words to be discussed again and again. Meaning is created through discussion, which develops an emotional bond and sharpens the statement. It is also not a marketing slogan and does not have to be 100 per cent understandable or sound nice to others. This work is similar to that of archaeologists: First you need coarse tools to dig away the earth, only then you have to work with fine brushes.

Phase 3: Purpose connection—Making the purpose tangible

Most people who have experienced a purpose quest are euphoric and do not understand why others do not react in the same way. Often you will even hear from non-participants: "What, it took you so long?" Your own experience is difficult for others to comprehend. The purpose statement is not just a sentence, it is an experience that makes the purpose of the organization clear. The purpose should be revealed to everyone anew. It has to be experienced and is not grasped by reading alone.

At our media house, we let the large group experience the Purpose Statement. By the way, the event was called "We want meaning!" Our invitation was: Help us to better describe the meaning of our existence! This was very well received by many, but not everyone was enthusiastic. That is also not necessary. What we wanted to achieve with this large group was, firstly, to win over many Purposers, as we call people who have experienced a Purpose process and carry it forward. And secondly, to bring the members of the organization deeper into the transformation process and to encourage them to participate.

The following principles were helpful in designing **Purpose connection**:

- Make the Purpose connection your own process that fits your organization and incorporates internal elements. It helps to set up an internal team to prepare and draft the statement. Cross-departmental work is essential here.
- This team is particularly effective and creative when it consists of an interdisciplinary mix of roles and different people.
- Make sure that future purposers have the opportunity to understand and deepen the strategic corridor.
- Use purposers by having them be interlocutors for future purposers and tell them about their experiences.
- Purpose is a dialogical intervention and needs many conversations.
- The Purpose connection is a wonderful participatory lever in the transformation process. Here many can experience the organization as their own organization.

Phase 4: Operate—Operationalize and organize the Purpose

This phase is about implementation, for which the following steps are helpful:

1. **Purpose hierarchy:** We like to start with the top management and the transformation team. They are the first to try out and test what energy this unleashes. Next, teams and roles are asked to describe their purpose and thus create the bridge between their activity and the organizational purpose. We recommend proceeding top-down, this way you create more momentum.
2. **Align initiatives in a purpose-oriented way:** Initiatives are defined on the basis of the strategic corridor. Each initiative is guided by the purpose statement and develops a specific purpose description for itself. We use the transformation team—which has its own role, the purpose steward—to steer this step, give feedback and pay attention to the purpose fit. Again and again, this role takes the perspective of the Purpose, for example, during a review where

current results are shown, and tells about the effect created and what is still needed more or less from this perspective.

3. **Develop Purpose practices:** One initiative is always to bring Purpose into the organization. For example, in the "We want purpose" event, the following teams were found: One team has the task to find practices and principles that support individuals, teams or areas to align their own work with the Purpose. Another team has the task of supporting meetings to become purpose-fit. Another team supports peers from different areas so that they have the opportunity to exchange with each other.

Phase 5: Monitoring

At some point, the Purpose development and implementation project comes to an end and the focus shifts. Now it is important to keep the Purpose well in sight. Now there is no need for a dedicated team, it helps to define your own roles that take on the task of the Purpose Steward: An outward-focused role and an inward-focused role. The outward-focused role pays attention to social developments and those of the relevant environments. The inward-looking role ensures that the purpose remains in view and that adjustments are made again and again.

3.3.3 Our recommendations for the Purpose lever

Purpose is not a panacea, but it is a good counterbalance to a one-sided efficiency orientation. The statement describes the contribution and the intended impact— "What do we want to contribute to the common good?"—are described. Purpose statements always describe a contribution and are not avoidance statements, such as "We are against environmental pollution". They restate the well-known motto "He who asks, leads" by calling it "He who contributes, leads" (Gomez, 2019). It is about a "for" and not an "against". They create meaning by connecting in the organization and to society.

We recommend using the Purpose for steering, especially in the transition from more traditional organizations to moving organizations. Firstly, it provides orientation, energy and support in difficult times, be it in a crisis or in the change itself. As one staff member put it in the middle of the Corona crisis: "The Purpose works like Bepanten (a wound healing ointment) right now". Secondly, it establishes a relevant connection to the environment which, if you take it seriously, will strengthen the organization's raison d'être in our society in the long term (see tools in Sections 5.2.7 and 5.2.8).

If you use Purpose for yourself in the conversion, pay attention to the following aspects:

- Involve different stakeholders in the purpose quest, and top management must be involved.
- Create a strategic corridor in which the Purpose is embedded.
- Use the participatory power that lies in this process.
- Make the Purpose process an individual and unique Purpose experience.
- Understand Purpose not as a marketing tool, but as an experiential process that is deepened through dialogue and only works through "connection".
- Develop practices that can be experienced in daily work.
- A purpose does not have to be 100 per cent beautiful and fit. It helps if it doesn't go down like oil, because that's how conflict happens.

3.4 Lever 4: Role-taking, role-making and role diversity

Some time ago, a blogger interviewed us on the topic of new work and asked us how organizations can integrate the whole person with all their facets. Our counter-question was: Do you really want that? Our counterpart was visibly irritated and at the same time we started an interesting discussion: Where does this desire come from and why does this concern fall short from our point of view?

We all live in a context that produces social and global dynamics. These developments are called megatrends and influence individuals as well as organizations. The most important in our context are[6]:

- We live in a knowledge culture: The fact that knowledge is not an exclusive good and is multiplying incredibly fast means that we need new forms of collaboration and learning so that we can make a meaningful contribution.
- Digital connectivity is fundamentally changing us: Digital networking and new communication technologies are shaping new behaviour patterns, demands and lifestyles. In order for individuals to keep up, other skills are needed with which to act in these networks without losing orientation.
- Individualization of our society: More and more people have the freedom of choice. This changes our values, ideas, consumption patterns and everyday life in our society. At the same time, this trend promotes, for example, the desire for a sense of togetherness. For organizations, this can sometimes be a

---

6   See: https://www.zukunftsinstitut.de/dossier/megatrends/ (retrieval date: 14.06.2020)

paradox: People want to develop themselves to the maximum and at the same time want to belong and feel secure in a group.

- New work and digitalization throw us back to our humanity: As more and more machines will take over our work and we as humans are not irreplaceable, the meaning of work moves more and more into the centre. If work no longer needs us, what do we need it for? It is less and less about rational decisions and more about the development of potential and one's own contribution. At the same time, this also creates uncertainty for many, because we as individuals do not know what our contribution can be in the future or how we can sustain ourselves.

These trends make it clear why we humans are looking for meaningful working relationships in which learning and development is possible, we need security and a sense of "we" should also emerge: For this, people and their needs must be at the centre. This is also one of the reasons why more and more concepts and methods that take up these aspects are attracting interest: Be it in Reinventing Organization by Frederike Laloux (2016), Theory U by Otto Scharmer (2020) or in Purpose Driven Organizations by Fink and Moeller (2018).

3.4.1 Differentiation between person and role

For decades, organizations have removed human aspects from the organization under the slogan of Taylorization (see Section 1.3.4) and trimmed it for efficiency. And now, one might think, people and their needs are returning to the organization. This is suggested by the trends mentioned above. But therein lies a danger. That is why we will take a closer look at the relationship between the person and the organization.

The success story of organizations shows that they have to focus on their purpose in order to remain viable, and, therefore, their members have to adopt this purpose. This is virtually imposed on them. From the organization's point of view, this is highly effective because the focus is precisely on what the organization needs. Organizations do not feel responsible for everything else that occupies people, all their private concerns, this should remain "outside" (Kühl, 2015, p. 69f). "Bring your whole self to work" would remove precisely this focus. Organizations would have to permanently take care of all the needs of their employees: From love and sexuality to domestic problems and the children's wedding. Total overload would be the result.

In this dilemma, exclusive purpose orientation and dominant person focus, the role concept and the active use of role-free spaces are helpful for organizations (Section 3.8.2). We want to turn our attention here to individuals and roles.

Individuals enter organizations through their roles and thereby become members. By defining roles, the context relevant to them is delimited and it is clarified what their tasks can be. Depending on who I appoint to a role, that role will be filled differently. And suddenly it becomes clear: Only through the differentiation of role and person do the personal parts of a person become visible. Only through this differentiation of role and person does it become observable that role performance can take on a personal style (Kühl, 2016, p. 108ff; Luhmann, 1997, p. 771f).

Even if this insight is not new, the distinction between person and role helps because roles are a central component in moving organizations

- People take on many (often between 4 and 20) different roles and do not have just one function, such as a marketing expert. This brings more accurate and diverse perspectives and observations to the organization.
- Roles help to make the purpose and requirements for the role bearers explicit and link expectations of the organization with performance. In other words, it is about consciously dealing with roles and expectations in the organization, which should always be adapted to the current context.
- Roles can be changed more easily and more frequently, allowing for more flexibility. A role rarely sticks to one person and is passed on in the sense of developing at the personal and organizational level.
- It also makes it easier to meet the developmental needs of individuals because certain roles can be aligned with their personal development.
- Roles are not all that occupy people, and people are not reduced to their roles. In a moving organization, time and space must be made available for the personal parts and abilities.

3.4.2 Roles in moving organizations

As the aspects of roles described above show, moving organizations is not about classic jobs or function descriptions. Rather, it is about multiple roles that are linked to explicit expectations and requirements, and are constantly adapting. In order for this to work well at the person level, it is important for people in moving organizations to differentiate personal and role-related challenges and to find a good way of dealing with them. The idea would be: "I am not one role, but I have several roles".

A good metaphor for this way of dealing with roles in organizations is the theatre: Plays describe roles and action quite precisely. The actresses, therefore, also move within this framework. From our point of view, this is similar in classical organizations. For moving organizations, we would choose improvisational theatre, figuratively speaking: Here the actors also act in roles. But they act in the uncertain and unplanned, they fill roles in the here and now, they cooperate radically in the respective moment, they change roles constantly and spontaneously, deal with mistakes with relish, resonate with the audience, allow themselves to be touched emotionally by the audience, are creative and continuously learn something new. What looks like an easy game on stage is practised by the actresses for a long time through certain practices until they are more confident in what they are doing. Interruption is not an option; it is important to stay in the flow. That is why all actors train for at least a year before they appear on stage.

And it is precisely these skills and attitudes of improvisation that role models need. This is also the reason why these principles of improvisation are now used in the work context. Here is an overview of the most important ones (Schinko-Fischli, 2018, p. 16f):

- Being in the here and now: Stripping everything away and focusing all your attention in the present moment—that's important when improvising. It's not about planning and thinking about how everything should go. The focus is entirely on the momentary interaction: Listening, observing, perceiving oneself, feeling one's own and other impulses. This means working with uncertainty, preferably with as little effort as possible.
- "Yes, and" attitude: Surely you know this: You make a suggestion and someone else says: "Yes, but ...". At that moment, you feel that the energy is out and you have little desire to continue the thoughts. Therefore, it is important to learn to accept and transform offers in order to adopt a "yes, and" attitude. This is how co-creation happens and the energy flows easily.
- "Let the other person shine": Co-creation and trust happens when everyone can be trusted to shine. By stepping back and allowing others to contribute and experience wonderful moments, you strengthen the whole system. It is not about individuals shining, but about creating something new together.
- Pleasurable failure: Anyone who is courageous and tries out new things makes mistakes and will also fail sometimes. The point here is to experience the joy of failure and mistakes, to find a good way of dealing with them and not to let yourself be blocked: This helps in situations where creativity and innovation are needed.

These four principles of improvisational theatre help us to clarify from the beginning how we understand roles in Moving Organizations: A role is embedded in a context that has a specific purpose, but is very dynamic, offers a variety of possibilities and requires a high degree of willingness to improvise. Therefore, people need a willingness to take responsibility for themselves and clarity in the role itself in order to be able to perform it well.

3.4.3 Role-taking and role-making

Role-taking is particularly successful when the process of *role-taking* is well designed. Therefore, people should not only be appointed, as would be the case in an office. Rather, it is about actively slipping into the respective roles so that they can fulfil them well in the future. We have had good experiences with creating rituals for new role assumption: An official act in a meeting so that everyone is aware of the new role.

Another step in role-taking is to make the expectations of the organization, the leader and the team members explicit: What competences are needed to perform the role, what ways of working are expected and what skills and competences are to be brought into the role and developed for it? We experience a deep examination of the purpose, tasks, expectations and scope for decision-making as very supportive.

In agile *role-making*, we place great emphasis on three things: The role description, the shaping or energizing of the role in daily activities and the dynamic clarification of expectations.

In a first step, we invite the employees to describe their own roles: What roles are taken? What is the name and purpose of the role? What activities and results can be expected from this role? What may be decided, what not? For this purpose, we usually use the framework provided by Holacracy with our clients (see Section 2.3). These collected descriptions are recorded, deepened in the teams and presented transparently in the organization: Every colleague should be able to see at any time what the tasks of the respective role are and what can be expected from this role.

The second task is to energize the roles in "daily business" and to use them as an anchor point on an ongoing basis. In everyday life, this is done by working through tasks and resolving tensions. Tensions are differences between what is now and what is possible in the future (see Section 2.3 for more details). The following practices help to make role-making a success:

- Next action of the roles: Next steps and/or projects for which each role is responsible and when they will be taken.
- Role self-reflection: Writing down what was done in the respective roles, what was achieved and what can be learned from this for the future.
- Transparent role reflection: An additional step is to make these reflections transparent to the team.

- Role feedback: Actively seek and encourage role feedback in teams or from peers.
- Role innovation: Creating space and time to rethink roles.
- Role-competence challenge: The role bearers can also develop their competences and link them to the roles. What else would be beneficial or helpful to support the purpose of the role and this team well? What can be learned?

The third task in a moving organization is to make the described roles transparent for everyone, to clarify them with the expectations of others, to adjust them again and again and to clear them out. Dynamic role clarification in moving organizations means clarifying what the role is supposed to do, what powers or rights the role has, what expectations need to be readjusted so that the purpose of the role and the team can be fulfilled. The core task is to make implicit expectations explicit, to clarify them in the team and to formalize this on an ongoing basis. In Holacracy, this is done through the governance meeting. In other organizations we introduce regular role reflections for this purpose (see also the Meeting mastery tool in Section 5.2.31). If this is done regularly, it has the character of system maintenance according to the motto: We check whether everything is still distributed sensibly and whether all the needs of our environment are still covered.

Again and again, we are asked what the difference is to job descriptions: Job descriptions are often far less concrete and hardly change. If organizations only did what is written in a job description, a lot of things would not work. In very few cases do these serve as points of orientation in daily work and are almost never developed further by the role holders or those directly affected. In traditional organizations, one is given a job and fleshes it out as one thinks it makes sense. Expectations of others are rarely made explicit. The job description is an entry-level document and sometimes provides support in cases of conflict. It is rarely an occasion for clarifying expectations, and does not provide an impetus for dialogue and further adjustment. In moving organizations, on the other hand, role holders have the attitude "many brains lead to a better result", and so expectations and tensions are permanently clarified. How this can be done and what skills are needed for this is described in more detail in Section 3.6 when it comes to development, individual skills and teams.

3.4.4 Perceive role diversity

In the moving organization, it is common for people to take on many roles—often between four and twenty roles. Some roles are very small, others are larger and more significant. It is important that you make use of this diversity of roles. Managing many roles is unfamiliar and can be confusing. Establish a system to have a good overview. Visualization helps: Digital overview of roles, analogue visualization on a board, place cards for the desk, cards to hang around your neck in meetings, and so on. At the American online shoe retailer Zappos, for example, each employee receives a batch for each role, which is handed over and hung around her neck when she takes on that role. Later, the batches hang on a hook at the respective seat and are taken to meetings to make it clear with which role one is currently participating.

In contact with others, it is helpful to clarify from which role one is acting. You can imagine roles like hats and put them on: "From my role in marketing I move …", "In my role as Happy Moments Manager I initiate …". This helps the others to identify the role from which the colleagues are currently acting. Conversely, someone may approach you and ask you what role you are currently acting out of.

People who have many different roles appreciate the variety of creative possibilities, as very different abilities and sides of the personality can be expressed. However, they also feel torn again and again, and this is the other side of the coin. They are servants of many ladies and gentlemen, that is, different roles with different role expectations. But what can be individually stressful for the individual makes sense for the organization as a whole. Therefore, it is important to always keep a good eye on dealing with role diversity and to establish routines as an organization that make it easier to deal with it (see Section 3.8).

3.4.5 Our recommendations for the role-taking, role-making and role diversity lever

A moving organization needs people and defined roles. Only roles create the necessary clarity in organizations so that people can act and different perspectives and perceptions of the organization are provided. The sensorium of the moving organization is broadened by roles, for example, ten people can become up to 100 roles.

We recommend that you rather define (too) many roles when new expectations arise, document them, and make the roles and how they are perceived a common topic again and again. It is helpful if you differentiate between two perspectives: The one on the person himself/herself with his/her personality, needs and competences, and the one on the role and the demands and expectations associated with it. Both contexts need different frameworks and discussion situations so that they can unfold well (see also Sections 3.5, 3.6 and 3.8 and tool in Section 5.2.11).

3.5 Lever 5: Organization as a resonance space for growth and development

Even if defined roles are a central feature of a moving organization, people must not be forgotten. On the contrary, people are given more and more space. They want to develop and pay attention to how their needs are taken into account. In a first step, we want to shed light on which basic needs of people are relevant in organizations. In the second step, we will delve into the concept of Deliberately Developmental Organizations (DDO) by Lisa Lahey and Robert Kegan (2016), who take up the development of people in the organizational context very consistently.

3.5.1 Basic needs of people

Moving organizations claim to take the concerns of their employees seriously, and in this regard a look at the basic psychological needs of people helps. Psychologist Klaus Grawe has further developed Seymour Epstein's theory of basic needs (Grawe, 2004, p. 187 ff; Epstein, 1990; Klinkhammer et al., 2015, p. 75f):

1. **Need for attachment:** Every human being needs attachment to other people. We are born into a social system, that of the family and the clan, and are embedded in it. From an evolutionary point of view, being part of a community is essential for our survival. Alone, we would be condemned to death, as humans themselves are physically too weak to face the challenges of survival. This need is deeply anchored in us and cannot be switched off. It is also the reason why rejection and refusal put us in a panic mode: Pain-like states are triggered by our brain because a subconscious existential danger arises for us. That is why every desire for attachment is also accompanied by attachment anxiety. Only through social behaviour do we strengthen ourselves, when the desire for attachment is satisfied, motivation is triggered, which in turn releases attachment hormones. This is why prosocial behaviour is also rewarded. At this point, moving organizations ask themselves how this need for community can be met. At the same time, they know that as soon as the question of membership arises, which is often the case in transformations, this fear dominates and makes much else unimportant.

2. **Need for orientation and control:** In order to gain security in our everyday life, we need points of orientation. We achieve this by creating goals and checking them again and again: Did we achieve them or not? We create our reality on the basis of these experiences. And we use this wealth of experience to make the consequences of our options for action more predictable. To do this, our brain constantly scans our experiences and tries to make predictions: "With whom do I go into confrontation—with whom rather not? In which regions am I safe, in which not?" Since errors can be a matter of survival, generalizations serve as a further point of orientation and thus seem to make situations controllable. This is why they are defended particularly tenaciously: "We have been doing it this way for years …", "We have never done it this way …". Moving organizations therefore think carefully: What are the safe zones that individuals can orient themselves to when there is a lot going on.

3. **Need for self-esteem protection and self-esteem enhancement:** Only humans have this basic need. It is only through social interaction and linguistic communication that awareness arises and one's own self-worth can be derived. Questions we ask ourselves in the process are: "What value do I ascribe to myself as a person?" and "What role do I play in the lives of others?" Again, rejection is perceived as pain and acceptance is rewarded by our brain. A strong driver in this is meaning in one's actions, knowing one's contribution to the bigger picture and growing in the process. Depending on what we experience, we protect or enhance ourselves. Moving organizations actively addresses this aspect: How can development be shaped by individuals and how do they experience their self-worth? What practices do the members have among themselves?

4. **Need for pleasure gain and displeasure avoidance:** We humans quickly distinguish between harmful and life-giving influences by making good-bad judgments. The feeling for this would be "woe" or "yay" and arises in milliseconds. We associate things, events and behaviours with either reward or punishment and therefore act accordingly. The danger aversion system sits in the almond nuclei of our brain, stores negative emotional experiences and develops avoidance schemes, such as not wanting to go to the dentist. The second system is an approach system: This part in the brain is the positive emotional memory, tracks down possible reward expectations and provides motivation for this through hormones. Through the interaction of both systems, different action designs emerge that lead to actions. It is at this point that moving organizations picks up on people's reflective capacities and creates spaces for them: When does this rapid assessment occur? What are

my personal trigger points and are they justified? When is my quick feeling useful, when is it hindering and not adequate?

5. **Consistency regulation and incongruence:** This is more a principle than a need. Consistency regulation means the compatibility of mental processes running simultaneously and concerns all basic needs. In principle, we can say that we humans prefer consistency and avoid inconsistency. In concrete terms, this means that we prefer our experiences and perceptions to be coherent and to make sense to us. If this is the case, positive feelings are triggered. If this is not the case, for example, by not achieving goals or perceiving inconsistencies, incongruence is experienced. This triggers negative feelings and increases the stress level. Such experiences, therefore, lead to approach or avoidance behaviour. Moving organizations are aware that a common purpose is supportive and they create spaces where people are given the opportunity to work through incongruities, as these are important for development.

The neurobiologist Gerald Hüther sums up the basic needs of us humans as follows: Experiencing connectedness with other people gives us safety and security and we need a "nest" that we can visit again and again. And at the same time, we want to be able to grow ourselves by exploring the world autonomously and freely. In doing so, we want to grow beyond ourselves and develop further by finding our own individual self-expression (Hüther, 2017). These two, at first sight contradictory, needs occupy us throughout our lives. Which of these basic needs is of particular importance to the employees of a moving organization and how they can be given space can be determined more precisely—as we will see in a moment—on the basis of the practices of a DDO.

3.5.2 DDO: Deliberately Developmental Organizations

The concept of Deliberately Developmental Organizations by Lisa Lahey and Robert Kegan (2016) focuses on the relationship between person and organization. It describes three aspects that organizations must take into account so that both the basic needs of people and the requirements of organizations are well integrated: Home, Edge, Groove. And they underpin these dimensions with practices and examples, which we would like to take up and also add to in the following.

Edge: The edge for development

"Edge" describes the boundary or edge that needs to be crossed for development to be possible (Kegan & Lahey, 2016, p. 87f). It is about the courage to leave one's own nest and comfort zones so that stretch for growth can emerge.

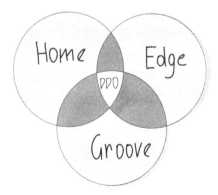

Fig. 3.6. DDO: Edge—Groove—Home according to Lisa Lahey and Robert Kegan (2016)

This development process is about overcoming hurdles, working on oneself and growing and learning in a community. A process based on four pillars: Better me + better you = better us, weaknesses and mistakes as a resource, development principles as a basic foundation and profitability and development are not contradictory.

Better me + better you = better us

The intention is to make this equation a shared premise of top management and leaders. For this we often use Carol Dweck's (2017) research on Fixed Mindset and Growth Mindset : In it she describes two mindsets of people who follow one of these two theories. Growth Mindset refers to the attitude that a person's skills and understanding can develop. That is, individuals with a Growth Mindset believe they can become more intelligent and talented through time and effort. In contrast, people with a Fixed Mindset believe that their abilities and intellect are not particularly changeable. They were just born into the world that way.

If we ask the managers how they see themselves and how they see their employees, the answer is: They see themselves and a few key employees in the Growth Mindset, the rest of the employees in a Fixed Mindset. When asked what their basic assumption is, most say: All people can grow. We then like to invite a change of perspective and ask: "If Alien were to observe this organization and describe the behaviour of the leaders, which Mindset would Alien recognize?" The answer to this question is then usually a Fixed Mindset. This phenomenon has been proven time and again by various research findings: If the basic assumption is a Fixed Mindset, it becomes a self-fulfilling prophecy (McGregor, 1982). It is important to break out of this spiral and implement interventions that promote growth![7]

Weaknesses and mistakes as a resource

In this principle, Kegan and Lahey (2016, p. 90f) describe what they see most people in organizations doing: They are busy hiding their mistakes and weaknesses and need a lot of energy for this—often as much as for the actual job itself. Organizations whose belief system is development, however, see it as an opportunity to learn. They see overcoming boundaries and limitations of individuals and teams as one of the most important aspects for moving forward. This requires good management of personal vulnerability on the personal side and practices that support openness to error on the organizational side. We have described practices that support this in Section 2.1.2 on HROs.

Development principles as a basic foundation

Deliberately Developmental Organizations (DDO) have one thing in their DNA: The whole organization orients its actions towards the development of all. In contrast to classical organization, there is not one department like human resource development that takes care of this, but each individual continuously contributes to it, in themselves and others. If feedback or an observation is withheld, this hinders the development of the whole organization and also of the individuals. DDO is based on the assumption that new things always emerge in life, skills grow or new ones are added, and individual and collective growth is always possible (Kegan & Lahey, p. 93f).

Profitability and development are not contradictory

With the DDOs, economic success is just as important as the development of the people. They need each other. DDOs can be found in all industries (Kegan & Lahey, 2016, p. 96). They work with key performance indicators, a typical tool of classic, efficiency-oriented companies, and also evaluate them. They also do not distinguish between these two perspectives, but integrate them. For example, they evaluate the performance of people in equal parts: Contribution to turnover

---

7   Suggestions can be found on this website: https://positivepsychology.com/growth-mindset-vs-fixed-mindset/ (retrieval date: 14.06.2020)

and contribution to development culture. Others continuously ask themselves, following Victor Frankl, "Have I acted in accordance with my own highest values today? Did we create or do anything important today? Did we care for others? Did we courageously face difficult circumstances?"

Groove: Practising together

Groove stands for a common further development. For this, practices are provided that destabilize constructively: "Mind the Gap" is the motto to counteract the tendency to hedge everything. DDO wants to create constructive unrest.

Destabilize constructively

It is assumed that learning can only be done well in motion and outside the comfort zone. If everything goes perfectly in one area, a new challenge is needed: If a role is filled perfectly, a new one is sought so that the person can develop.

This approach prevents us from serving the natural, conservative side of us humans: In principle, we like to arrange our lives comfortably and reduce complexity. However, this often leads to less attentiveness towards systems and fellow human beings. To counteract this, DDO has developed a formula: Pain + reflection = progress. And whenever pain is involved, it is also about one's own vulnerability and the willingness to deal with it personally in order to learn from it. The scientist Brene Brown deals with this topic intensively and also entertainingly in her Ted Talk "The Power of Vulnerability" (Brown, 2011) and says: Vulnerability can cause feelings of shame, unworthiness and separation, and at the same time it can also be the beginning of joy and creativity (Kegan & Lahey, 2016, p. 100).

Mind the gap

Gaps are differences that should prevent organizations from driving on autopilot. "Mind the gap" means use the differences and spaces in between. Gaps are conversations that don't happen, topics that are not discussed, contacts that are avoided because they might be uncomfortable. They occur between:

- what we do and what we say,
- what we feel and what we say,
- what we say in confidence and what we say officially in the meeting,
- how we assess a person's performance and how we provide feedback to the person concerned,

- what we know about the organizing principles and how we apply them, and
- what we know to be the purpose of the organization and how we actually act.

Seeking out these in-between spaces and connecting them again and again is the daily task of every single member of the organization. In Holacratic companies, this is called picking up tensions. Everyone is called upon to bring them in.

Leaders or their own roles are responsible for establishing frameworks such as conversation routines and support formats for their members so that they can

- gain access to the most important core issues of the organization,
- overcome the pain that can arise when one's own weaknesses become visible,
- get a framework in which interpersonal disagreements can be dealt with openly and authentically.

It's like successful coaches of professional sports teams who, even after winning a game, look for the gaps, the places where the team can develop further.

Focus on effectiveness instead of efficiency

At first it seems more efficient not to address some things or to pay less attention to a gap. After all, you reach your goal faster. But efficient is not development-oriented and often distracts from the essential. It's similar to sport or healthy eating: At first you don't feel like it because it might not be pleasant at the time. In the long run, however, it makes sense so that we are healthy and full of energy.

When we work in organizations, one of the most dominant issues is: Little time. If such thrust directions are worked on, the question quickly arises as to when and how to integrate this into daily activities. It is not uncommon for us to wrestle with management boards and executives over this very issue. In most cases, it is a second-order change: Doing something fundamentally different so that development is possible (see Section 4.5).

For second-order change to occur, most people need support in this transition: Formats such as Immunity to change are ways to support one in such a transition (see Section 5.2.28; Kegan & Lahey, 2009).

Turning the camera around

You probably know the video of the astronauts that Otto Scharmer uses to launch Theory U (Scharmer, 2012; Peter Senge 2011, p. 439). The astronauts have only one goal, namely to explore the moon. All attention is focused on this and when they arrive on the moon, the unbelievable happened. All of a sudden, they see their own home planet. They are touched by the beauty and visible vulnerability of the earth, which is only protected from space by a wafer-thin layer. Only when they turn around and look at it do they realize what connects, what is interrelated and what is worth protecting. Only by reflecting on one's own and relating to oneself does one become aware of what needs to be done: To protect the earth so that it can be a planet worth living on in the long term.

When development is the focus, this is exactly what it is about: Keeping an eye on and developing one's inner life and attitudes so that a good and meaningful contribution to development can be made in the organization, turning the camera not only on others but on oneself and stimulating learning: What is happening on the inside that can affect what will happen on the outside? What are individual automatisms, patterns, beliefs? What will be most difficult, meaningful, rewarding or significant tomorrow?

In addition, another step is also considered: Which of my own psychological factors will play a role the next time, for example, because I am particularly agitated or easily upset by the person. We also know some of the practices described in DDO from another context, the resilience described by Weick and Sutcliff (2016) (see Section 2.1.2), who, however, have not so much worked out the next aspect Home.

Home: Ensuring safety

To be able to bear all this well, I need a nest where I can experience belonging, connection and trust. And this space is called home. For flourishing and lifelong learning to succeed, there needs to be communities of work where people value each other as human beings, hold each other accountable and are involved in genuine and sustained dialogue. Principles that support the nest feeling:

1. **Leaders have no privileges:** They are challenged and encouraged just like any other member of the organization. They are questioned about why they say things the way they do and what their real concern is. They get feedback on what the way they approach things says about them and at the same time about you.
2. **DDOs are a meritocracy:** Titles count for little; expertise is recognized as a "mild power" if these ideas are shared honestly, and ideas are welcome from all.
3. **Everyone is responsible for staff development:** This is a strong cultural feature of DDOs that does not reduce development support to a few roles. Everyone takes responsibility for it and contributes. Interesting practices include taking on unfamiliar roles: Facilitating others' meetings, onboarding boys, transmitting values in person or leading seminars. Others facilitate a

daily reflection process of their staff and also evaluate this regularly so that development is visible and conscious.

4. **Community and team:** In order for growth and vulnerability to be worked on without interruption, containment is needed for each individual. And this framework is created by teams: Each person is in demand as an individual, one is personally interested in the others. Private and personal stories have just as much space as topics from the job. There are role-free spaces. The self-image of such crews can be described as follows: Pain and vulnerability combined with reflection in a very trusting environment creates meaningful developments and progress.

5. **Each individual actively shapes culture:** As in all organizations, there are routines and practices that shape culture. This is an invitation for everyone to participate and contribute, because culture is everyone's business (see Section 3.2).

3.5.3 Our recommendations for the lever "growing and developing in the resonance space"

If you have a desire in your organization to improve the relationship between people and organization, the DDO framework can give you valuable clues as to where to start. Causes may be too high staff turnover, a lack of subject matter experts, low motivation or little willingness to change and dynamism in the organization. Perhaps you have the feeling that you do not have the "right" staff. With DDO you can change the question: Do we have the right organizational set-up for this staff?

This concept is not only based on the assumption that there needs to be a balance of attention to people and organization, but that everything should be thought of in the service of the development of both.

For development, there needs to be restlessness and security, comfort and excitement, performance and learning. For this, every organization has its own practices that regulate belonging (Home), enable learning and development (Edge) and provide collective routines (Groove). How are these dimensions developed in your organization? Which fields do you master particularly well? Which ones less so? How would your employees answer this? (cf. tools in Sections 5.2.13, 5.2.14 and 5.2.15).

3.6 Lever 6: Ten skills that individuals need

Anyone who has been involved in agile change processes or upheavals in companies knows the difficulties. We are so used to planning and sticking to familiar routines that it is difficult for us to adopt a different way of working. In agile transformations, a new competence is needed: To drive on sight, because past decisions cannot be built on, and to trust that meaningful things will come out.

3.6.1 Two logics in companies

In the shift to agility, two worlds collide, which can be summarized in two logics (Gebauer, 2017, p. 88f). In logic one, individuals see social systems as technical systems and assume that the future is predictable. Through planning, uncertainty in the system is hedged and risks are reduced. In this logic, people usually opt for techniques, processes and rules. They focus on controlling what can be expected, preserving and stabilizing. Systems are equated with trivial machines (cf. Section 2.4.2).

The second logic is based on the assumption that the future is uncertain and the unexpected has to be navigated. This requires stability of expectations via rules, processes and routines (as an important function for organizations and people), but these are constantly adapted. For this, a sensorium—organizing collective mindfulness—is developed that permanently deals with uncertainty, detects deviations and continuously makes adjustments. Social systems are seen, according to H. V. Foerster, as non-trivial machines. The capabilities for this are learning and adapting.

These logics are based on the considerations of Weick and Sutcliffe on High Reliability Organizations (HRO), which we have already described in Section 2.1. There, the necessary practices of the organization are described in order to be

Table 3.1. Two logics in organizations based on Gebauer (2017, p. 89)

	Logic 1	Logic 2
Perceived challenge	Solving complicated and computable problems	Dealing with complex unpredictable situations
Description	Technical/trivial system	Social/non-trivial system
Destination	Maintaining and protecting security	Dealing with perceived risks
Way or approach	Creating security through technique, routine and repetition	Dealing with risks and uncertainties by organizing collective mindfulness
Focus	Preserve/Stabilize	Learn/Renew
Effects	Doing more of the same: Rigid loop that conveys security	Continuous vigilance, reflection and evolutionary loop thinking

able to deal with the unexpected and risks. This is exactly what needs to be practised and learned at the individual level, which is concretized by the ten skills
described in the following.

3.6.2 Ten skills for individuals in moving organizations

Ten skills or development areas for individuals that we believe are helpful for individuals in dealing with the challenges and uncertainties in moving organizations:

1. **Creating variety and dealing with paradoxes:** We humans like to catego-
    rize and simplify. Therefore, it helps if we learn to develop an aversion to
    simplification by establishing routines for it. For individuals, this means
    constantly creating and allowing variety and diversity, opening topics and
    contexts wide and being able to close them again at the right moment. This
    also requires a sensible approach to paradoxes and ambiguity (Weick &
    Sutcliffe, 2016).

2. **Focus on errors and processes:** Because we tend to negate deviations or
    consider them normal and strive for consistency as a matter of principle,
    we need a meaningful, differentiated and mindful approach to errors and
    differences as compensation. Therein lies both development and innova-
    tion potential. We pay little attention to operational processes and they
    quickly become routine. Rarely are connections or consequences for others
    considered and deviations recognized. This is why individuals need more
    sensitivity for operational processes and joint action in these (Weick &
    Sutcliffe, 2016).

3. **Striving for resilience:** Resilience in individuals is helpful when a situation
    requires resilience: Something threatens to tear apart and is then supposed to
    find its way back into a shape. It is rarely clear what this future will look like.
    Because we tend to give too much importance to our own experiences and
    adventures. We often lull ourselves into a sense of security by carrying out
    processes again and again without questioning them, forgetting that we have
    not seen or experienced most problems in exactly this way before. Resilience
    means thinking about what might be needed in the event of disruptions, such
    as competencies, resources, reserves or adapted processes. In this way, indi-
    viduals can learn to adapt themselves and their contexts, and at the same time
    work on their adaptability (Weick & Sutcliffe, 2016, p. 90f).

4. **Respect for expertise:** Respect for expertise means that we pay attention to
    which role and person has the most expertise in the context. Authority is
    attributed to this person (see Section 3.7.4). So I can be an expert in organi-
    zational development, but the people in the organization themselves know

better how things work. Therefore, decisions are not firmly anchored to one role, but wander contextually. In addition, it is important that experts are aware of their own authority and how it affects others. As in the example mentioned in Section 2.1.2, a fire chief assumes that he knows nothing every time he goes into action. This attitude leads him to more important information, because it means that everyone around him sharpens their perceptions and makes them available (Weick & Sutcliffe, 2016, p. 109f). In other words, we recommend a humble approach to your own expertise and authority. We show how you can work on this in Section 3.7.4.

5. **Loop work and self-organization:** When it comes to new solutions and integrating the unplanned, we need other competences: Self-organized and process-like work in loops. Expertise alone—see the fireman again—will not get us very far. This new form of working, which is timed in short iterations, proceeds prototypically and always has only the next step in mind, provides security. For this to bring security, it needs practice and a sense of achievement. In the process of walking, security emerges and we realize that this approach helps us to keep moving forward and to trust that good results will emerge. This also requires the skills to let go and immerse ourselves in the context.

6. **Radical cooperation in teams:** Moving organizations do not rely on individual heroes, but use the intelligence of several. That's why working in teams is a central aspect: We often work in diverse, temporary teams that demand high levels of attention and performance. Each individual contributes to the whole. Radical cooperation becomes more important and everything that is a hindrance is used to learn together how to become better. This is especially demanding in virtual cooperation. A significant lever for developing cooperation is to promote the team's ability to play (see Section 3.8.3) and to bring up difficult issues (tools 5.2.16 and 5.2.22).

7. **Performance:** In many places in this book, it becomes clear that this is a new way of playing the game. Especially in agile work and also in preparing for crises, it is about being mindful and making sure to be playable. It makes a difference whether I am prepared for the ball to be passed to me at any time in a basketball game or not. Agile working is about being able to be proactive, to maintain a higher level and pace of work for a time, to show perseverance and at the same time to make bold decisions (see Hübschmann & Nagler, 2015). In order for this performance to be achieved, individuals need a basic rhythm that includes both recovery and activity phases. Virtual collaboration, home office and also meaningful meeting formats are suitable containers for creating a good rhythm.

8. **Actively shaping roles:** In Moving Organizations, we take on more and more different roles with explicit expectations. As a person, I need a conscious approach and options on how to shape and energize my own different contexts by constantly sharpening and consciously developing my roles (see also Section 3.4).

9. **Creative work and innovation:** We are not used to seeing our own work context as a hotbed of innovation, as the focus of organizations has long been on efficiency. Today, organizations need more creativity so that innovations can be developed. They want members who have an appetite for new things, who can be creative in the uncertain, who are willing and able to perceive new things and thus take courageous, unconventional paths. And if you fail, then with as much relish as possible. This competence must be practised and also needs a framework that allows this.

10. **Reflection and developmental learning:** All these requirements and skills demand a lot from us: It is about continuous development. And time for self-reflection and personal development is essential. Moving organizations also provide intrapersonal spaces for this. You know how important it is for individuals to have time to question and recognize patterns and to be able to continuously adapt to new challenges. But that is not the only reason: It also takes time to reflect on one's own basic needs, to strengthen oneself and to be able to recharge.

3.6.3 Differentiated language as a metacompetence: clear leadership

"When people work in a diverse complex environment, they also need diverse complex sensors with which to sense the complexity in their environment. Simple expectations produce simple perceptions that fail to capture most of what is going on" (Weick & Sutcliffe, 2016, p. 61). That last sentence has to be read on the tip of your tongue: Simple expectations produce simple perceptions. But how can we better equip ourselves with complexity and develop sensors for it?

The Clear Leadership Model by Gervase Bushe (2009) helps us to do this. It is based on how individuals communicate and contribute to the environment. The starting point is the person himself and his contribution to cooperation and how we prevent and hinder it. Two beliefs play a role in this:

1. Every single person creates their own experiences and creates their own world. In the descriptions, however, many assume that others create these experiences.

2. We humans are sense-driven beings. That is why we are constantly inventing stories about what we do not yet understand, where there are gaps in our knowledge and where things are not yet 100 per cent clear to us.

These two aspects lead to an interpersonal mush that poisons partnerships and teams (Bushe, 2009, p. 19f): We are constantly interpreting countless impressions, considering why one person reacted like that, the other person looks like that, the person next to us said that and how that affects us. From an evolutionary point of view, there are good reasons why we almost always assume the worst and tend mainly towards negative interpretations. This negative mush leads to exactly what moving organizations do not need: Individuals feel victimized, interactors fail to recognize the consequences of their contributions, their own projections are the order of the day, little to no shared learning takes place and problematic patterns are repeated over and over again.

The antidote is to separate these mixes and mashes and make them workable. Two basic assumptions help us to do this: Firstly, to see collaboration as true partnerships and secondly, the belief that within these relationships, all participants are responsible for the success of the common, overarching purpose.

We can do this by having learning conversations. Talking and dealing with each other in a way that clarifies how events are perceived and how they affect the relationship and the work. A set of skills helps to be able to articulate this. But first a basic competence is needed: A self-differentiated self.

Self-differentiation

Self-differentiation integrates two contradictory basic human needs, namely to be able to separate and connect at the same time (Bushe, 2009, p. 63f; see also Section 3.5). We humans want:

1. self-determined individuals and
2. at the same time be a beloved part of a community with a higher purpose.

So, on the one hand, we want to be recognizable as an individual, develop ourselves and decide everything for ourselves as much as possible. At the same time, however, we also want to be a valued member within a group and contribute to a larger whole. To understand this "I versus We" well, it is helpful to look at the two extremes of it: On the one hand, total fusion in the we, and on the other, total separation from each other. As Table 3.2 shows, fusion results in too strong a connection with other people: One's own boundaries or those of others are not recognized, interactions are reactive and one's own experiences are projected

Table 3.2. Comparison of fusion, self-differentiation and demarcation based on Bushe (2009, p. 80)

Merger	Self-differentiation	Separation and demarcation
Too strongly connected	Separated and connected	Too strongly demarcated
No limits	Optional limits	Rigid borders
Reactive in interactions	Conscious decision-making in interactions	Reactive towards people
Own experience based on the experience of other people	Would like to know what others are experiencing and experiencing while remaining true to themselves	They don't think about what others experience, they stay with themselves.

onto the other person. If, however, people primarily set themselves apart from others and are strict and rigid in setting their own boundaries, then they are reactive towards other people and do not consider how others experience situations, but only proceed from their own point of view.

Self-differentiated people integrate the strengths of both poles: They can separate themselves and connect with others at the same time. They are aware of their boundaries and deal with them consciously. They also consciously decide how to engage in interactions, taking an interest in what others are experiencing while remaining true to themselves.

Practising self-differentiation means finding and testing your own healthy boundaries for yourself and at the same time focusing on the energy in contact with the circle of people in the here and now. You already have one of the best support mechanisms for this: Your body, which helps you to trace and interpret your perceptions in each moment. The process that arises is a permanent clarification process: What is here and now, how does it feel, how do others experience it, what does it do to me, what of it is my own part? Asking oneself these questions means choosing permanent clarification, which is sometimes exhausting: It means going into conflicts and being able to step on others' toes without losing sight of the contact with the other person and the bigger vision for the organization (see tool in Section 5.2.17).

Leading learning conversations—the experience cube

The learning conversation (Bushe, 2009) follows a pattern consisting of four dimensions: Observation, thoughts, feelings and volition. It helps decode our experience and prevents everything from mixing into an interpersonal mush.

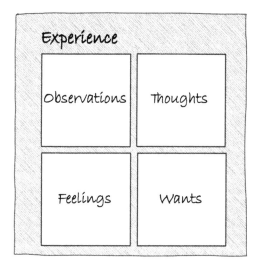

Fig. 3.7. Experience cube according to Gervaise Bushe (2009)

Apply four elements of the experience cube

Applying the four aspects of the experience cube doesn't sound so difficult: First I tell what I have observed, then what thoughts I have about it, what feelings it triggers in me and finally I say what I want. The good news: Yes, that's how it works. The bad news: If it were that simple, there wouldn't be so many conflicts, misunderstandings and problems in this world. That is why it is important to understand more precisely what is so special about these distinctions. The first step is already a challenge: To separate observations and thoughts from their interpretations (cf. tool in Section 5.2.18).

Separate observation and thoughts

"I see that you are committed to your work!", "I observe that he is tired", are all not pure observations, but already contain some interpretation. At this point, it helps to take a different perspective, as if you were a camera: How would it capture this situation? Then perhaps something would come up like: "I observe that your voice gets louder and you use your hands more than usual when we talk about this topic. This triggers the following thoughts in me …". This form of observation and also the separation of observation and thoughts is a process that has to be practised again and again: Being present in the moment and participating and at the same time observing what is right now.

Include own feelings

Making one's own feelings available in the conversation and also naming them is also part of the experience cube: How do I experience these situations, what feelings are triggered? If feelings are not named, they often get lost in the interpersonal mush, which becomes more and more viscous as a result. The challenge is to get to the bottom of one's own feelings and put them into words. Because it was not desired in the professional context for a long time, we stopped tracking them down. At the same time, emotions and feelings are an automatism that we cannot switch off. At breakneck speed, our brain stem has a feeling about the situation, while our mind takes much longer to evaluate the current experience. How does it feel right now? How do I feel when we talk about this? Where do I feel the emotion? Our body supports us in noticing feelings: A sinking feeling in the stomach, heat in the legs, energy is suddenly there or gone, pleasant warmth in the hands, a heavy head, etc. By addressing your own feelings, you enable the other person to understand why you are acting the way you are. In connection with the thoughts that arise through observation, this also becomes more comprehensible. At the same time, one's own image is sharpened at that moment: How did I get this feeling?

Formulate the want

The last step is about clarity of our expectations: Being clear in what I need in the here and now so that I can move forward. It is about a clearly formulated request. Some people feel they are being too demanding or selfish in expressing what they want in this step. This is about being clear about what we want from others and asking for it so that they can respond.

With these four steps, the model helps to conduct conversations in such a way that all participants are open to new turns and can learn in the process (Bushe, 2009, p. 47f). Problem solving is supported, conflicts can be managed more easily, decisions become more transparent, cross-hierarchical communication becomes easier, and so on. This succeeds because stories and experiences of individuals are productively transformed into communication. Especially in a context where interpersonal mush is very spread out, these four steps help to come out and develop a different culture. And here, too, practice makes perfect.

How do individual experiences come about?

The basis of communication is always concrete experiences that we have. Therefore, it helps to understand how these are composed, which is also shown in Fig. 3.8.

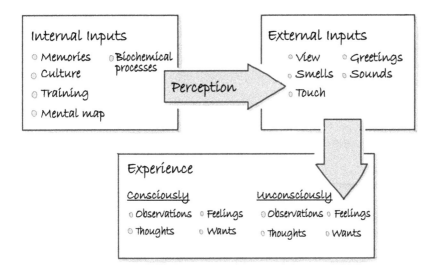

Fig. 3.8. How experiences are created; based on Bushe (2009, p. 93)

Here we distinguish between internal and external inputs. Internal inputs are shaped by personal memories, one's own culture, education, one's own mental map, biochemical processes of the brain, perceptual distortions and much more. With this imprinting, external stimuli are interpreted through what I see, smell, taste, hear or touch. The whole then makes up the experience itself, which is experienced both consciously and unconsciously (Bushe, 2009, p. 93).

The opportunity of this processual logic of experience and this pattern of conversation is that our counterpart and we ourselves learn to understand how some conclusions and feelings are reached, and this enables constructive energy for action. An important point is also once again the distinction between conscious and unconscious: We do not always act the way we say we do or the way we think we act. Experienced and observed always drift apart. This is where the espoused theory and the theory-in-use come into play: The espoused theory describes the world view and the values that people pretend to act according to. Theory-in-use means the worldview and values that are implicitly visible through behaviour, or the internal maps that these individuals actually use to act. Applying this distinction between a theory-in-use and an espoused theory to oneself has great potential for learning. In the Clear Leadership Model, one asks about the theory-in-use, that is, the implicitly action-guiding backgrounds, and these always hold surprises for all of us!

Clear leadership supports one's own development, sharpens one's own awareness of what is happening and brings this to the fore. In this respect, it is not only
a communication model, but also an attitude that is transported through it. In
order for this attitude to be sharpened, four ego states must be distinguished:

• the conscious self
• the descriptive I
• the curious me
• the appreciative I

In the following, we will briefly explain these states and explain practices so
that you can practise them. Before we do this, we would like to share with you
another experience that became particularly clear to us during the Corona crisis.

Communication for us in this crisis, as for most of you, was mainly limited to
virtual collaboration. All of a sudden, without being able to prepare, we were also
at home. And the only connection to our colleagues and clients were video conferences. This change was very emotionally demanding for many of us. That was
noticeable, but somehow it was no longer so easy to talk about differences, problems and conflicts because of the distance. Especially because one thing became
clear: The other person can withdraw from the dialogue quite quickly by closing
the laptop, the internet connection suddenly stops working or the camera is
turned off. Contact was difficult, spatial proximity, skilful communication interventions were suddenly no longer possible. This experience left us perplexed
at first. But then we remembered the above-mentioned attitudes and models,
especially the appreciative and the curious I emphasized at the beginning of the
virtual meetings. By practising these attitudes more consciously for ourselves,
more difficult virtual conversations and meetings became possible. This created
a good basis for staying in contact, even if the physical proximity was missing.
Our urgent recommendation is therefore: Practice (cf. tool in Section 5.2.19).

The aware self

In this attitude, I know my own experiences, recognize my decision-making possibilities and know which decisions I have made myself. This awareness supports
in action and in the assessment of one's own self-efficacy and is promoted by the
following disciplines (Bushe, 2009, p. 109f):

1. **Apply experience cube:** As a person, I am aware in the here and now of what
   I observe, think, feel and want, and can also separate and name it. This requires practice and also includes consciously dealing with fears and shame,
   one of the strongest drivers of behaviour and decisions.

2. **Use clear language:** As a person, I use clear language so as not to confuse others or make them happy with my impressions. I speak from my own position instead of using generalizing phrases: I say, "I think it's nice that you're here" instead of, "We think it's nice". Or I say: "I am cold in this room" instead of: "It is cold in this room".

3. **Speaking in the here and now:** Self-reflection is a part of the conscious I, but the clearly larger and more important one is learning in the interactions themselves. That's why I am fully present in conversations by directly taking up what is right now, and not by referring to something else, for example, what has happened in the past. I am trying to make a difference now: I don't talk about the colleagues who could do something better, but with the people involved now about what has happened, what feelings and thoughts this triggers in me and what I therefore need.

4. **Identify your own mental maps:** We all have many different mental maps, about how we understand the world, how things should work and also about people. The advantage is that I can quickly refer back to them. The disadvantage is that it controls my attention. That's why it helps to identify your own maps and be open to changing them as well. And I pay attention to what is in that moment and where this comes from: The theory-in-use guides me in learning.

The descriptive self

In this ego state, one knows that one's own experiences are no more or less true than those of others. In this state, a person tells what is going on in their head so that others understand them better (Bushe, 2009, p. 145). This can be practised using four criteria:

1. **Be transparent without being intimate:** Transparency is not about telling everything about your private life. It's about being transparent about what's going on or what's holding you back, and about what's important in the work context. This can also mean saying that some things should not be said. It is not about sharing everything amicably, but about being honest about what is going on.

2. **Make statements before you ask:** First say what your concern is before you ask questions. This will prevent your counterpart from asking: "Why exactly is she asking me the question? What does she expect from me? What expectation do I have to fulfil? What is the consequence if I answer incorrectly? What happens if …?" Questions trigger people to ask questions about why they are being asked. Therefore, it is helpful to say in advance what is going on inside

you and why you want to engage your counterpart. This also increases the likelihood that they will get an honest answer about their counterpart's experience—because they have shown themselves beforehand.

3. **Describe the effect before you answer:** At the moment of a conversation, two things happen at the same time: We talk about the content and at the same time we have an experience of the conversation itself. This means that we are constantly evaluating the content of what is said and/or the other person— automatically. That's why it helps to describe your own assessment of the conversation and only add your own perspective in a second step: "Franz, I would like to have a learning conversation with you about the presentation of the turnover figures and about the fact that the current form does not meet my expectations."—"I can understand that. At the same time, I realize that when you say it like that, it makes me tense and uncomfortable because I have already invested a lot of time and I get the idea that you don't see what has already been done...".

4. **Describe your experience and not the evaluation:** If we want to be open and honest, we often give our personal evaluations, which can have a high potential for offending our colleagues. Therefore, it helps not to judge but to name your own experience. Here is an example: Variant 1: "I don't think you are really trying, you don't care about this project." Variant 2: "The story I'm making up in my head is that you're not trying very hard in this project. Is that so? ... Let me briefly describe how I get this impression ...".

The curious self

The point here is to be open and curious oneself and not to close off too soon. I am closed when I roll my eyes, stop listening, put my counterpart in a drawer and am no longer in contact and relationship with my counterpart, but in my own individual world (Bushe, 2009, p. 171f). You can practise the following points in order to succeed in remaining curiously open:

1. **Be inviting:** Invite others to be self-descriptive. To reduce the fear of this, show yourself vulnerable, then your counterpart will also dare to show themselves. It helps to listen, to remain curious in order to better understand the other person's experience. It is not helpful to give advice or to try to solve problems immediately.

2. **Park your reactions:** We are all human and have red buttons that, once pressed, lead to quick reactions. This quickly creates reactive ping-pong conversations. Therefore, it helps if you feel these reactions, put them aside for a while, a breath and stay in a curious mode to first understand the other

person better. When we are no longer curious about what the other person is saying, we are also no longer in our curious self, but completely with ourselves in our patterns. And as far as the red buttons are concerned: Here, too, it helps to curiously explore which of one's own buttons one has, when we ourselves project our feelings onto others and what these red buttons want to protect us from.

3. Make an **effort to gain insights:** Try to understand different perspectives on the basis of the experiences described. If, for example, a colleague has repeatedly failed to hand in results by the given deadline, the variant of direct confrontation is rarely helpful. If, on the other hand, the moments of agreement are discussed, it is possible to find out how these discrepancies came about. Only when both have a similar picture of the process do both have enough insight into what they have experienced.

4. **Listen through the experience cube:** Listening actively and being able to paraphrase what you hear is the first level in listening. In addition, it is about understanding the position and experience of the other person. As a curious me, I use the experience cube in learning conversations and try to understand what my counterpart has observed, what thoughts have arisen as a result, what feelings this has triggered and what the person wants as a result. An additional step can sometimes also be to learn more not only about the experience, but also about the person themselves and their map: What did you observe about yourself during this experience? What did you think or feel about yourself in this situation? What did you want from yourself? This form of listening is similar to Listening Level 4 by Otto Scharmer (2015a; 2015b), except that the focus is more on person learning (cf. tool in Section 5.2.20).

The appreciative self (ego)

This side of the self creates a context through which others are happy to learn along, gives courage and conveys the value of successful and flourishing partnerships. Here it is not a matter of valuation, but of appreciation that makes contact possible (Bushe, 2009, p. 201f). There are also four disciplines for this, to which we add Positive Leadership

1. **Promote an appreciative mindset:** If the common mindset is that the glass is half full and not half empty, then a lot has been achieved! Unfortunately, it is not that easy to move from a deficit-oriented mindset to an appreciative one. We are so well trained to become better and better and to solve problems that we don't always see the positive. In this respect, it is important to keep an eye on what more is wanted, to strengthen what is already going

Table 3.3. From deficit-oriented thinking to appreciative thinking (Bushe, 2009, p. 215)

Deficit-oriented mindset	Appreciative mindset
What I do not like	**What I appreciate**
She always emphasizes what doesn't work without offering alternatives. She just gets cynical all the time until I'm in a bad mood.	I notice the intelligent points in what she says, there is usually some truth to it! I also like the passion and care behind the criticism.
How can I solve the problem?	**Identify what I need more**
How do I get her to talk less so that the energy of the whole group is not lost?	I wish she would make more constructive suggestions and bring her passion to the whole group in a meaningful way.
Noticing one's own contribution so that the pattern does not change	**Taking responsibility for one's own experience**
I have done nothing to change the situation with her. When I examine my real needs, I recognize a part of me that wants others to be just as frustrated with her and thus marginalize her.	Time to grow up! I will make an appointment with her before the next meeting to hear her concerns and challenge her in a constructive way. This way she can deal with the issue in advance without having to do so in the meeting.

really well. An example of how such a transformation can succeed can be found in Table 3.3.

In addition, it is necessary to believe that in principle every person in the company has positive intentions because they all want to be good at what they do, even if you cannot see much evidence of this. This form of approaching others increases the chance of partnership. And here, too, the self-fulfilling prophecy works!

2. **Align with a positive intention:** As a matter of principle, assume that everyone is acting out of a good intention. Even if it doesn't feel that way. People rarely think about how they can show another person up. In this attitude, it is easier to find your way into the conversation and also easier to work.

3. **Find what is needed, point it out and document it:** It helps in creating more of what you want or desire and that way it increases transparency. By being appreciative, we believe in new things and it helps us highlight every little progress that effect.

4. **Increase what is new:** What arises and succeeds needs to be strengthened so that it can grow. Cross out what more is needed, blow into the embers that are already there. Here it helps above all to describe the experiences that have triggered something positive.

5. **Strengths-based leadership:** A helpful approach to strengthening positivity is Markus Ebner's strengths-based leadership, which is based on Martin Seligmann's (2014) PERMA model (Ebner, 2019). Positive psychology has been dealing with the question of what contributes to people feeling life satisfaction and how people flourish for more than 20 years. The PERMA model is an acronym and represents five dimensions that contribute to a successful life: P stands for positively perceived emotions of people; E stands for Engagement and means using one's strengths and experiencing flow moments; R stands for Relationship, as successful deep relationships contribute to life satisfaction; M stands for Meaning and explains that meaning-oriented and spiritual people are more satisfied with life than others; A stands for Accomplishment and clarifies that people who know their own self-efficacy and contribution to life are more satisfied than those who do not notice this. Strengths-based leadership takes the perspective of the company and the employee leader and asks: What can I do so that my colleagues have positive experiences? How can I make sure that employees know their strengths and use them? How can I strengthen relationships with each other and how can I be well connected with everyone? Is everyone clear about the purpose of our organization or team? Does everyone know the purpose of their work and tasks? Is everyone clear about how they contribute to the success of our results and is this appropriately celebrated or made transparent? Based on these questions, interventions are researched for their effectiveness. For example, a positive gratitude check-in is highly effective and has a lasting impact on the well-being of teams (cf. tools in Sections 5.2.19, 5.2.20, 5.2.21 and 5.2.22).

3.6.4 Our recommendations for the "ten skills" lever

We have presented many models in this section. You will not be able to apply them all at the same time. First think about what you need and want to develop: Certain skills, conversation skills, self-awareness, the ability to diagnose patterns. What do you want to strengthen individuals in? Then use the appropriate model and choose a focus. For example, if you want to start with some of the ten individual skills, we recommend going step by step: Start with one or two skills that come easily, that quickly generate energy and interest, and that also have great leverage. This way, learning is associated with pleasure and people become curious. Once one area of development is running almost routinely, move on to the next. At the same time, we always connect the learning of new skills with content initiatives and routines so that a connection to everyday work can be made and the new skill is practised. Learning a new language, as we describe it in the Clear Leadership Model, flows into the whole process and also develops step by step. The persons thus sharpen their language skills more and more and thereby learn to deal with more complexity.

3.7 Lever 7: Leadership, power and the transition

A practical example: A manager heads a department with 3,000 employees whose task is to keep the roads and motorways in good shape. The managers reporting to her are, among others, motorway maintenance officers, whose job it is to ensure that their respective section is maintained in summer and winter. They are each responsible for about 30 employees as well as tools and machines with which the motorway is maintained. They identify with their part of the road network, are proud, and are treated like little princesses by others.

Among other things, it is their job to mow the grass strips at the edge of the motorway. Each motorway maintenance officer has only one machine available for her section of the motorway, as it is quite expensive. The mowing process always causes traffic jams, several times: The machine mows one strip, then has to turn around and mow the next strip up, and then the next strip up again.

The manager now wants to reduce the amount of congestion and wants the motorway mowers to cooperate. If three mowing machines were to drive one after the other in a staggered manner, each could take over a strip and there would only be one traffic jam. The manager wants the neighbouring motorway mowers to coordinate and borrow each other's machines and drivers.

The goal is clear. And yet there has been no cooperation for years. The manager therefore turns to us. It turns out that it is due to the traditional understanding of leadership that cooperation does not take place. Throughout the organization, there is a view that does not allow much flexibility: Leadership is only linked to certain positions. It is the leader's job to develop solutions and then enforce them. Deviations are seen as mistakes and decision-making power is located in only a few positions. And so it can't be otherwise than that the motorway managers delegate responsibility upwards and there is a solidification of power relations.

3.7.1 Leadership in the moving organization

As already explained in our introductory hypothesis, moving organizations is about changing the top-bottom relation of leadership to an inside-outside relation. In other words:

- *More leadership is* needed, because situations in which leadership is necessary are increasing, not decreasing. Therefore, self-organization is not a helpful term, as it suggests that power can be eliminated. However, this is impossible.
- The situations in which *leadership* is necessary are *differentiated*, increasingly diverse and require different know-how. For example, in everyday life, different leadership is needed than in a crisis; with customers, different leadership is needed than when dealing with part-time employees. These differences need to be utilized and coordinated.
- Leadership is directed both *inwards to the* employees and colleagues and *outwards to the* clients and stakeholders. An increasingly important task is that of boundary management: What belongs to the system, what should remain outside (temporary workers, regular customers).
- The demands on leadership are temporally *unstable*. What was valid yesterday is outdated tomorrow, that is, redundancy is decreasing. It is becoming increasingly difficult to refer to precedents; more and more often decisions have to be made on a case-by-case basis. The principle of "predict and control" is being replaced by "sense and respond".
- Concentrating the decision-making authority of leadership in a few *roles* is not a good idea in view of this situation. Modern organizations need to distribute influence (power) and leadership roles and therefore speak of distributed authority based on expertise.

Let's come back to our motorway maintenance department. We decided, together with the manager, to hold a series of workshops with the female motorway maintenance workers to work on the obstacles to cooperation together. All the workshops were attended by the manager herself and the regional managers, who are the direct supervisors of the motorway maintenance workers, to show them the importance and appreciation. All the objections were discussed and solutions were worked out, which enabled the motorway maintenance workers to plan the mowing operations themselves. This intervention has been successful, because today not only do the mowers drive one after the other, but the motorway maintenance workers cooperate without their manager interfering.

The leader has refrained from using the powers of power, such as instructions, allocation or withdrawal of resources or disciplinary measures, and has instead relied on dialogue. Power is a form of influence. But there are also alternatives to power that achieve the same thing: Trust and understanding lead just as much to increasing security in the team and successfully exerting influence. The manager succeeded in doing this with her motorway maintenance workers. This takes

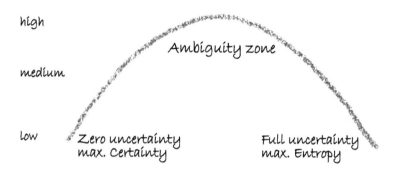

Ambiguity zone

medium

low   Zero uncertainty   Full uncertainty
         max. Certainty   max. Entropy

Fig. 3.9. Zones of uncertainty and power according to Zirkler (2019)

time, but it pays off and is also the way to move from a traditional understanding of leadership to leadership in the sense of the moving organization.

The function of power in social systems is to reduce uncertainty. This is vividly illustrated by Zirkler's curve (2019; see Fig. 3.9). At one of the extremes, at zero uncertainty, where everything and anything is predetermined, at absolute coercion, power is just as low and ineffective as at absolute indeterminacy and uncertainty, where anything is always possible. In one case, power is not necessary because everything is regulated; in the other case, it fizzles out. Between the two poles, power works and serves to reduce uncertainty.

Crises in particular are phases of great uncertainty, in which people often reflexively call for power. But there are other forms of exerting influence: Trust and understanding (Luhmann, 1968). These also serve to reduce complexity and have their advantages and disadvantages compared to the use of power in terms of time, risk and resilience. In practice, all three forms of influence always occur together with the others, that is, always in mixed proportions (Kühl, 2017b, p. 19 ff).

Classical power theory starts from the case of conflict and assumes that there is a struggle for scarce goods. In day-to-day business and in the normal operation of organizations, however, power is much more distributed, subtle and systemic; it does not need the case of conflict (Luhmann, 2012b, p. 23 ff). The moving organization uses this knowledge. It too is exposed to much uncertainty, but it practices dealing with this phenomenon differently: By making power transparent, distributing it and combining it with trust and understanding. This is also true, and especially so, when a moving organization is in crisis. In this phase, there is often a desire for centralized power and a call for the strong man or woman. For some women managers, this is a great temptation which they find difficult to resist without help. Irritation and uncertainty among staff are quite normal. In crises, decisions and clear communication are needed. Teams that can communicate openly are a good container to manage crises. In the toolbox, we have described some tools that show how you can work with them. Good communication that is not dominated by the desire for power is, as they say in English, "the proof of the pudding" of a moving organization.

Leadership uses all forms of influence. It cannot do without power, but at the same time it must build trust and ensure understanding. Practice shows that the transition to this understanding of leadership is extremely difficult for many organizations. After a short excursion into the theory of power, we will discuss this.

3.7.2 What is power?

Power, to our surprise, is almost absent from the relevant literature on change management, although an understanding of it is so important in order to deal with it and change the power structures.

The new theories of power (Arendt, Foucault, Luhmann) see power as embedded in social relations; people cannot possess power just like that. A corporate boss on a desert island has no power. For power, she needs several people and situations in which there is freedom *and* coercion. In both extremes, with absolute freedom and with total coercion, there is no power. Therefore, following Max Weber's definition, power can be described as "the ability to assert one's own will within a social relationship, even in the face of resistance" (Rudolph, 2017, p. 10f). Three aspects are important for our understanding of power.

No social system without power

Social systems need power for their community building. Power is an exchange relationship that is always reciprocal and asymmetrical. Complex systems need more power than simpler ones (Luhmann, 2012a, p. 31). However, power relations are changing: Increasing complexity reduces the influence of those in power and the controllability of organizations (Crozier & Friedberg, 1993, p. 44 ff).

Function of power in organizations

Why do organizations need power ? Power has a "peculiar ordering capacity" (Luhmann, 2012, p. 39). Power serves to reduce uncertainty and ensures that the system remains viable. Firstly, power ensures that the system-environment relationship, the boundary of the organization to the outside world, is maintained, for example, by deciding who is a member or not, who is invited to a meeting, which supplier to cooperate with or whether to expand the product range. Secondly, power ensures that decisions can be followed up, that is, decisions must be followed by decisions or, in other words, decisions must have consequences. Power thus helps to maintain the viability of a system.

What is power in organizations based on?

Power is possessed by those agencies or persons who can influence the zones of insecurity of others: Examples include the customs officer who can simply refuse entry to travellers crossing the border, or the supervisor who may or may not decide on the transfer of an employee.

In organizations, the zones of insecurity can be captured more precisely (Crozier & Friedberg, 1993, p. 51 ff), therefore, bodies or persons have power that is

• have specific knowledge (e.g. experts in controlling, IT) and can thus contribute relevant expertise;
• who are intermediaries and translators for important environments (e.g. key accountants, lobbyists) and have exclusive access to important stakeholders as relays;
• can pass on, colour or filter information due to their position in communication networks (e.g. personal referees, employees for their boss) and as gatekeepers thus exercise control over information channels; and
• can decide on rules and can use rules to expand or restrict resources and thus the fields of action of others (e.g. hierarchy, boss function).

3.7.3 Working on the transition of power

All of us know stories of conflictual transitions of power. They are always challenging because uncertainty increases rapidly. Because power is supposed to help reduce insecurity, a change in the power constellation leads to more insecurity. These are moments that threaten to slip out of all control, and at the same time we easily fall back into old patterns of action in phases of great uncertainty. This is what makes these transitions so exciting and so challenging. Moving organizations must learn to work with their leaders on the transition of power. It is important to actively face this issue and to discuss the implementation again and again. This is not easy and requires special discussion formats so as not to end up in escalations and accusations straight away. External counselling that is aware of its own role and power (see below) can be extremely helpful here (cf. tools in Sections 5.2.25 and 5.2.26).

Holacracy is one of the few formats that provides rules for dealing with power and has created a constitution for this. This is very valuable and creates transparency in decision-making. Many organizations do not have a Holacratic constitution and yet want to become more agile. We recommend that they discuss the way they are led and work on it continuously and transparently.

When it comes to working with power, the following interventions can be useful (Zirkler, 2019):

- Make zones of uncertainty transparent and reduce them as much as possible.
- Agree on rules for dealing with power, similar to the constitution in Holacracy.
- Set up teams that are given the chance to experiment with the transition of power.
- Make power change an issue, that is, set own meetings with agreed rules of the game (see Holacracy).
- Rewarding new forms of exercising power.
- Making visible examples of the transition of power and relapses into old patterns.
- Enable personal coaching in the transition period.

3.7.4 New authority

It is important to accompany the transition of leaders and help them gain a new understanding of the leadership task. However, you should not plan to do this during the crisis. Here the uncertainty is too great. The work on the new authority needs a reasonably stable context. The *model of lateral leadership* (Kühl, 2017b), which works with the distinction between power, trust and understanding described above, or the *model of new authority* by Geisbauer (2018), can help here. This model proposes to examine the concrete practice of leaders and to reground (leadership) authority. It uses Luhmann's concept of authority: Authority is attributed to that person whose communication is "adopted as a premise for decision-making without examination of its correctness" (Luhmann, 1994, first 1968, p. 103; Fischer, 2004, p. 60). Authority is attributed to someone from outside and is a form of influence on others that does not presuppose a superior relationship. Experts have authority they cannot confer on themselves, they receive it through attribution from others.

According to Geisbauer, we use certain relations (see below) to make a diagnosis and derive concrete thrust directions and actions (Geisbauer,

2018). This supports leaders and creates security in the new way of leadership performance.

Social level

- **Relationship—presence versus distance:** The new authority of leaders develops from closeness, interest and care. Distance, in turn, weakens authority. The source of new authority is called presence and that means: "I am here and will stay until a meaningful solution is developed." Presence also means that give and take are well balanced. You form appropriate relationships with relevant system partners.
- **Reparation and understanding—de-escalation versus escalation:** Leaders play a key role in dealing with conflicts. Through their behaviour, they decide how a conflict can be resolved, maintained or solved. In the process, new spaces can be opened or relationships can be destroyed. In order to prevent escalation, leaders need a set of tools for conflict resolution and professional reflection so that they recognize their own part in conflicts.
- **Coalition—networking versus hierarchy:** Leaders are often in competition with each other and work against each other for tactical reasons. New authority means closing ranks with other leaders. It is no longer the lone leader lording it over subordinates, but a member of a working community that draws strength and legitimacy from mutual support.

Factual level

- **Information—transparency versus obfuscation:** Leaders who are transparent manage to communicate information directly and simultaneously. This creates a resonance space that enables viable solutions and builds trust. Too many one-on-one conversations conducted by leaders look like mousing from the outside and therefore promote compartmentalization, which in turn establishes taboo zones.
- **Boundaries—decisiveness versus dominance:** Leaders with new authority can set boundaries or consistently ensure compliance with boundaries and rules. If they recognize rule-breaking, they demand compliance. In doing so, positional power and dominance are renounced, instead emphasizing what is not tolerated: "I do not tolerate this behaviour because …" instead of "Because I am your leader, I command …". Safe structural spaces and clear relationships are created.

Fig. 3.10. New authority according to Wilhelm Geisbauer (2018)

Temporal level

- **Understanding time—persistence versus urgency or impatience:** New authority is based on a new understanding of time. As a leader, dealing with time constructively creates authority and is appreciated. Patience is required, coupled with perseverance: Persistent goal orientation creates continuity.
- **Reflection—Self-leadership versus control:** Leaders lead themselves first and foremost. And self-leadership requires a high degree of impulse control, self-mastery and reflection. Trying to achieve control over employees or their actions is an illusion. Through self-leadership, leaders gain respect: "I am reliable" and "I really do it" are the corresponding implicit messages.

3.7.5 Power of the counsellors

Since external consultants and trainers also have power, it is important to know what this power is based on. For this, you can make good use of Crozier and Friedberg's (1993) sources of power, because depending on your assignment and competence, whether as a technical or process consultant, you control different zones of uncertainty. Have you ever thought about what your power is based on and how you work on power issues?

- As a process consultant, you work in workshops on roles and competences, on openness of communication and help to uncover taboos.
- As a technical advisor, you use your expertise to help create an ideal image (balanced scorecard, Scrum roles, etc.) and thus provide the organization with orientation for its development.
- Sometimes you get a job because you provide a special approach.
- They moderate a meeting in which it is decided which employees will be included in project teams.

You can also ask yourself whether you are really taking advantage of the opportunities you have in your roles. We have developed a tool for this purpose, which is described in Section 5.2.26. Either way, we want to encourage you at this point to look into this topic.

3.7.6 Our recommendations for women advisors at the levers of power

Those who act in organizations act in a context of power. Through every change project, this becomes significant. Therefore, in conclusion, a few recommendations that help us when we work on power issues:

- Ensure equidistance, that is, ensure impartiality with regard to the issue and the persons.
- Create radical transparency about what was given (what was decided, who was there …).
- Do not enter into covert alliances, hidden agendas or secret meetings.
- Make the issue of power discussable in the client system, if that is possible.
- Work on the willingness to create alternatives.
- Use non-judgemental language.
- Provide space for reflection and for relief.
- And lastly: Modesty and knowledge of one's own relative importance cannot hurt.

3.8 Lever 8: Agile teams

Teams are currently experiencing a powerful renaissance. In this chapter we ask ourselves what the reasons are for this and how agile teams differ from "normal" teams. To become a moving organization, you need agile teams. Under certain conditions, these can both meet the performance expectations of the organization in different contexts and fulfil important needs of individuals. Together, teams can meet both requirements better than any alternative, such as managers.

To do this, however, teams must first be empowered and what is special about teams must be understood. We use current research results and show what we—here in the Neuwaldegg consulting group—do to remain agile as a team.

3.8.1 Agile teams: Flexible, open, ready to learn

Google, international consultancies, NASA and many others are currently intensively researching the conditions that make teams particularly efficient. Where does this current great interest come from? Teams are nothing new. We already experienced a boom in the 1980s. With group dynamics and the famous semi-autonomous working groups in the automobile industry, teams were intensively studied. Don't we already know everything and is this now just old wine in new bottles? The answer is no, because the prerequisites for teams and what is expected of them have changed. What we understand by teams today and what expectations they have to fulfil is something different than it was back then:

- **Complexity** has increased, and well-functioning teams have shown that they can deal with complexity better than individuals. Not all teams can do this, now one wants to find out what makes teams powerful.
- Organizations are confronted with **paradoxes** much more often nowadays; this is also a consequence of complexity. Dealing with paradoxes is one of the strengths of good teams. If they have learned to decide, they can deal well with high volatility and acute crises.
- The understanding of **leadership is** changing. Instead of all aspects of leadership being concerted in one role, they are being divided: Responsibility for the outcome and the process, for individual and collective learning, including decision-making, is distributed. It is no longer up to one role, the leader, to handle everything and thus become overburdened.
- Teams are the place where **learning** and development of individuals in organizations can take place. This is where mistakes can be made under observation, where not only actions but also one's own assumptions can be questioned, enabling more intensive learning.
- Teams can fulfil the need for **home.** In good teams, individuals feel welcome. Their needs are perceived and respected by others. They offer protection and visibility at the same time.
- Teams are more open and integrate **outsiders** at times. In agile teams, female clients are integrated early. The involvement of others is handled flexibly.

When teams meet these expectations, they are powerful and useful for organizations. And they are very different from the previously known working groups, department and project teams, management and steering boards. Teams have their own routines and criteria of composition. They are stable in terms of their structure and the tasks to be performed and need their own setting to function well.

For the transformation to a moving organization, you need agile teams. These are only superficially similar to our traditional picture of teams; on closer inspection they are quite different: These teams are "a small number of individuals with differences and complementary skills who share a common purpose, goals and approach to which they are mutually committed" (adapted from Katzenbach, 1994). They are liaisons between the individuals and the organization. They serve not only to meet the performance expectations of the organization, but also the developmental needs of individuals (Kegan & Lahey 2016).

Agile teams are characterized by the fact that

- the participants belong to several teams at the same time, often of equal value.
- the affiliation is only temporary.
- membership is identified via roles.
- expectations of the teams in terms of results and process are unstable and always need to be "renegotiated".
- early involvement of the customers takes place.
- the teams are deliberately composed in an interdisciplinary way.
- the members are highly interdependent in the completion of their tasks; they plan, solve problems, decide and check progress together.
- the sense, the purpose of the team, is supported by all and provides orientation and a framework to be and remain capable of action.
- the way of communication—how openly sensitive issues are addressed and how listening is done—is of great importance.
- individual needs and talents are respected and promoted.
- disruption is valued. It is not harmony in the team that is sought, but destabilization that helps the team and individuals to develop (see also Weick & Sutcliffe, 2016).

Communicate like astronauts

Good teams have to be developed. Some successful teams manage to reconcile completely different requirements, but not all succeed. Relying only on the personal skills of individuals and a great diversity in the team, as was still assumed by large management consultancies, is not sufficient (Williams & O'Reilly, 1998). International research in recent decades has explored the question of what needs to be considered when teams are expected to perform excellently in exceptional circumstances, such as outer space, in order to draw conclusions for the exceptional situations that agility brings.

As part of the "manned Mars flight" project, NASA explored the conditions and requirements for selecting the suitable six astronauts. Being dependent on each other for better or worse for two years in a confined space in a hostile environment requires a very special team.

One has to take this into account: NASA still has the shock of 1972 in its bones, when the astronauts in space interrupted communication with the base in Houston for 20 minutes and went on "strike". They felt that the Space Centre in Houston did not value them enough and cut off the connection. They wanted their peace first and no further instructions. An interruption Houston had not expected and which must have lasted an eternity for them. Later they asked themselves: How could this have happened? How could we not have realized that the astronauts had had enough of us? What signs were there that were overlooked? What can we learn from this, because on the way to Mars this must not happen again under any circumstances. How can we learn from this if virtual teams experience something similar? NASA's goal—as for all organizations and leaders—is to maintain communication, especially in difficult circumstances.

Long simulations conducted in the Houston laboratories identified four factors for a successful team in exceptional circumstances:

- Capability, that is, the individual skills that each person brings to the team.
- Diversity, the variety and heterogeneity of the team.
- Reliability, the degree of dependability, that is, how much one can rely on others.
- Psychological safety, the safety in the team to also be able to take interpersonal risks.

The above four factors overlap and complement each other. Some, such as the skills of team members and diversity, can be determined through a careful selection process. They are particularly relevant when putting together a team. Others are difficult to test in advance. These include psychological safety, in other words the degree of freedom from fear in a team. To what extent is it possible to address uncomfortable questions and conflicts in a team or to speak out on issues that are not well received by others. How can someone have a completely different opinion and still be appreciated by the team?

NASA as well as Google (to be researched under the keyword Project Aristotle) emphasize the importance of psychological safety. They base this on the research of Edmondson (2020). Psychological safety is the framework for successful communication in teams, and five preconditions must be in place for this to happen:

- Different opinions can be expressed openly and confidently.
- The members' share of speeches is approximately evenly distributed over time.
- Everyone can make mistakes, experimentation and learning are more important than looking for culprits.
- Empathy, that is, social sensitivity for the needs of others, can be experienced.
- Individual talents are valued and encouraged, not deficits highlighted.

Psychological security is a good example of how quickly certain concepts can make a career for themselves when they point to prominent companies, such as Google in this case. The critical sides of this concept have been described by researchers, albeit less publicly, for years. Some bristle at the methodological flaws (predominantly questionnaire-based research, where "positive" results are preferentially published; Meyer et al., 2018, p. 15). Others are surprised that neither the extensive results of trust research are taken into account, nor that there are references to the origin of this concept (e.g. Ed Schein, 2017, and Kurt Lewin, 2012).

Psychological safety is primarily about trust, an important component of successful teamwork. That is why it is important for agile teams to continuously clarify how open their communication is, how they distribute speaking parts well and how they can learn from mistakes. In the following chapter, we show in which contexts this works best.

3.8.2 An agile team operates in four spaces

There are many reasons why teams often fail to develop their full strength. Sometimes it is because of the skills of the members and the lack of diversity among them. We also come across teams that somehow do not function as one would imagine. They report a lot of idle time and conflict and are far from the team playability that everyone wants. This usually has many causes, but often one reason for the insufficient playfulness is the lack of clarity regarding the purpose. In other words, the purpose for which this team exists and how it helps to realize the organization's purpose is not clear (see Section 3.3, lever 3). A clear purpose creates focus and makes it easier to distinguish what the team's tasks are and what they are not. However, this alone is not enough. Because teams as a social system have to cope with even more tasks: It is about information, about decisions, about developing content, about visibility and recognition, about relationship and also personal issues. All this automatically occupies the members and it is often not clear what is "on" at the moment. Mixing these different tasks and purposes makes teams inefficient and emotionally tedious (cf. tool in Section 5.2.31).

Four spaces of agile teams

Agile teams are masters at differentiating which different contexts they need to fulfil their purpose. This gives clarity and establishes focus. Therefore, a first step after developing the purpose is to identify and separate the different contexts with their purposes. Robertson (2015, p. 200) uses the metaphor of "space" to better separate them. He distinguishes four different spaces. The spaces serve the different purposes and we have continued to think about them in our daily practice:

1. **Operational space:** This is about the operational business, about the what. The purpose is to coordinate one's roles, to synchronize through information and enquiries and to develop something new. Two formats are of particular importance in this context. One is called *synchronisation or tactical meetings*: These can be held standing up, should be as short as possible and always limited in time. The aim is discussion and synchronization, the result clarity about next steps and projects. *Creative formats* are another form: Here the focus is on content-related solutions, on clarifying open questions together, on a problem for which a solution is sought. We also call these *focus meetings*.

2. **Organizational space:** In this space, rules of the game, powers, roles, structures and directions are set. This is where decisions are made about where to go, what to be for and how to work. Meeting formats that work on the rules of the game are called *governance meetings* (Holacracy) or *game rule reflection meetings*. These formats need good facilitation and clear rules on how decisions are made (see Holacracy and decisions). The goal is integration and organizing, the outcome clarity about roles, responsibilities and rules of the game.

   Another meeting format is the *strategic room*. Here we work on the strategic focus. It is about the future direction, about guidelines for further decisions, that is, about coordination and preferences. Since these topics require a different approach and need to be opened up, many teams have become accustomed to using a different location for this and have chosen a workshop format. The goal is more focus, the result preference rules and strategic initiatives.

3. **Interpersonal space or tribe space:** This is where people interact and relate to each other. It is about contact, visibility, shared learning and reflection. This is where culture, language, conflicts, values and successes are lived.

Fig. 3.11. Four spaces of teams based on Brian Robertson

A traditional meeting where everyone sits around a table is not very condu-
cive; it is better to have separate, alternating settings. The aim of this space is
to resonate and develop understanding for each other.

4. **Intrapersonal space:** The individual relates to the organization and the team.
The focus is on the individual. With what is experienced, with one's own
development, values, own performance and also competences. The aim of
this space is personal clarity, the result suggestions for personal development.

Fig. 3.11 visualizes the different rooms for teams with the respective important
meeting formats.

This form of differentiation alone is unusual for many teams. We often find
that the first two spaces, operational and organizational, are frequently mixed.
This is one reason for lengthy meetings. Interpersonal and intrapersonal spaces

only happen informally, if at all, or once a year in the form of a team building session. As a result, they "creep" into the other spaces, becoming an interpersonal mush and making meetings unproductive and tedious. In addition, rooms can be differentiated according to regular communication, for example, so-called jour fixe, which take place at regular intervals and are also intended to pursue a specific purpose. Creative and strategy rooms, on the other hand, are convened on an ad hoc basis and less often. They tend to use workshop formats because otherwise it is difficult to achieve the desired purpose.

To develop a team's ability to play, we recommend separating the rooms and using all of them continuously and incorporating them into the regular meeting routine. At the Neuwaldegg Advisory Group, we have a separate role for the architecture, that is, the planning of the four rooms. This role sets the agenda for our home team days (one day jour-fixe every fortnight). It constantly sets new interventions so that no two days are the same. All meetings are held on the home team days, including the Holacratic Circles (first and second rooms).

All rooms can be used on the same day. We divide some rooms and meetings into different days and decide which formats, virtual or face-to-face, make more sense. In this way, we interweave operational work with work on the organization and with learning. We make a point of ensuring that interpersonal and intrapersonal spaces also have their place on each home team day. These are more open, creative and varied. Depending on demand, strategy and creative spaces take place or we schedule extra days on these days and on extra fixed dates.

In summary, it is important to give the different purposes that a team pursues the appropriate spaces. To stay with the game metaphor, different playing fields are opened up and team members have to learn where which game is played. This has made us faster and more efficient (which can be seen in the number of decisions), improved contact with each other and made the team livelier. Virtual collaboration creates an additional context and also challenges for organizations and teams. We deal with this specific influence separately in Section 3.9 on social innovation. At the same time, these approaches also apply in the virtual context. Here too, once the space has been created and its purpose is clear, a new field of development opens up—dealing with barriers in the team. We will turn to this question next.

3.8.3 Develop the playing ability of a team

A systemic approach that promotes playfulness in teams and that pays particular attention to interpersonal and intrapersonal spaces is provided by System Centered Training. This approach supports teams in solving conflicts together and integrating differences. To achieve this, barriers are removed.

System Centered Training (SCT) describes the most common barriers of teams as follows (Gantt & Agazarian, 2018, p. 14): Team members do not recognize what information is relevant to others, they do not recognize that there are opposing viewpoints and cannot use them productively, or they withhold information.

To counter this, the following approaches can be used:

1. People, roles and the team: moving from person-centredness to team focus.
2. "Functional Subgrouping": Using conflicts and differences in the team for development.

Decouple problem and person to generate solutions faster

Unlike in the anonymous organization, the great advantage of teams is that people and roles can be experienced. Often, the team is the most important reference point for employees in terms of their well-being and development. The organization is abstract and comes into play through the functional roles. All team members have functional roles , such as controller, assistant, and store manager, which they have to fill and also bring to bear in the team. Successful teams need to balance both aspects, people and their needs, roles and their expectations.

When problems arise in teams, we can observe that they quickly personalize, that is, they put people in the foreground: In what they do, where they cause problems, how they irritate or how they develop or hinder teams. This view is of limited help to teams because it limits the possibilities for solutions and the team as a whole learns less. To avoid this, teams need to learn to develop a system-centred language instead of a person-centred language. This process takes place in four steps:

Step 1: From self-centredness to observing system-centredness

The aim of this step is to be able to take a bird's eye view in order to recognize the effect and origin of your own actions in systems. For this it is helpful to observe when you take a self (person) perspective and when you take a system (role and member) perspective. You can also ask yourself what the role needs and what the person needs. The distinction between thoughts and feelings helps (see also Section 3.6.3): Which feelings do I have that arise in the here and now based on this current reality and experience? What thoughts arise on the basis of my fears about the past and possible future and what feelings does this produce? A good exercise that supports this differentiation is the distraction exercise, which approaches the team from the outside and creates resonance (see the tool "Distraction Exercise" in Section 5.2.29).

Step 2: From observation to membership

The aim of this step is to move from observation to participation. This is achieved when you can hold your own emotion by first creating resonance with yourself and then moving into resonance with others. Resonance occurs when you feel what is happening on both sides of the relationship. Teams thrive on members taking on roles in the team. The member role in the team does not mean a functional role like accounting or marketing, but the specific contribution that role makes to the realization of the team purpose. The extent to which team membership is pronounced can be seen in how easily team roles are taken on and the criteria of psychological safety are lived.

Step 3: Use subgroups in the team

Every team has functional subgroups, groups that are closer to each other because of their functional roles, that is, all market-related or all assistance functions or all those who are currently working on a big project. The emphasis here is really on "every team", because not all groups are or function the same. This fact leads to subgroups having similar perceptions and assessments among themselves, which are often different from those of other subgroups. In this third step of the STC process, these subgroups are made visible in their differences. This is especially important in tuning in and resonating with the other members. This results in a change of perspectives and of one's own roles, because both the similarities and differences become clear.

This process of subgroups gives people security and promotes vigilance and readiness among all members. A conflict in the team can now also be viewed from this perspective. Common differences in evaluation often become visible, making it difficult to attribute them to individuals. Paradoxically, making this distinction discussable creates a connection with other subgroups and raises members' awareness of their social role in the team. It becomes harder to "take things personally".

Step 4: From the subgroups to the organization

The aim of this step is to be aware of the context in which the person and the team are currently located. The team is a subgroup from the perspective of the organization. Shuttling between the perspectives of the organization, the team, the subteams and the roles is an important skill for team members. The team serves as a platform to explore and integrate differences that cause conflict rather than reject or exclude them. This is where organization and person come together. Instead of leaving the "cold" organization outside and presenting the team as a good ideal world, it becomes the focal point for the development of persons and the organization. For this we use the method of "functional subgrouping", among others.

Functional subgrouping to exploit conflicts and differences

We use "Functional Subgrouping" when there are two views on a topic in a team, but at least one "Yes, but …". The aim of this method is to name conflicts and differences and to prevent fleeing into passivity and lukewarm compromises. It is about learning to deal with similarities and differences (Gantt & Agazarian, 2018, p. 24f). The term "functional subgrouping" clarifies the concern: It is functional for teams to group around differences within the team, that is, to make different opinions on a topic socially visible and to set the norm that one is allowed to have different views here.

Functional subgroups are formed around differences in a dialogue form: When there are different points of view or a contentious issue, people assign themselves to one point of view and form a functional subgroup. A functional subgroup first focuses its energy on exploring the similarities in its own group, which automatically makes diversity visible in its own subgroup. Several subgroups make the different forces in the whole team visible: Each of these groups has a different function. Similar to a football game, defensive players, midfield players and offensive players are needed. Recognizing this and making it workable increases the ability to play: The development steps are separating, holding, integrating and transforming differences in a team as a whole.

The dialogue follows the following steps:

- A "Yes, but …" is the indication of at least two points of view. The facilitator takes up this situation.
- The first opinion of a team member brought into the conversation is taken up and supplemented by similar views: Thus, the first subgroup is formed. In this part of the dialogue, people explain what moves them. Similar views are found by asking: "Who else sees it this way?" Everyone else listens attentively. Only those who are of a similar opinion get a turn. Those who do not see it that way are invited to listen carefully.
- Through this dialogue, similarities but also subtle differences and variations within this subgroup become visible in the course of the conversation. In these conversations, it is important to ensure that the language does not take up abstract generalizations. The point is to address and express one's own experiences, feelings and thoughts in concrete terms.
- If the first subgroup has nothing more to illuminate, it is the second opinion's turn. Again, a subgroup is formed and given space to explain. Again, everyone

else listens attentively. When there is nothing more to say, new differences are opened with a next subgroup.

- By discussing these differences, members realize that each perspective has different qualities and functions in the team. In the course of the process, bridges are built that enable one to integrate different aspects, let go and agree on next steps.
- Other ways of integration: If these bridges are not strong enough, there are other ways of working further:
  - One variation is to open up the group as a whole and talk in a dialogue about what has just been learned and which aspects have become clear or what is still unclear, open or totally new. For this, next steps can be agreed upon.
  - Another possibility is to formulate different goals and purposes and from the dialogue to jointly formulate a force field analysis (see Section 5.2.27). Here, too, it is important to agree on the next steps.

Example "Functional Subgrouping"

When we found the common purpose with a management team, there was a strange mood in the room. One member said: "Actually, we should all be happy now, but somehow the mood is not like that. I think a lot of things will not change because of this Purpose." In response, another team member said, "Why, I don't understand you, it's perfect like this!" A good moment to apply this method!

Counsellor: *"It seems like there are several opinions in the room here! We would like to deepen and clarify these opinions with you. To do this, we ask that in the first step you only speak up if you have the same opinion, and if you disagree, to listen very carefully. Important: Everyone is allowed to say what they think here in this round as soon as it is their turn. Mr. Müller, you were the first ... Does anyone else see it the same way as Mr. Müller? Please make sure that you bring in your experiences along the experience cube.*

B: *If I'm honest, yes! When I look around here, there is hardly any energy. That makes me feel insecure. I realise right now that I can't trust that this will make a difference now. Too often I have experienced that we have made agreements that we have not looked at afterwards. I need concrete commitment and also implementation measures.*

M: *I also feel insecure. For me, it triggers the thought and also the question of whether everyone really wants to move here. The change is already big and I have a lot of respect for it and somehow it feels too cosy.*

After some time of exchange on this opinion, a new perspective comes:

G: *I see it differently. I think this purpose fits perfectly. I just realise that I first have to understand what it really means. I haven't had time to think about implementation yet.*

Y: *Yes, I feel the same way. I am a bit overwhelmed by this situation. So far I have no idea how to apply it to my area, with so many employees. My head is spinning.*

Z: *I can see that it's a big step, but it's true. I'm not euphoric because we have to prove it first, but I'm confident. Only when we see the first successes can I be really happy.*

The conversations in this example went on like this for a while. As you can see, more and more perspectives are added. And although opinions were far apart at the beginning, it quickly became visible what common steps need to be: It still took time to think about implementation measures, about next steps as a team, but also for the individuals.

In the course of such a dialogue, the team members gain more and more understanding for the differences. By being able to exchange their own views in a protected way and by being heard, relaxation sets in. By listening to others, it becomes clear that the other points of view also have different facets that are not so difficult to interact with.

Using differences is important for the vitality of the team and is a signal that differences and conflicts can be dealt with here. Integrating them is necessary because integration has a stabilizing effect. Teams that have learned this are proud of their ability to deal with differences; the importance of individual opinions recedes into the background. A good result for these teams is that a result emerges that no one could have imagined before, and concrete steps can be derived.

3.8.4 Our recommendations for the "agile teams" lever

Agile teams are at the heart of a moving organization. As we were able to show, these are demanding to use, because each participant is a member of several teams, acts there in different roles and the teams meet in different formats. This cannot be achieved without professional facilitation of the meetings.

Therefore, our first recommendation: Train all staff members in facilitation, because once everyone takes on the facilitation role, they will better understand what it means to lead a team. Our second recommendation: Distribute the steering of the teams among different shoulders, that is, give new members a chance to practice once they have settled in a bit and rotate regularly—according to the motto, everyone gets a turn.

Thirdly, we recommend that you work on the teams' communication skills regularly, that is, at least once a month for half a day and not once a year at a team development workshop. This succeeds through variety, playful elements and reflection in the interpersonal space. And fourthly, check whether communication relevant to the organization and the individuals takes place in the teams, or whether it is channelled past them externally. Agile teams are characterized by their ability to have difficult conversations (cf. tool in Section 5.2.27 to 5.2.40).

3.9 Lever 9: Social innovation

While we have been writing this book, the Corona crisis has hit us all. The impact on the economy and society is not yet foreseeable. But it is changing society. It slows down or prevents some developments, while others are promoted by it. One of the developments that is being promoted is digitalization. This is experiencing a boom. Those who are digitally equipped can communicate, those who have digital offers can sell, and companies that have started the conversion to the digital age in time are at an advantage. Digitalization is showing its potential under the special conditions of the contact ban. Much is not possible without the digital infrastructure.

On the basis of the crisis, digitalization shows above all that it is not just a technology, but a social innovation. It intervenes in social events, structures, intervenes in communication and opens up possibilities that would not have existed without it. Even after these limitations, the technology of digitalization and social events remained intertwined. This intertwining will not only stay with us, but will get a boost. Where there has been hesitation to digitize, there is now a shift (Reeves et al., 2020).

In order to use digitalization, other social customs and routines are needed. People and systems have to take up these opportunities. We call this change social innovation and the whole book is dedicated to this in relation to organizations. In this section, the ninth lever, we first want to clarify the understanding of digitalization and then turn to the connection between digitalization and social innovations.

3.9.1 Digital transformation—three phases

Digitization refers to the use of bits and bytes instead of analogue media and information. This concerns content, products and processes. Digital transformation goes further than the pure digitization of content and processes. Familiar problems are seen and solved differently through the new technical tools. Digital transformation is a game changer. It changes our ways of seeing and working, it leads to an immense acceleration and forces organizations and society to make radical adjustments. Digital transformation has the character of a force of nature and seems to be almost impossible to influence (Kelly, 2011).

Organizations can experience digital transformation in three stages (cf. Fig. 3.12):

You know the first stage as working from home, the home office. The second stage is something that some organizations have been able to expand during the crisis by offering and delivering products and services over the internet. The

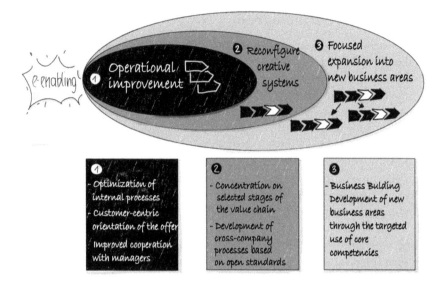

Fig. 3.12. Three stages of digital transformation

third stage is used by companies like Mural, a virtual communication organization that is itself virtual. How organizations handle digital transformation affects their competitiveness and their position in society. Even public authorities cannot escape this process, although the type of digitalization can often occur in different forms within the same organization. One and the same organization can go through all three stages in different areas. It is often a question of balancing the different dynamics and reconciling this with the analogue world. This is rarely a question of "either digital or analogue", but a smooth transition, for which one of our clients has developed the image of a slider to sensitize leaders to the different requirements. What is needed is ambidextrous leadership (cf. Fig. 3.13).

In one case, the slider is relatively far to the left, in the familiar environment of the efficiency-oriented organization. In the other case, the slider is far to the right in the foreign, digital world. In most cases, the slider is somewhere in between. The message of this model is: It needs the skills from both worlds. Most leaders can build on what they have done successfully so far, and they need to learn new things.

For women technicians—who shape the culture of this company—the model with the slider is reassuring because it promises control. At the same time, it is a call for change and learning, for social innovation. Without this, that is, only with a different technique, they will not be successful.

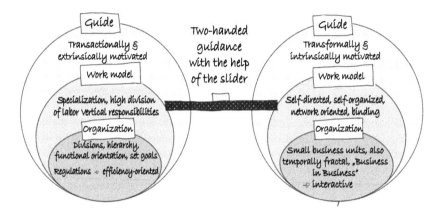

Fig. 3.13. Ambidextry: Ambidextrous leadership in a digital transformation

3.9.2 Social innovation in the virtual world

You can recognize successful economic innovations by their return on investment: At the end of the day, your investment must have generated more than
you put into it. You measure success by the financial return. Following this
idea, social innovations can be recognized by whether they change social processes, relationships and behaviour patterns and thus create a social return on
investment. According to Josef Hochgerner (2016), social innovation is new
practices to address social challenges that are adopted and used by affected
social groups.

In both cases, the investment is measured by the return, in one case with
money, in the other by the impact in the social environment. Economic investments are easier to measure, for social investments many metrics lend themselves. These will vary from case to case. But whichever one has chosen, a moving
organization is not conceivable without ongoing social innovation. Moving
means social innovation, and the moving organization needs tools that make
this possible and contributors who can manage it.

When communication in organizations is even partially switched to virtual
media, things change. We were able to experience what happens in the virtual
world during the crisis. It was a kind of training camp. In the Neuwaldegg advisory group, we communicated a lot in virtual meetings and were able to learn as
we practised. At the beginning, we thought that the virtual format was mainly
suitable for factual issues and that it was difficult to work on conflicts in the team.
We have learned. In the beginning, meetings were also held in smaller teams of
up to 12 participants (later over 20), and lasted up to one and a half hours. Later,

we worked for up to three hours with a short break, we were able to discuss different opinions, work on conflicts together and used this experience for client projects.

Do you remember the section in the first chapter (see Section 1.4) where we presented the four dimensions of communication: Factual, social, temporal and spatial? The special thing about virtual meetings is that the dimension of space is omitted. This has an impact on the social level in particular, as the possibility of varying proximity and distance is eliminated here. What you can express in the real world through distance, your posture, your seating arrangement, your facing or facing away, is hardly communicable virtually. This does not mean that emotions cannot be conveyed and difficult conversations cannot be successfully held, it is just more challenging. It needs a good framework. What you should avoid, however, is trying to exert pressure. Verbal pressure, threats of consequences and the like are not good tools in virtual meetings! It is too easy for your counterpart to distance himself, stop listening or hang up; there is no space to hold back.

It is helpful if you know the people involved personally beforehand and have already worked with them. But exceptions prove the rule, sometimes sympathy for strangers arises spontaneously even in a virtual setting. To make this productive, it is important to set a clear time frame and to moderate the meeting. Structuring the meeting into phases, such as check-in, input, questions, reactions, next steps and check-out, is just as helpful as setting rules. Rules help to determine how you want to communicate here. One of our colleagues has introduced netiquette for this, a set of expectations for each participant that she sends out beforehand. It contains rules like: Please make sure you are not disturbed; put on silent when you are not talking; test the technology beforehand, etc. As a facilitator, inviting an appreciative, open attitude and doing a small exercise for it will also be beneficial. Invite to bring the curious I into the meeting instead of judgements. Allow for mistakes and use every meeting to get ideas for improvement and ideas. Much of what we have written to you in the previous chapters on skills of individuals and agile teams also applies here.

We are still at the beginning and are constantly learning. The technical possibilities are also developing rapidly. The leap from conference calls to virtual meetings is not that long ago and makes a big difference as we can see people and work on documents together.

An example: Advertising on the move

We briefly take a look inside a creative agency that could no longer work without digital tools, that thrives on constant innovation and is transforming itself as an organization in the process, that is, the way employees work together is also subject to continuous change. Almost 80 people in this agency are working on agile transformation at the same time, experimenting with prototypes, trying out new processes, deepening analyzes and bringing in ideas. Within a very short time, vast amounts of ideas, analyzed data, new processes are created and quickly implemented. It is important that the different teams learn from each other quickly and build on each other. That's why the teams are interested in each other, interfere, demand information and critically want to know if everything always pays off on the common ground. As you can imagine, this place is really humming.

There are two crystallization points where you can feel this. The first is the monthly review, where the different results are coordinated and decided transparently. Through this form of transparency, many people can understand how further impulses come about. The second is the common digital platform: All files are stored there, each team has a chat for exchange, there is a video function that is mainly used for stand-up meetings when you are not in the main building. Every team channel is visible to the other teams, because everything is transparent. And everything happens on this platform! Every meeting is visible, problems with prototypes are pointed out, new results are documented, everything is done through it.

Then the following happens: Little happens on one channel, immediately others ask what is going. Team members look at the intermediate status of other teams, are thus pre-informed in the reviews and can ask targeted questions. Prototypes can only start if all prototype members communicate via this platform. This is also monitored and commented on: Positive feedback or constructive help is offered. In the meantime, the management team has also moved communication to this platform.

Something has changed here: Individuals act differently and they have a new understanding of how good collaboration works. This organization uses its digital platform to communicate openly. Without this tool, without this new way of working together, this progress and shared learning would not have been possible. The agency lives social innovation, there is no end in sight to this process.

3.9.3 Our recommendations for the "social innovation" lever

We understand social innovation here as the ability to use digitalization for organizations. This requires good knowledge of the possibilities and conditions of use of digitalization, but also the ability to change social processes. Systemic approaches and tools are made for the complex situations of the digital world.

Social processes need to be designed in such a way that they are useful for people, the organization and society.

Moving organizations have no role models, because every organization is unique. It is important to bring out the uniqueness, oriented to one's own purpose. If you would like to see an example, go to the Mural homepage.[8] You will be amazed to find little of what organizations usually present to the outside world. The form of orientation towards top performers, as in efficiency-driven organizations, does not help.

Being part of it is a lot of fun and extremely demanding. It requires skills from completely different worlds. Both the opportunities and the performance expectations in such organizations are high, plus everything is in motion. Individuals will not be able to meet these demands: It takes teams and well-trained people who are capable of working in teams. The conclusion: The lever for social innovation is us, is you. Therefore, our final recommendation for this last lever is: Educate yourself, practice, create. With your skills, with your whole person, you are the lever for social innovation. Read books like this one, go out and create communication, have courage! You are the social innovation.

3.10 The key messages of this chapter

Getting an organization with a long tradition and track record moving so that it can cope well with the digital and uncertain future is a challenge. It is about becoming more agile and crisis-proof, but where to start? From our experience, the nine levers are a good starting point to move these organizations in an agile transformation:

1. The starting point is a common, fundamental understanding of organizations and how they make decisions. The Neuwaldegg Triangle creates a good framework that shows where to start and how connections are made: Through programmes, communication channels, personnel and culture.
2. For many, the culture lever seems to be the most obvious lever for the new cooperation to succeed. Organizations invest a lot of time and money precisely for this purpose. From a systemic perspective, we know that culture can only be addressed indirectly. Nevertheless, it is important in an agile transformation to keep an eye on it: Which patterns play into our hands and which ones hinder us? What and who do we want to be in our moving organization? These considerations flow into other measures indirectly or directly.

---

8   See: https://mural.co/about-us (retrieval date: 14.06.2020)

3. Purpose accomplishes several things at once that are important for organizations in complex and turbulent times: It provides orientation and is a beacon to reach for. It creates identity and values what the organization has achieved in the past. And it also connects people and organizations emotionally.

4. The levers of role-taking, role-making and role diversity address the needs of agile organizations to increase flexibility and clarity: By explicitly distributing roles and responsibilities and clarifying expectations, and by having role bearers make decisions based on their expertise. By constantly clarifying and adapting expectations and requirements, the roles evolve and so does the organization.

5. But it is not only about the development of the organization. If that were the case, people would starve with their own needs. That is why moving organizations create resonant spaces that make it possible for people to grow and develop. Teams create the home so that individuals feel safe and familiar, and on the basis of this, spaces for development are created in which the following applies: Growing and developing is the shared belief system.

6. Agile working requires specific, or more precisely ten, skills from individuals in order for innovations to emerge, uncertainty to be dealt with constructively or radical cooperation to succeed. All this and more can be practised step by step. One metacompetence for this is understanding and language: Learning a "new" kind of language that supports cooperation, that establishes understanding and contact and that perceives and makes available observations for development.

7. A central lever in an agile transformation is leadership and power, but not in the traditional sense. Here, it is mainly about distributing them. And such shifts in power relations automatically lead to great irritation in organizations. If they are not actively and carefully addressed, the chances of transformation fade. We often observe that precisely this issue is underestimated or not taken into account. It is, therefore, important to pay attention to how more understanding and trust can be established and that leaders are well accompanied in the transformation of their own role.

8. Agile teams are the heart of moving organizations. As key players in agile working, they are the engine for development and progress. However, this only succeeds if they know the game and can act in a differentiated and context-related way: Meetings are structured and focused and always aligned with what is needed at the moment. Agile teams also work on their relationships and the way they work together by being able to address fears and conflicts and strengthen each other.

9. Digital transformation only succeeds when organizations also develop social innovation by working, thinking and communicating differently. This not only creates new ways of working, but the job itself, the work processes and also the business models change. Above all, virtual collaboration is a related characteristic that many of us have experienced in recent years.

4 The process of agile transformation

Let's get more specific now. In the first three chapters, you got a good understanding that agility is much more than a structural change. A paradigm shift is needed for your organization to become a moving organization. Chapter 3, in particular, illustrates *where* you can make a difference. Now we show you *how* to proceed and *what* an agile transformation actually entails. While we offer concrete tools and steps in Chapter 5, in this fourth section, we show you those power tools that start at a meta-level and have the whole picture in mind. Here we describe how you can use them in and for the transformation process so that you always keep an eye on the connections. Because relying on just one method does not do justice to the complexity of these projects. A good interplay of different approaches is needed. How this can be achieved is explained here.

First of all, we want to describe what concerns us in agile transformation, what needs special attention and which of our own assumptions we had to correct in practice.

Then we present the Neuwaldegg loop. For us, it is the model that describes the stations that need to be considered in change processes and puts them in a sequence. The first station in the loop, the reception of information, is dealt with in detail in this chapter. After the second station, the formation of hypotheses, we turn to the third step in the loop, the development of thrust directions and especially the change architectures.

The chapter concludes with the transformation map. In this map we locate the different types of change projects, from reorganization processes to business reengineering and organizational development to agile transformation. We often use the map at the beginning of our work to map out their change process with clients and derive the specific requirements from it. Here it serves as a summary at the end of the chapter to once again clarify the differences of agile transformation.

4.1 Transform agilely

Do you still remember the first chapter and the "Derivations for agile transformation and why we no longer say change management"? We have deepened these differences using four dimensions (cf. Fig. 4.1): Factual, social, spatial and temporal.

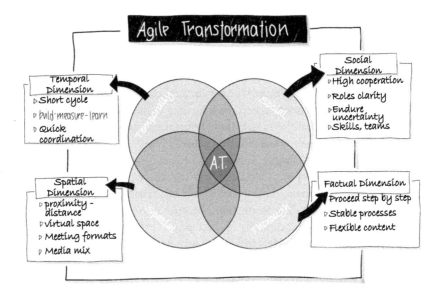

Fig. 4.1. Four dimensions of an agile transformation

Now the question is how to effectively orchestrate these dimensions. One thing right from the start: Almost everything revolves around dealing with uncertainty and unpredictability. Moving organizations must learn to deal with this and remain capable of acting. The agile transformation process creates the right framework for this, because uncertainty is fundamentally at odds with our need for security and the ability to plan. This is also the big difference to the traditional approach: We can plan a little in advance. We know it and accept the uncertainty. The feeling of security that a plan can provide is absent. Instead of security, we look for novelty.

A good example is the media company mentioned in Section 1.4, which initiated an agile transformation process to integrate digitalization into its business model. Different teams worked on different topics, one achieved the breakthrough: The target image of a new digital editorial office. Everyone in the organization was excited by the bold and clear proposal and celebrated this team. Diligently, the other themes and teams were aligned with it, and put to the test. The enthusiasm continued, but after a few months of happy work, new data experts were hired. Their main task was to analyze existing data, find correlations and prepare them for the teams. That's what they did, and before long it was clear that 70 per cent of the existing digital target image did not match these analyzes.

At first, this was a shock for everyone. Now there were only two options: Either talk down the clues or rethink a lot of things from scratch. Fortunately, the second option was chosen. Within four weeks, all prototypes were aligned with the "new dynamic target image". This experience had an impact on the whole process.

It could also have gone wrong. The particular challenge in agile transformation lies above all in the process of constantly picking up and letting go, and that is not so easy. Agile methods do help, but without experience from the outside, it will probably be difficult to succeed. As organizational consultants, we also experience similar things, sooner or later throwing overboard some long-held assumptions that we will describe in this chapter.

We have also experienced surprises in the course of writing the book and have been caught up in the Corona crisis with our projects: We asked ourselves how much the suggestions we give here apply in such a crisis situation. The answer was formulated by a client as follows: "The previous agile transformation process was like a dry run for the Corona crisis." The crisis only intensified the requirements; the approaches were right. Therefore, the next step is about one thing above all: What are the elements to manage such a process in an agile way?

4.1.1 Elements in the agile transformation

The most important element is a functioning team that really energizes this transformation process. In our experience, agile transformation is not possible without this. Only the interaction of different skills, expertise and personalities makes this special form of learning and cooperation possible. Therefore, we recommend paying special attention to the composition of the core team. This is the heart of every transformation. It not only develops the necessary impulses, but it already also lives the desired future. The core team is the nucleus of the agile transformation.

We have summarized our experiences so far on the basis of the four dimensions of factual, social, temporal and spatial. The order does not represent a valuation, as this differs in each individual case.

Factual dimension

When we are invited to support an agile transformation, the first step is to work on one thing: An accepted *case for action with the* decision-makers. This describes the motivation, the commitment and the reason why this project is being launched. The starting point for a Case for Action can be a drastic change in the market, as in the case of the media company due to digitalization, or a slump in sales that disrupts the entire organization, or a completely new competitive situation. The development of the case for action is usually a process in itself that takes time and for which learning journeys are helpful. Decision-makers need to be sure of the "why do we want this change".

Another important element is to consistently align the decision-making programmes, more precisely to sharpen the *strategic corridor* and the purpose. An agile transformation needs a *strategic* corridor that indicates the direction of development. The first step in arriving at this is to create a dynamic vision. This is not thought of here as a fixed quantity that must necessarily be aimed at and to which the resources used and the time available must be subordinated, but rather it is a blueprint that quickly loses its meaning. To be honest, we start with the goal picture mainly because it would be too irritating for most managers not to formulate goals at the beginning.

In an agile process, however, decisions are guided by the *strategic* corridor, which is continuously underpinned with figures, data and facts, and a *powerful purpose*. The organizations that set out on the path always demand this. The purpose grounds the organization and its members in all turbulence. It makes people aware of their own strengths and promotes pride in what has been achieved in the past. It connects the members with their organization and creates awareness of why this organization exists. Both the purpose and the strategic corridor help to make decisions, for example, by adjusting the key figures again and again, giving meetings a new focus and prioritizing projects.

The factual dimension naturally also includes the formal structures, such as the organizational *and procedural structure*. Questions and suggestions about this come up again and again. They are important and we treat them like prototypes that can be revised later. So we don't follow the rule "structure follows strategy", where a strategy has to be in place first, but stay true to the principle "build—measure—learn This is always challenging: To think about roles and positions without people attaching their own hopes to them and thus really thinking "greenfield"—entirely in the sense of the organization and the mission.

Such challenges and other organizational issues are worked on with the core team using the Neuwaldegg loop (see Section 4.2). With the core team, the *central patterns of the organization* are continuously described, checked for their functionality and new measures are taken if necessary. In the media house, for example, one department found it particularly difficult to switch from print to digital. This could be seen in the fact that print topics were always dealt with first in meetings and there was hardly any time left for digital issues. The use of digital media was also very low. When the core team realized this, the tools were changed (among other things, Microsoft Teams was made mandatory for communication and documentation) and the order of topics in meetings was turned upside down. By the way, this is an example of how we work with culture change; we "play across the board" (see Section 3.3) and we use the communication channels (meeting format and the communication tool) to influence the interaction and culture in this department.

As progress is made, more and more measures and prototypes emerge that need to be integrated. In order to keep the whole thing going well, it is essential that *roles are* constantly sharpened, *meeting and coordination structures are* adapted to the new requirements and relevant outputs are well documented. This demands a lot of discipline and requires a certain form of perseverance in managing the process, which is not only sympathetic. It is important that individual ways of working do not dilute the common approach. Gradually, the advancing process connects with the operational day-to-day business. As it walks, the organization readjusts itself based on the prototypes and is permanently in motion. **The agile transformation process becomes a moving organization.**

The *logic of the* process steps is based on *Scrum* (Section 2.2.2). This creates security and a good rhythm. However, intervals are adapted to the respective context. Sometimes two weeks are too short, sometimes too long. But we do not forgo the alternation of sprint and retrospective with sufficient duration.

Our own way of working is also influenced by this. In our role as *external facilitators,* we not only act as process consultants, but we also permanently share our experience and know-how with the different interaction systems, that is, with the agile teams, management board and core team. We contribute our expertise wherever it makes sense. We also contribute content and help shape the transformation process. This is very challenging for us, as we have to take good care of our distance-and-proximity relationship with the clients. This is not possible without reflection in the advisory team.

In the Corona crisis, many of these aspects intensified once again: As process facilitators and core team, we were challenged to work virtually and to integrate the current developments on a daily basis without forgetting what the purpose and also the strategic corridor were. In most of the projects already underway, the case-for-action had intensified: It was still about digitalization, agile management and transformation. The challenges were mainly in the social dimension, which we describe below.

Social dimension

As already mentioned at the beginning, *agile teams* are the essential component of such transformations. The core team, which has a content-related and steering function (see Section 4.4 on architecture), occupies the central position. Unlike in change management, the size of the core team changes with the tasks at hand, as members join or leave. It breathes with the different challenges. In addition, there are expert teams and temporary teams of all kinds, which are made up of members from different areas and positions in the organization. They work on content in a prototypical way, using agile methods to bring knowledge and desired practice into the organization. The composition of the teams is also essential: Cross-functional teams with different expertise are needed. Sometimes it is not so clear beforehand what task individuals can take on. We experience cases like this again and again: A controller has the brilliant idea for marketing or the warehouse employee for a new product.

One of the sticking points in agile transformation is the *commitment of the leadership* and especially the top management to work on themselves. This is an essential difference to the classical approach: As a leader, you are an essential part of this change. Leadership is not abolished, but your role and the necessary skills change: To distribute power and decisions more, to think and act in iterations and loops, to see yourself as a facilitator of social processes. This has to be learned first, for which there are many possibilities in agile transformation. As a leader, your actions are often under the scrutiny of the whole organization, which constantly checks and evaluates the coherence of behaviour and decisions. Almost everyone has an opinion on this. This does not mean that you have to comply with everything all the time. But you have to learn to transfer the strengths of leadership from the past to the new and to be a pioneer for the new. And this is where external support, if you are careful with your own power, is almost always needed (see Section 3.7).

As a result, some roles are particularly exposed and people who fill them get stressed. Imagine: All of a sudden you get permanent feedback on your behaviour, which you are just practising. This can sometimes be very irritating, needs to be dealt with adequately and means patience and tolerance from many sides. Roles that are responsible for a particularly fundamental change are also constantly challenged, which unsettles their role bearers. They all receive special support and are by no means left alone. Paying attention to this and developing appropriate measures is the task of the core and advisory team.

What is still true is that a lot of attention is paid to the *way communication flows*. The focus here is often on meeting formats, the quality of conversations and the way people interact with each other. It is important to discuss patterns of behaviour and observations and consider whether they are helpful or dysfunctional. Everyone notices that the way "one deals with each other" is observed and has consequences. Therefore, reflection on the progress and the way of working together is an integral part of every meeting.

In addition, such projects require maximum transparency of the results for all parties involved. With all the uncertainty, one must be able to trust that one is up to date and not communicated tactically. Therefore, new communication and interaction formats come to the fore: Members of the organization become process bloggers, new communication platforms are introduced and town hall meetings are also held again and again.

What runs through all these aspects of the social dimension: It takes courage to fill in the gaps! Again and again, questions arise that no one had expected and that cannot be answered right away, for example, What do we do when the new female experts for a digital application break our salary scheme? There is no other way to get them, but how do we deal with the differences? Everyone must be able to endure this uncertainty and lack of knowledge. The rule is: Let's work in the present moment with what we think is a good next step and not let our fears stop us. These will be addressed when they actually occur. This is where leaders are particularly challenged, and also exposed roles and advisory teams.

This is even more true in a crisis like we experienced with the Corona crisis: It takes real courage to take gaps. Organizations that had already tested these steps were happy and were able to adapt more quickly than others. In the virtual context, the particular challenge lies above all in social interaction and leadership: What does leadership look like in times when so much is uncertain? There is a great danger of falling back into old, hierarchical patterns. The challenges are greater in the virtual world. Physical presence often makes it easier, because a connection is created more quickly and you can feel what is having an effect. In the virtual space, many things are filtered. That's why we have been using all four spaces for teams during this time: Especially the tribe space, to be able to share fears and challenges and to connect with each other. Virtual collaboration demands even more discipline: In meetings, in addressing differences, in sticking to patterns, in developing and adapting roles, in making decisions transparent. But above all, the joint review was the linchpin in the process: It helped to move forward in terms of content and was the fire that warmed and energized everyone.

Time dimension

One thing quickly stands out: Agile transformation is a *process of short cycles that* is highly structured. Regular meetings, short consultations and mini-workshops are proving their worth, and are constantly timed into the daily routine.

A wide variety of formats take place almost every week. The meetings themselves are tightly planned when it comes to coordination and varied when it comes to reflection and the development of new ideas. And they are always prepared, moderated and well documented. This kind of structure creates security in the process. We hear participants say again and again: "I realize again that I am uncertain about what will come out today. But in the meantime I can trust that the process and the procedure will take us well forward!"

And that is exactly what it is about. It's about moving forward step by step and keeping the next step in mind: What is new is quickly tested, evaluated, discarded or taken up. Most things are unfinished for a long time, 80 percent solutions are sufficient because they change anyway.

In a crisis, as during the Corona pandemic, time becomes even scarcer. Virtual votes are now even more frequent, almost every two to three days, and are shorter for that. Next steps are even smaller, are voted on more quickly and adapted more quickly. Everything that had already been practised before is helpful: Meeting formats, role clarity, transparent communication, digital tools. This kind of transformation would not be possible without digital tools that ensure fast and transparent communication, which in turn requires experts who know how to use them.

Spatial dimension

There is probably a fairly universally observed rule here: *Agile transformation workshops* are held outside the usual meeting rooms, outside the organization or in a special room. If you want to develop something new, don't use the rooms where you regularly meet. Space influences communication. Emotions and status differences are expressed through space, spatial proximity conveys intimacy and connection.

We use this in agile transformation by seeking out spaces that can be designed. They must be friendly, open, equipped with all technical media and with good facilitation material. We also value analogue elements, even Lego bricks, music and good food. However, we do not like large, fixed tables, as they restrict mobility. A circle of chairs or in a U-shape, where everyone can see each other and find equal conditions, is the setting of our choice. We like to change this depending on the goal and topic—it is important that the space can be designed dynamically. We also use different locations because themes are associated with them—people often talk about the "Sierning Future Paper" years later—and we "stage" each sequence of a workshop in the space. Even walks in nature are a good intervention.

In the *virtual world,* these forms are taken away from us. When we sit in front of our computer, our own space is (almost) always the same and it is difficult to separate the different topics, meetings or even groups because we lack spatial anchors. Virtual communication restricts and opens up other possibilities. We pointed this out in the ninth lever.

The third context besides workshops and the virtual world that is important in an agile transformation are the *meeting formats.* These were described in Section 3.8, and you can find tools for them in Sections 5.2.31–5.2.38. Here, too, it is advisable to use different spaces for different formats or at least to change them. For example, we like to use stand-up meetings for synchronization in the operational room. It is helpful if we can use and design all contexts, include them in the architecture of the transformation (see Section 4.3) There are workshops inside and outside the building, carefully designed large group events in our own spaces, many virtual meetings and meeting formats in the meeting rooms. The spaces support the transformation process and make it a rounded whole.

4.1.2 Bye bye beliefs

As already mentioned, we are constantly learning in agile transformation and have already had to change some of our long-held beliefs. We notice this whenever we come to new decisions. We had certain principles, beliefs that we were guided by and that now stand in our way, that is, do not help us to achieve the desired effect. These beliefs that we had to change included:

- "The core team with which we work intensively should be stable and not too big, that is, have a maximum of eight members." Because the core team is the heart of the transformation, we have always realized that it can make sense to include more roles and people.—Today, we sometimes work with teams twice as big as usual. In addition, these also change.
- "In principle, not very many leaders of the 'old' organization should come into leadership roles of the new organization (e.g.: product owner), so that the new can unfold."—We often see "old" leaders enthusiastically driving the agile transformation. The organization has changed, although the leadership staff is still the same but has changed. They now have different roles, a new understanding of leadership and act very differently. They can act as accelerators because they can quickly create focus in groups.
- "Top management must be fully behind the project in every phase of the transformation. Above all, it must not show any doubts."—Today we understand better that uncertainty in leadership is normal and see it as part of the

process. And we have learned: Not everyone has to fully agree at all times. When the process is broadly supported, even top management can wobble for a while. Nevertheless, we work with them on an ongoing basis in the form of many discussions, coaching and visits to similarly affected managers.

- "Project reviews serve to determine where we stand. You find out where the various tasks stand and can make adjustments."—Today, many more employees are involved in the review meetings. They sometimes have the character of lively community meetings, where the whole village comes together to find out what is going on, and we try to use them as "magic moments". Besides the content, the character of community building has become more important.

In dealing with our own beliefs, we have become aware of one thing above all: In times of crisis, it is more important than ever to have a good theoretical model as a reference point for the debate. This helps to pay attention to concrete effects and to deviate from beliefs when this seems to make sense. This is not an invitation to do just anything! It is about reasoned interventions and attentive observation of the consequences of our actions. There is no escaping beliefs, we cannot do without them (except perhaps in unintentional meditation). We find, and this is also a belief, that it is more helpful to be aware of them and reflect on them. We will show how we have implemented this belief in the following section using the four steps of the Neuwaldegg loop.

4.2 The Neuwaldegg loop

All transformations follow a spiral development. A spiral is different from a flow chart. In the latter, step follows step in a predictable sequence. In the loop, you don't know what exactly is coming and you watch what develops. For us, change projects are not linear but disruptive, which of course must also be reflected in the process model (Boos et al., 2017).

Our model is the Neuwaldegg loop. It has helped us in countless change processes, which is why we like to call it the mother of all process models. The Neuwaldegg loop has four steps that are followed in a transformation: We take in information, form hypotheses, determine thrust directions. From these we derive concrete interventions. Based on the reactions to be observed, we take in information again and thus enter the next loop. Change is, therefore, an ongoing process and the loop is a procedural model, a process guide.

Distinguishing between these four steps is important because, unlike in everyday life, transformations are about stepping out of familiar pathways and, as we will show here, this can be supported in each of the steps.

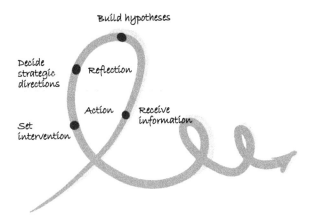

Fig. 4.2. Neuwaldegg loop (Boos & Mitterer, 2014, p. 33)

In a change process, *taking in information* means making oneself known, asking questions, measuring and recording data. This **first step** can be compared to a doctor who asks a new patient questions during anamnesis, listens, measures and looks. In processes of change, the art of this step is to ask the right questions.

For us as external counsellors coming to a new client, this first step of gathering information is particularly important. We first have to familiarize ourselves with the location, as was the case with an internationally active cultural institute that asked us for help. It had just got new management, was now very successful again and wanted to grow further. Suddenly, however, they were confused because there were a few staff resignations. The staff and the leadership were noticeably irritated. Sickness, excessive demands and the type of leadership suddenly became an issue. Was it possible to stay the course? Who had to change? Had the leadership overlooked something? People feared more departures and wanted to understand what was happening.

We were called in and spoke to the management and all the staff in the form of personal interviews. We wanted everyone to have the opportunity to present their views, expectations and concerns in a protected circle. Our task was to listen and absorb the information.

The same is true for anyone starting a project internally. For example, two initiators who are about to start a process can ask themselves: What are our assumptions? Why do we want to initiate this process now? Who should be involved? How much time and resources do we have? What ideas do we have about the goal? At this point, it is helpful to adopt a questioning attitude and gather the available information.

The **second step** is what we call hypothesizing. At the cultural institute, after we had conducted all the interviews, we went back for this step and worked out hypotheses. We describe exactly how and which ones in the next section.

Forming hypotheses means pausing and not acting immediately. They should help to question one's own assumptions. Hypotheses have the function of providing orientation, promoting self-reflection and recognizing patterns. In this way, they promote other ideas and prevent hasty action.

The **third step** in the loop is *the thrust directions*. They are based on the hypotheses and determine how to proceed in principle. To stay with our example: It was agreed that neither new staff nor new leadership was needed for further development, but that the aim was to use the existing resources differently. The thrust was to be more open and flexible with each other.

The thrust directions are not measures, they are more general and describe a direction. Developing them is easy if the hypotheses are accepted, because then the thrust directions are on a solid foundation. We therefore recommend to spend more time working with the hypotheses, you will reap the fruits later.

The **fourth step** is interventions. *Interventions* are concrete measures that are meant to make a difference. One of the 20 or so interventions agreed upon at our cultural institute was to change the seating arrangements in and between the rooms. This had been rigid for a long time and had led to the formation of subgroups that were able to isolate themselves from each other, solidifying their assumptions about the others. This was also true of the leadership. Now people had to move, including the leadership, and adjust to a rotating seating arrangement.

From a systemic point of view, we understand interventions as interventions in a system with the aim of changing the communication in the system. Communication is always the eye of the needle (Luhmann, 1990). At the institute, it could still be observed months after the workshop that the agreements made were kept and that motivation had noticeably increased.

Social systems are not trivial machines (see Section 2.4.2). We do not know how they react to interventions. Therefore, we observe the reactions, gain new information which in turn helps us to sharpen the hypotheses or develop new ones: We rethink the thrust directions and ask ourselves what the next interventions could be. Step follows step, loop follows loop.

The loop as a model helps us to be open to the surprises of a development process. It helps to separate action from reflection. It needs both. Most of the time is short and resources are lacking; but what should never be spared in agile transformations is time for forming hypotheses. This is what the next section is about.

4.3 Form hypotheses

The term "hypothesis" comes from the Greek and means as much as assumption or set assumption that would still have to be proven. We use hypotheses as assumptions that help us understand the situation and develop ideas on how something could be worked on in the context of a transformation. We are not interested in proving them right or wrong, but rather in offering a perspective on a problem or issue. For us, hypotheses are observations (and not truths) that are meant to provide stimuli for further thinking.

Two hypotheses at the cultural institute were:

1. "Staff commitment to the Institute is strong, it just seems thin in some places: Needs such as parental leave, recognition for services rendered or further professional development opportunities are difficult to discuss. Probably the existing communication formats even hinder this."
2. "The leadership is aware of its role and strives to keep work and private life separate. The role could be called 'emergency doctor': It creates structure in a crisis, finds replacements quickly when someone leaves and stays healthy when everyone else gets sick. The leadership puts its own needs aside for the benefit of the organization and expects the same from everyone else."

These hypotheses were presented together with other hypotheses and then the institute was asked to react to them. It was possible to agree, modify or reject the hypotheses. The aim of this step was to bring the relevant and sometimes difficult, because they are subject to accusations, topics into the conversation and to indicate a direction as to what a solution could look like, without immediately proposing measures. Hypotheses, then, are the talking points for the next round, in which perspectives and points of view are exchanged. Often it is about different points of view, associated feelings and disappointments. Everyone had been strongly engaged again and again, but this was hardly noticed by others.

The second hypothesis suggested a direction that could contribute to the solution. In the first hypothesis, the assumption was that an improvement could be achieved by changing the type of communication, that is, no more staff talks or team meetings. Deliberately, no suggestion is made here as to what this other form of communication might look like. Only after everyone had agreed to the hypothesis and the related experiences had been shared did we come to the proposals and thus to the interventions. These were a moderated conversation still in the workshop, later walks in pairs without mobile phones to a coffee house appreciated by all, and the change in the seating arrangement already described.

4.3.1 Setting and flipping hypotheses

We all use hypotheses all the time. Without hypotheses we would not find our way. In everyday life and routine mode, we don't need to discuss them either, because we have settled on a set of common assumptions that we function well with. We are on the highway of our assumptions. But when there are changes or in completely new situations, we need to exchange hypotheses. Then it is necessary to clarify to oneself and to the others which assumptions one is working from, to check them and, if necessary, to correct them.

In the field of startups, testing hypotheses is part of daily business. We have already described an example in the first chapter in thesis 2: A company that successfully sells e-bikes wanted to launch an electric wheelchair on the market. The development team originally assumed that the market launch would only be possible with the support of insurance companies. The hypothesis was that wheelchair users cannot help themselves; they are dependent on insurance benefits. They had not thought about women wheelchair users who are travellers or athletes who want to help themselves and not depend on others. The team had to rethink—"to pivot" is what this rethink is called in the startup scene—and come up with other hypotheses to bring the product to market via a different distribution channel.

4.3.2 Hypotheses for change

Hypotheses are helpful in a transformation process in many ways:

- They provide *orientation* and clarify what is at stake. With a hypothesis you set a topic, such as leadership or staff retention, or name a conflict. Therefore, we think carefully about which topics we address and turn into hypotheses and how many are tolerable. Our rule of thumb is that between 4 and 12 topics are still manageable.
- Hypotheses help to *distance oneself from the system* (problem, persons). We recommend formulating them in such a way that they describe, do not judge and do not take sides. Taking the first hypothesis as an example, it is: "hinder the existing communication formats." We could also have evaluated the nature of staff and team discussions, probably causing feelings of guilt on the part of the leadership.
- Hypotheses are effective when they *encourage self-reflection*, that is, make the participants think. This can be done through reinterpretation, as we intended by calling it "leadership as an emergency doctor".
- Hypotheses also help to *see the bigger picture* by explaining the temporal and social framework. For example, the intention of the phrase "staff commitment seems to be tenuous only in some places" in the first hypothesis was to create

a positive frame (staff and leadership are committed). It was only the form of the previous attempts that did not achieve the goal. Hypotheses also clarify the time dependency and help to understand why this issue is on the agenda right now. What explanation is there for this?

- Finally, hypotheses focus on *potentials and support the change of perspective*. It is about naming the strengths and possibilities (An emergency doctor has a lot of competence) and inviting to develop a different view (Does it make sense as a leader to always appear as an emergency doctor?). The change into a different view serves to loosen the attitude and one comes a little closer to the solution.

4.3.3 Developing hypotheses

Hypotheses are not truths, but offers of interpretation. For hypotheses to be able to do this, they have to be worked out, that is, prepared like a good dish. Peter Gester used a helpful distinction many years ago: everyday and change-friendly hypotheses (Gester, 1992). Everyday hypotheses are developed every day, usually quickly and without much thought. They serve as explanations and are intended to fulfil the desire to explain behaviour (that of others and one's own). They are usually evaluative and rarely useful for solutions in more challenging cases. They are more like fast food and satisfy simple hunger.

Table 4.1. Typical design principles according to Gester (1992, p. 143)

Typical construction principles of everyday reflection	Design principles that promote change
Inner qualities: "He/she is just like that".	*Interpersonality*: "Everyone participates" (co-perpetrator principle instead of perpetrator-victim-perpetrator principle).
Causation: "This had to happen because …"	*Functionality*: "Everything has a use, even if it is hidden".
Past-oriented: "He always does this".	*Future orientation*: "Focusing on what there is something to shape".
Time stability: "That was always true".	*Dealing with time*: "Nothing is always valid and nothing is eternal".
Deficit-oriented: "Negative descriptions lead to resistance and take away energy".	*Open positive evaluation and contradictions*: "Positive descriptions give energy".
Without context: "That's the way it is" (no situational reference).	*Illuminating the overall context*: "Everything has a background".
Conventionality: "That's what we're used to".	*Unconventionality*: "A new look brings new ideas".

To be helpful in change, hypotheses have to be constructed differently. This is shown by the comparison in Table 4.1.

Change-friendly hypotheses are an invitation to slow down. To do this, they have to be worked out step by step. In practice, at the cultural institute described at the beginning of this chapter, it went like this: There were two of us, the advisory team. We each wrote our hypotheses on post-its, off the cuff. Everything that preoccupied us could and should come out here. We clustered the post-its into topics and checked them for relevance to our mission. There should not be too many topics, but also not too few. In this case there were ten. Then we worked through hypothesis by hypothesis and described them in complete sentences according to the rules mentioned above.

We know from many trainings that it is not easy to formulate hypotheses in a change-friendly way. Change-friendly means that they pick up the addressee and motivate him to take a different view without immediately thinking of concrete measures. We recommend formulating them in complete sentences, even if they are not to be presented to someone else. The change-friendliness of hypotheses also has an effect back on those who create the hypotheses and helps to adopt a more open attitude. This can be learned, but needs some practice.

Before you get to work, here are a few tips:

- Have the courage to be unconventional, a new look brings new ideas.
- Play with alternative possibilities! Perpetrators become victims. Luck becomes misfortune. Everything has two sides.
- Change the radius of vision! Small to large, short term to long term.
- Remember: Everything has a use, even if it is hidden! Find the functionality: What is the good in the bad? Who gets what out of it?
- Visualize the flow of time! What does the present have to do with the past? What are possible futures?
- Pay attention to existing contradictions! In which patterns are conflicts balanced?
- Translate thoughts into images or metaphors. Analogue language also captures latent dimensions.
- Start with resource-oriented hypotheses. These are usually more difficult to find than team-oriented ones and train a good eye for the positive.

As the Neuwaldegg loop illustrates, forming hypotheses is not a one-time act, but a process that takes place continuously. In transformation processes, it makes sense to form hypotheses again and again. In agile transformation processes, this is even a necessary prerequisite for moving forward. Only agile teams that have learned to form change-friendly hypotheses together at short intervals are successful. They enjoy it and defend the time for joint reflection. For them, forming hypotheses is like flying in a helicopter: Get in, climb up, look at everything from above and get a picture of the connections. When the helicopter has landed again, the team goes on to the next tasks strengthened.

4.4 Determine thrusts and develop the architecture

The next step in the loop is to work out the directions of thrust and how to manage the transformation process. The result of this step g is what we call architecture. The architecture of a change process has six different dimensions.

1. **Steer and decide:** Steering the transformation should ensure that decisions are made. This concerns decisions about necessary resources, about the involvement of the organization as well as determining in which direction the transformation should proceed. Often these tasks are fulfilled by a steering team or the Product Owner. It is about the role of the commissioner. In contrast to classic change management, the intervals between coordination meetings are shorter in agile transformations and this function is more intensively involved in the process, since it is also part of the change itself.
2. **Work on content:** This is about working on the essential tasks of change: Developing something new, being creative, working out alternatives. This happens in workshops, through learning journeys and the involvement of experts. It needs careful planning and its own social space, for which a so-called core team has proven its worth.

    The composition and working methods of the core team are therefore of great importance (see Section 3.8). In agile transformations, the core team is even more important than usual; it is the nucleus of change. The core team stands for the new. What doesn't work here, certainly doesn't work in the organization. The way the core team acts must reflect the state that the agile transformation has set as its goal; it is the prototype, the biotope of agility. This is what makes the function so challenging and exciting.
3. **Communicate:** This function does not only describe the communication of information, which only comes from the core team as in a one-way street, but it means two-way communication, that is, involving the participants and stakeholders in an engaging way, that is, they not only get information but also have a voice. This can be done via social media, IT platforms or large group interventions. Planning these is one of the tasks of the core team in agile transformation.
4. **Test and simulate:** The aim of this function is to test the effect on a small scale for the whole system and to gain experience for implementation. Typical

examples are test phases, pilot projects, experiments or simulation workshops with users. In agile transformations, this is used as often as possible to learn quickly.

5. **Further development of competences:** This function is essential in agile transformations, as the steps are not planned for a long time, then tried out and implemented later, but kept as short as possible: Build, measure, learn. Everything that is done should serve to learn. Everything that is done should have the same focus: How can we learn something from the next step? The goal is to develop the necessary skills and provide sufficient support. Examples of this are training on and off the job, communities of practice and coaching.

6. **Giving and receiving resonance:** This function is about feedback on transformation. It is about how the changes in the organization are perceived by the stakeholders and what emotions they trigger. The very fact that resonance is asked for makes a difference. Methods that are often used here are focus groups, surveys and sounding boards. This is a helpful vehicle for dealing

Transformation architecture

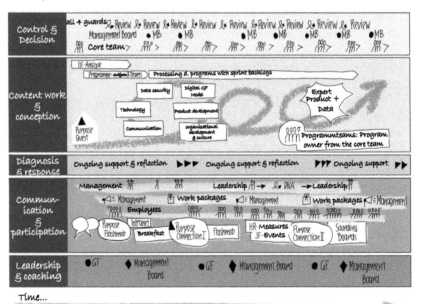

Fig. 4.3. Transformation architecture

with the dynamics of emotions in particularly emotional transformations, mostly second-order change (see Section 4.5 on the transformation map).

4.4.1 Architecture in practice

How does one arrive at a good architecture? Creating it is a task that is sometimes done by external consultants, sometimes done by the steering team, but often done in several loops in the core team and with key stakeholders. The architecture is a powerful intervention, so it should be agreed upon by the core change promoters. It sets the direction and is the basis for further transformation. Everyone can orientate themselves by it and it is easy to see the nature of the transformation.

You can literally feel the pressure and the agility in the process and the challenge of close interlocking. Much of what we have said about agile transformation is illustrated here. The architecture was developed in many discussions and workshops with the core team, with significant input from us as external consultants. It is a draft that changed during the process and was adapted again and again. This was a task of the core team.

Of course, there is a lot of work behind the different levels and individual steps. To describe them would go beyond the scope of this book. However, we would never have arrived at this governance architecture if we had not worked on the structure and interaction of the teams, which ultimately resulted in the structure shown in Fig. 4.4.

It shows more clearly than the architecture how responsibility is distributed and how the teams are networked, whereby we have used elements of Holacracy here (e.g. cross-linkin the voting circle) to enable better dovetailing of the circles.

4.4.2 Quality criteria of an architecture

In order to be able to check whether an architecture is fulfilling its purpose, we have defined five criteria that we use during the development and later also during reviews to make corrections and develop further interventions:

1. *What opportunities are there for participation?* Often the focus of the core team is entirely on the content of the transformation and the involvement of others is seen as a step to be taken later. In agile transformations, the nature of stakeholder co-creation needs to be at the very beginning. The questions are: "How can employees co-design during the process? Can they influence the content and is there room for co-creation or is everything worked out by experts? What steps are planned to move from "knowing" to "being able"?

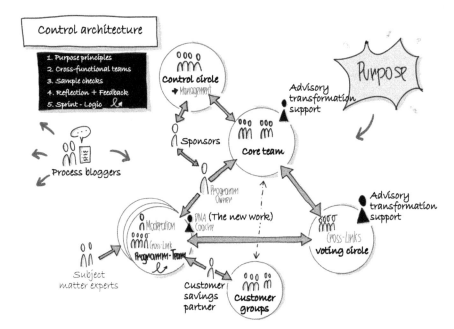

Fig. 4.4. Control architecture

2. *How does the organization and its development as a whole remain in view?* How does the transformation help the organization? This requires an open dialogue with the steering team or Product Owners to involve them in the process and to discuss issues together such as: What interactions can be observed? What effects were intended and what unintended effects can be identified?

3. *How is the environment of the organization taken into account?* This is about the system-environment relationship. Dynamic transformation processes in particular create a world of their own and tend to neglect other things. That's why in Scrum the Product Owner wears the hat of the customer, the "buyer" of the project, to bring the outside world back in. Here it helps to put yourself in the position of stakeholders and observe the transformation with their gaze. It is about the internal or external customer focus, about owners or the competition.

4. *How much disruption and innovation occurs?* As already explained in Chapter 3, it is helpful to distinguish between first-order change (further development and improvement) and second-order change (disruption and

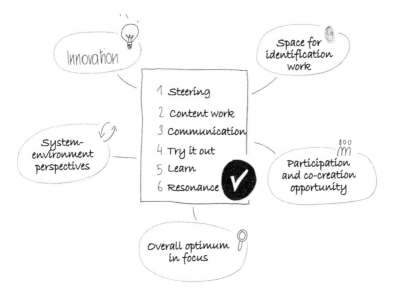

Fig. 4.5. Quality criteria of an architecture

radical change). Agile transformations are second-order changes. Here, many things are broken with that have been the norm up to now, in all dimensions of the triangle of organizational development. It is a matter of reorganizing, relearning and strengthening the new. Can this be seen in the architecture?

5. *How and through what is the engagement with the identity of the organization?* This is the other side of the same coin. What does second-order change do to the identity of the organization? Are the history and achievements appreciated? Is the purpose being worked on and given meaning and significance to the transformation? When important things are left behind, is there space for farewell and mourning?

4.5 The transformation map

At first, Mr. Brenner, the head of the sales organization of a financial services provider with over 200 employees, was not very pleased when we asked him to locate his major change project on the transformation map. He had probably assumed that—after he had explained the initial situation and his objectives—we would immediately propose a concrete approach. It was a very demanding project: The closure and merger of some branches, the resulting reduction of 15 per cent of the staff, the restructuring of the sales processes and the associated change in the tasks of the field and office staff. The goal of the whole project was to make sales more customer-oriented and efficient. In addition, this change had to be carried out during ongoing business; the sales targets were unchanged and the entire company was watching the sales department during this change.

It was understandable that even an experienced salesman like Mr. Brenner was under a lot of pressure. We were able to put ourselves in his shoes and asked him to place this project—symbolized by a small circle made of cardboard—on the map we had prepared. The two axes: "need for change" and "ability to change" (cf. Fig. 4.6) helped him to do this.

For its better orientation, we briefly explained both dimensions: *Need for change* describes the urgency, the pressure that this organizational unit has to change. Whenever the need for change is very high, it is a matter of survival. *Change capacity*, on the other hand, describes the competence and readiness of an organization to make that change. There are two dimensions, horizontal (the view inwards) and vertical (the relation with the environment), which can also be considered separately to determine a starting situation.

After a moment's thought, Mr. Brenner put the circle at the top left of the sheet. The pressure was obvious and there was great concern that his own organization would not cope well with it. There had been no major changes for a long time. For many years they had been more successful than the competition, but now they had become too slow for a number of customers, had lost large projects and the margins had collapsed. Something had to be done, and it had to be done now. At first glance, the situation seemed like a case for restructuring. In the further course of our conversation, the resources and abilities of the previously successful sales department became apparent: After the first setbacks, they

Fig. 4.6. Axes of the transformation map

had been shaken up and had started to conceive first ideas for a new beginning. Above all, it had become clear to all employees in the sales department: "We have to change a lot in our organization! Therefore, Mr. Brenner moved the circle a little to the bottom right".

Already this was no longer a rehabilitation project, but a kind of project that we call a reengineering project. But doesn't it make any difference whether Mr. Brenner is talking about a rehabilitation project or a reengineering project? Not at all, because the difference is serious. In a reengineering project, metaphorically speaking, the call goes out for the fire brigade. You need someone who knows how to assess different fires, who can tackle emergency situations, who has the knowledge and experience to deal with tricky situations and who remains capable of acting in unforeseen situations. A rehabilitation project needs short decision-making processes and clear communication. The goal is survival.

A reengineering project, on the other hand, as the name suggests, needs the engineer, or rather the engineering approach. Here we measure, analyze, develop a plan and construct. Here, dependencies have to be recognized, important things have to be separated from unimportant ones and an ideal sequence has to be defined. A concept is developed that is logical and justifiable, depicts an ideal state and can be transferred to reality like a blueprint. The goal is: The greatest possible efficiency.

Whether we start from a reengineering or a restructuring project has far-reaching consequences for the decisions on how to set up a change project. It is, therefore, better not to call an expert for reengineering projects into a reorganization case and vice versa! It is not so much about the expertise that is called in. It is about processes, communication and expectations. The whole approach is different and the result will be completely different. Whether Mr. Brenner conveys the image of a reorganization case to his management and staff or that of a planned reorganization will trigger completely different reactions.

By combining the two axes of need for change and capacity for change, a matrix is thus created which we call the "transformation map". It was originally developed by our colleagues Jarmai and Heitger (cf. also Heitger, 2014, p. 35ff). It enables us to distinguish between different types of change projects (cf. Fig. 4.7). These are:

- Redevelopment management
- Business Process Reengineering
- Going agile
- Organizational development
- Quality Management (QM)
- Continuous improvement process (CIP)
- Transformation

Fig. 4.7. Transformation map

4.5.1 Change is not equal to change

What can be seen on closer inspection: Projects with a low need for change (which are located on the Y-axis below the solid line in Fig. 4.8) are projects that want to increase efficiency. It is about doing things better, making the workplace safer, getting quotes out faster, ensuring documentation of repairs is consistent, and so on. It is always about gradual, evolutionary improvements, about optimizing the system and about constant learning in everyday life, which is why we also speak of "first-order change" here.

We call projects that are above the line "second-order changes", because here the demand for change is different. Here it is not about improvements, but about radical changes, about doing things completely differently. It is about changes that shake and question the previous self-image and are likely to trigger an "identity crisis". To stay with Mr. Brenner's distribution: In the future, the office staff will be able to process standardized orders themselves and thus the division of roles between office and field staff will be completely changed. The switch from a warehouse in production to just-in-time deliveries, resulting in the dissolution of the warehouse, is another radical change, as is the move to a new office building.

Second-order changes refer not only to what *is* now done differently, but also to *how* something is done. The way of doing things, the distribution of roles, the self-image and the identity are at stake. Whatever is created by the change, it will be different afterwards. It is like a metamorphosis, the caterpillar becomes a butterfly. Second-order changes are more exciting for those affected because there is more at stake. Instead of learning something new, it is about relearning. On a personal level, the changes are accompanied by questions such as: Can I really

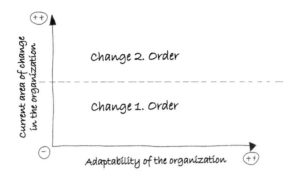

Fig. 4.8. The transformation map, first and second order change

do what is then expected of me without embarrassing myself? Do I even want this transformation?

Second-order change rarely comes alone. Second-order changes often come as a package. They bring about or trigger other changes that need to be thought about. For example, if the office staff can now handle certain orders themselves (so that the field staff spends more time with the customer), this will have an impact on the bonus system for both the office and the field staff.

When distinguishing between first-order and second-order change, it should be borne in mind that it is a gradual transition (some may be more in the nature of second-order change than others) and the assessment should usefully be made from the perspective of the individual concerned.

4.5.2 Not all leadership is the same

The type of leadership can be inferred from the graph if it is divided vertically as shown in Fig. 4.9: All procedures in the left half have a programmatic character, that is, there is a concept, a model of the right procedure. One already knows in advance what is to be done, what is right, and this model has to be implemented (and possibly adapted somewhat to the concrete circumstances). Not only the objective, but also the model is usually already in place at the start of these change projects.

This has implications for the successful nature of leadership and governance. In the left half, a form of management that we call "direct management" has proven to be helpful. This is about top management being close to the change process and familiarizing themselves with the details of the change, understanding them and following them through in implementation. This applies to Mr. Brenner just as much as to the reorganization manager,

Fig. 4.9. Transformation map: Programmatic and contextual leadership

who would massively weaken the change process if he had to ask a committee first for every decision. The fire brigade has a clear hierarchical decision-making structure because this is necessary during operations in order to be able to act quickly.

In the lower left quadrant, the positive effect of directive control is not immediately obvious. The constant small steps of change are only adopted sustainably and thus become part of the culture when the system senses that the leadership is behind it. Steps such as cleanliness in the workplace, the exact documentation of irregularities that have occurred in the night shift, and the ongoing maintenance of manuals are just a few examples that show that the challenge of change here is not in the one-time action, but in the consistency. How do you make these actions part of the daily routine? In order for the desired behaviour to become part of the culture, the leadership must give attention and importance to these actions. Over and over again.

In the right half of our map, on the other hand, the direct involvement of leadership often seems disruptive. This is due to the fact that no blueprint, no model for change exists here yet. This has to be worked out first. What is right only emerges as we go. Things have to be tried out here, not every suggestion has to fit immediately. In the lab and during the first experiments, you don't want the board to be there either. The early attention to detail can prevent the unfolding of the creativity that is needed in this kind of change.

In these types of changes, leadership has another important function. We call this form "contextual leadership". It is about providing the framework, enabling conditions (staff, resources, access) and also providing the protection and calm that these changes need. Leadership creates space for innovation, but is not the expert.

The distinction between the two quadrants of the right half denotes the extent or depth of the change sought.

The change projects such as the learning organization in the lower right quadrant are now associated with agility. Examples of this are very innovative companies that constantly create something new for their customers. Leadership takes a step back, provides the framework and enables innovation, as Mural and Spotify are already doing successfully.

The upper quadrant is about developing something new with a lot of risk—agile transformation. Often it is about a new business model. An example would be Mannesmann, which transformed itself from a steel company to a mobile phone provider, or Nestlé, which developed a new product, a new distribution channel, a new business process with Nespresso. Not much is recognizable after the transformation of the old identity. Change processes of this kind require some courage from those responsible. Either the pressure is already very great and they see no future in what they have done so far (Mannesmann) or they are so enthusiastic about the vision that, as with Nespresso, they accept setbacks and only succeed in the second attempt.

The agile transformation approach is radical. The essential difference to the other approaches lies in the assumption that there is no suitable model and that this must be developed by the organization itself. High pressure to change is paired here with high willingness and ability to change on the part of the organization. The security of an already proven process model, as in reengineering, does not apply and must be developed in the process itself. Change triggers for organizations are usually radical upheavals in the markets. A new business model appears necessary. The priority is on innovation and working for the future. The media company mentioned repeatedly in this book is a good example of this kind of transformation.

Naturally, the models are not uniform in practice, as experimentation and trial and error are in the foreground. The motto is: "safe enough to try". Steering and leadership are also themselves subjects of trial and error. Therefore, a framework, a meta-competence, is needed that defines the field in which the experiments take place and can be further developed through reflection.

Leadership is challenged in two ways here. On the one hand, it requires the courage to question the previous business model or to throw it overboard, which is always accompanied by uncertainty. On the other hand, leadership in this model sees itself less as omniscient, determining where things are going, but more as enablers who take a back seat and provide the framework conditions so that the new can emerge in the organization. It is a paradox: Leadership leads without knowing where the journey is going.

One difficulty this type of change has to deal with is the change in power structures. To become more agile, decisions have to be made differently. And to be able to decide differently, a different distribution of power is needed than in the classic hierarchy. This makes it difficult for most organizations to become truly agile. Power does not simply disappear, but it must now be distributed differently.

4.5.3 What do we use the map for?

Not all transformations are the same. It is therefore important to distinguish right from the start what kind of project we are dealing with. The map illustrates the special position that agile transformation occupies. A traditional approach does not make sense; it needs a radical approach right at the beginning. This is not always clear to everyone involved. The assumptions about the starting situation and objectives are different, but should be aligned before things really get started. To achieve this, the map can provide valuable services.

The bad news first: In practice, different classifications of approaches are the norm. Management teams have different basic assumptions; we have yet to meet a team that was equally united on this. The good news is: If teams exchange their different views at the beginning and use a framework like the map for this, they develop a much more differentiated picture of the situation and a solid starting point for their decisions. Essential here is the understanding of the degree of change: Are we expecting an improvement or a profound change (second order change)? This is also a benefit of the map: It helps to clarify expectations. It shows in appropriate complexity the challenges ahead and provides the basis for many discussions and decisions.

5 Tools for moving organizations

In this chapter, we have compiled for you different tools and interventions that we as the Neuwaldegg consulting team have used and tested in agile transformations. This is an arbitrary selection. We have tried to give you several suggestions for each chapter so that you can choose for yourself. Most tools pay off on different levers. Evaluate for yourself and adapt the interventions to fit your context. We would like to take this opportunity to thank our colleagues who have actively supported us or inspired us to do so. We have tried to mention everyone who contributed in the tools themselves. We hope we have not forgotten anyone!

We wish you a lot of curiosity in implementing it!

5.1 Tools for topics in Chapter 2

5.1.1 Producing variety and resisting simplification

Purpose	Develop practices that create variety despite uncertainty and avoid simplification
Goals	• Create awareness about variety and uncertainty • Check work processes for apparent safety • Establish and apply concrete use cases
Special features	The members learn to consciously deal with paradoxes and permanently deal with the fact that they cannot plan.
Section links	2.1, 3.5, 3.6
Source	Own development (Buzanich-Pöltl) based on Weick & Sutcliffe (2016, p. 67f)

Being able to act in uncertainty and complexity as a person and a team is one of the main challenges in moving organizations, because the only answer is diversity. The art is to create it, to be able to hold it, to keep it open as long as possible and to make a choice in the end. Besides the possibilities described at the person level, it helps to develop different practices in everyday life that destabilize again and again, so that some contexts do not seem too safe.

Table 5.1. Overview of described tools and linked sections

Tools	Section
Producing variety and resisting simplification	2.1
Error: Establish "spirit of contradiction"	2.1
Dealing with mistakes and own stress patterns	2.1
Respect for expertise and leadership understanding (or co-creation expertise and leadership)	2.1
Develop sensitivity for operational processes	2.1
Integrative decision-making process	3.1
Decision-making systemic consensus	3.1
Deciding in the electoral process	3.1
Patterns and beliefs	3.2
Digging for insights	3.2
Culture Soundings	3.2
Purpose quest with the Ikigai	3.3
Purpose connection—we want meaning	3.3
Learning journeys	3.3
Stakeholder interviews	3.3
Ongoing role reflection and feedback	3.4
The role-free space	3.4
Edge—Belief Set "Grow Fixed Mindset and Growth Mindset	3.5
Location and goal: Belief "better me + better you = better us".	3.5
F#: Feedback—Impulse—Tension	3.5
Practising here and now to be playable	3.6
Practise self-differentiation	3.6.1
Clear leadership: Using the experience cube	3.6.1
Clear leadership: Practising appreciative and curious self in extreme situations	3.6.1
Curious Me: Four levels of listening	3.6.1
From a deficit-oriented mindset to an appreciative one	3.6.1
Describe experiences and do not judge	3.6.1
Journaling	3.6.1
Noticing game	3.6.1
Status flexibility: Power in high and low status	3.7
My power in my roles	3.7
Team and role diagnosis: Force field analysis	3.8
Immunity to change: Overcoming personal obstacles in a team-oriented way	3.8
Check-in exercises in teams: Shaping the transition of people and members	3.8
Create a map	3.8
Meeting mastery based on the four rooms	3.8

Tools	Section
Role marketplace: Aligning team and roles with purpose	3.8
Tactical meeting	3.8
Governance meeting	3.8
Virtual focus meeting	3.8
Team agreements for virtual cooperation	3.9
Lustful tribe space in virtual space	3.9
Retrospective in teams	3.9
Twin Star—reteaming[*]	3.8
Strengthen feedback and cooperation between teams	3.8

Direction

In the context of a workshop or meeting, you as a facilitator can use these questions again and again to develop targeted practices that will be incorporated into daily work. Start the session with a warm-up by having participants have a piece of paper and a pencil at hand: "Please draw a house with a garden in one minute." After everyone has drawn, these pictures are shared with each other. Often the pictures look very similar. Discuss why this is, whether these drawings correspond to reality, what other shapes and variations there might be, and so on. The aim is to create a sensitivity for simplifying and also the number of possibilities.

Then explain why working on these issues—diversity and avoiding simplification—is important by explaining the aspects from Section 2.1.2. Form small groups to look for existing practices and how to deal with them:

- How do we deal in principle in the team with holding complexity and diversity? What promotes and what hinders?
- Which work processes in daily activities support non-simplification? Which are obstructive?
- How do we act in uncertainty? What are typical patterns of ours? Find concrete examples of successes and failures.
- How would we describe doubt in ourselves? How do we deal with it?

The small groups share their findings and then go one step further by forming one or two small groups around one question each:

- Adapt existing work processes so that they do not lead to simplification. Make concrete proposals.

- Which projects and routines can we name differently so that the working titles do not become fixed? Make concrete suggestions.
- What do we need to do new/different to get better at this skill? Suggest how concretely you want to do this.

After the small groups have worked out suggestions, it is important to clarify which of them should be put into practice and which should not. Fix a date by which you want to practise the new practice in order to evaluate it.

5.1.2 Error: Establish a "spirit of contradiction"

Purpose	Establish a "spirit of contradiction" at the personal and organizational level so that mistakes are a constant source of development
Goals	• Establish good error handling
Number of participants	3 to 80 people
Section links	2.1.2, 3.5, 3.6
Source	Own development (Buzanich-Pöltl) based on Weick & Sutcliffe (2016, p. 55f)

Establishing a spirit of dissent means confronting people with different points of view, stimulating discussion and criticism, looking for controversies, discussing them, looking for anomalies and addressing them. The opposite of this would be an "approval spirit" and would not be useful for moving organizations because it means that learning and adaptation opportunities are lost. The spirit of dissent has errors in focus!

Direction

As a facilitator, you explain what the purpose of this exercise is and what causes mishaps or big mistakes most of the time: Someone did not anticipate them, the deviation was not registered in time or the persons did not deal with the unexpected event sufficiently or have no form for it. In order to deepen this topic and connect it to the participants' world of experience, an exchange takes place in small groups: Which mistakes and mishaps have already been experienced in the organization and what are the possible causes behind them. After some time, the findings are shared in the group and the facilitator looks for patterns or red threads. In the second step, the practices described in the chapter on resilience and agility are used to discuss how this form of doubting can be used constructively in one's own organization. Depending on the size of the group, in plenary or in small groups:

- Expectations are expressed so that deviations quickly stand out and provide a frame of reference.
- Raise awareness of vulnerability and ask about risk so that the environment is sensitized to vulnerability to mistakes and surprises and wants to learn from them.
- Look for bad news and communicate it. Make it clear that only good news or no news is "bad news".
- Do not conclude mistakes too early and look for connections.
- Near-accidents or "just barely made it" are considered failures and must, therefore, be actively dealt with.
- Establish dealing with mistakes as a strategy. If someone says: "This is my strategy; this is what is important to me", it translates to: "These are the mistakes I don't want to make! This is where I need reliable performance!"

Based on this discussion, the participants derive concrete measures and practices that are implemented in the company and are constantly reflected upon and further processed.

5.1.3 Dealing with mistakes and one's own stress patterns

Purpose	Create conscious handling of errors at person level
Goals	• Reflect on own behaviour patterns in the context of mistakes • Practising concrete conversations in the context of mistakes
Special features	Working with mistakes is usually very exciting for individuals.
Number of Participants	6 to 20 people
Section links	2.1, 3.5, 3.6
Source	Own development (Buzanich-Pöltl/Jarmai)

You quickly hear yourself saying: "Mistakes are part of the game. Mistakes are human. A mistake should only happen once." Often, however, the opposite is experienced: Many justify themselves when mistakes occur or are particularly critical when others make mistakes. What is said and what is observed often diverge. The reasons for this are manifold: In school, many of us were and are still pointed out mistakes with a red pencil, and that rarely meant anything good. Because mistakes are often associated with punishment and shame, fear arises as a self-protective reflex (Kline & Saunders, 1997, pp. 19, 34). This also has to do with the fact that we are Catholic in our society and rule violations are associated with punishment. The whole thing is made more difficult by the fact that our brain perceives negative biases more strongly. With all this in mind, it helps to question one's own stress patterns so that a conscious approach to mistakes can take place that promotes development.

Direction

As a facilitator, start with a mind map on the topic of mistakes, which the participants call out to you: What comes to your mind on the topic of errors and dealing with them in organizations? On the basis of this, you can create a first opening round and sensitization for it. Then explain the two-step process: First, reflect on your own behaviour and how you deal with mistakes. Then the handling of others.

Step 1: Person level

People have about 30 minutes to think about the following questions and write them down in the sense of journaling:

- Mistakes made by others: What is a mistake for me? How do I react to mistakes made by others? Why do I react differently to mistakes? How does it feel? How do I feel about the question of who is to blame? What differences can be made at all? How do I address mistakes? How do I deal with the setbacks of others?
- Own mistakes: What were my own mistakes in the past? What different categories of mistakes can I identify? How do I feel about them? What have I already been able to learn from mistakes? What new things have already been created? How do I deal with my setbacks? How strict am I with myself? What mistakes do I definitely not want to make in my different roles and also as a person?
- Fault tolerance: What does that mean for me? How resentful am I? What contexts do I create where mistakes are desirable? How do I allow for mistakes from the outset? What are my beliefs about mistakes? Where do they come from?

After this self-reflection, you form pairs that share these insights. Each creates their own stress pattern profile based on personal experience. The insights are shared and deepened if necessary. In addition, each is given the opportunity to share a mistake and how it affected them emotionally. Afterwards, emotions are discussed and how they are related to mistakes. Often the topic of guilt, shame or vulnerability comes up at this point.[9]

Step 2: Dealing with the mistakes of others

After a break, the focus is on dealing with other people. The productivity of mistakes and setbacks also depends on how the other person reacts to them. Therefore, it helps to experience different situations by practising the delivery of bad news. As a facilitator, you collect "bad news from the company" that the participants can think of. These situations are the starting point for the next exercise. It is best to form groups of three with the following roles: A bearer of the bad news, a relevant counterpart and an observer. The trios change their roles after each round and also the way of reacting to the news. In the first scene, the search is on for the guilty person: Who is to blame? In the second scene, the problem is to be solved quickly: How do we solve the problem? In the third scene, the focus is on learning: How can we and others learn sustainably from this situation? After this exercise, the different experiences are shared and first measures are derived.

   "When someone tells you about his setbacks, he usually wants to know from you what you think of his experience. With a gentle conversation and carefully chosen words, you can help him get over his setbacks," say Furman and Ahola (2014, p. 109). They suggest an approach that is carried out in the context of another role play, based on the current examples:

- Show interest and listen.
- Accept the emotional weight of the mistake.
- Show understanding for his reaction to the mistake.
- Show empathy for the fact that it takes time to overcome this mistake.
- Messages like: "It'll be all right!", "It's not really that tragic!" or "It'll be good for something" are not very helpful. All this distracts from what is. Stay with your counterpart, listening is often enough.

---

9   A helpful impulse for this is provided by "Brené Brown on Blame": https://www.yout ube.com/watch?v=RZWf2_2L2v8 (retrieval date: 14.06.2020).

5.1.4 Respect for expertise and understanding of leadership

Purpose	Use expertise sensibly and establish a suitable attitude towards it
Goals	• Establish practices that support respect for expertise • Sharpen and practise attitude regarding leadership and expertise
Special features	• Work on the basis of own concrete situations and derive practices • Be able to describe critical situations of the organization
Number of participants	unlimited
Section links	2.1.2, 3.6
Source	Own development (Buzanich-Pöltl) based on Weick & Sutcliffe (2016, p. 73f)

Respect for expertise is often misunderstood: Many understand it as a shift of power from managers to experts. That would be too limited a view: Firstly, managers are also experts, just not for everything. And secondly, it is about distributing authority and decisions in a meaningful way. In this respect, it is clear that work is being done on structures and also on the understanding of leadership. In order to be able to shape the diversity of this ability, it helps to prepare this approach in such a way that you can deepen it with the participants (see Section 2.1.2).

Direction

As a facilitator, first prepare the topic by letting the participants associate freely: What could be behind the statement "respect for expertise"? What can it be useful for? What is it harmful for? What does all this have to do with leadership as well? You can write down the main messages. Then tell the group how you understand this topic and show the different perspectives on it. In a first discussion, this topic is deepened and hypothetically applied to your own organization: How do we experience this in our organization? What could it mean? What barriers do we recognize and what favourable conditions do we see? How does this affect our current understanding of hierarchy? Summarize the current state and underline that in the future it will be about making decisions where the highest expertise is at that moment to make a good decision. A moment when such decision-making structures take effect quickly is a challenging situation. Look together in the group for challenging situations: Those that succeeded and those in which you (almost) failed. Small groups then have the task of looking closely at these situations:

- Describe observations: What was the situation like? What was the great uncertainty? How did who behave? Who made decisions? What observable mechanisms occurred?
- Hypotheses: What dynamics and patterns have emerged from our perspective? Who or what has provided security? What are possible reasons for failure or non-failure?

In the whole group, the different observations and hypotheses are shared and commented on. Together they outline patterns related to respect for expertise and leadership and then describe new or complementary patterns that may be helpful in the future. They then move into developing practices and actions that will be built into future everyday life. At this point, we recommend also working through the issue of power, including the high and low status exercise (see Section 5.2.25).

5.1.5 Develop sensitivity for operational processes

Purpose	Develop mindfulness towards operational processes
Goals	• Making people aware of their own contributions to the team as a whole
	• Focus on and analyze processes
	• Develop own practices for this
Special features	Input and moderation
Number of Participants	6 to 20 people
Section links	2.1.2, 3.6
Source	Own development (Buzanich-Pöltl) based on Weick & Sutcliffe (2016)

Direction

Introduce this idea, which is described in Section 2.1.2, as a facilitator to the group and briefly deepen together what this aspect can be useful for. Once a common view has emerged, work in three steps, if possible in small groups:

1. What is the big picture for us and what is my contribution? The small groups present their results, which are discussed and reconciled in the whole group. It is important that everyone is heard.

2. What are our operational processes and where are the interfaces with other areas, stakeholders and systems? Where are we influenced, by which processes are we affected? How well do these work and where are the critical points? Why? Who is responsible for what? This step is an analysis step and can take longer. It may help to divide it up according to certain criteria. This step can take several loops and does not have to be done all at once.

3. Strengthen sensitivity: How do we want to give ourselves feedback in the future and when do we do it concretely? What are our expectations in relation to our resources such as curiosity, body awareness and differences? The language of the Clear Leadership Model also helps here!

It is important that after each step, concrete derivations and measures are made with each other, which are incorporated into the daily work.

5.2 Tools for topics in Chapter 3

5.2.1 Integrative decision-making process

Purpose	Clarifies whether objections are valid or not in the sense of the Holacracy Constitution.
Goals	• Takes different views on a potential expectation or rule and checks whether they make sense for the whole circle • Integrates meaningful objections transparently • Involves all members of the team/circle to create rules of the game that are effective
Special features	• Includes many clever questions that clarify personal assumptions and thoughts at the person/role interface • The idea is: More brains come up with better solutions—even if it doesn't always feel that way.
Resources	1. Role facilitator consistently guides through the process. 2. Role secretary writes visibly and transparently for all. Supports the facilitator by interpreting the rules.
Duration	5 to max. 15 minutes per single-wall round
Section link	3.1
Source	HolacracyOne

The Integrative Decision Making Process (IDM) reviews objectors' objections for validity and validity. The facilitator role asks questions and engages the objector to clarify their tension. At the same time, the facilitator role takes care to comply with the governance rules under the Constitution and to avert proposals that violate the governance rules.

Direction

The following questions are asked step by step by the facilitator in case of an objection. If they are answered with "yes", the question is continued; if they are answered with "no", the objection is not valid:

- "Is there any reason why applying this proposal could cause harm or set us back? If so, how is harm done?" This step is about better understanding harm and sensitivities. Often concerns are explained and gut feelings are discussed in more detail.
- "Is your fear that this proposal will cause harm, *or* do you fear that this proposal is unnecessary or not complete?" Here we clarify whether the circle's capacity will be limited in order to fulfil the circle's purpose. If the proposal does harm from the perspective of the objector, it moves on to the next clarification question. However, if the proposal is considered unnecessary, it is not a valid objection. Only tension bearers can evaluate for themselves whether this suggestion is necessary or not. The proposal is also not valid if it is assessed as incomplete: It is a better idea that can be brought to a governance meeting at any time.
- "Does your objection arise because of this proposal, *or does* this problem already exist if this proposal is not applied?" This question clarifies whether applying the proposal creates new tensions. If this is the case, we move on to the next question. If this is not the case, the objection falls out of the process as there is no direct link between the proposal and the objection and the objection is not valid. Tip: This is a resource for new tensions to be resolved!
- "Do you know that this effect will happen, *or* do you anticipate that this effect will happen?" If the effect is fixed, we move on to the next clarification question. If the effect is anticipated, another clarification question is added: "Can significant harm be done by applying this suggestion *or* is this suggestion "safe enough to try", knowing that this suggestion can be adjusted again at any time?" If significant harm is done, move on to the next question. If not, then it is an invalid objection. The purpose of this two-step is to find out whether there is already fact- or data-based experience that predictable harm can be done and to what extent.

- "Would this proposal limit one of your roles, *or* are you trying to help the circle or another role of this circle?" The former would be a valid objection, the latter question would not! It is not the responsibility of any role or person to protect others. It is the responsibility of each circle member to do so themselves.
- Valid objections must be integrated into the proposal. This means that both tensions have to be resolved and both work productively on this solution. Once a common solution has been found, the objection process must be repeated in turn (including the proposers). After that, there is a re-processed governance.

5.2.2 Decision-making process: Systemic consensus

Purpose	Find a decision for different solution variants and pay attention to a good balance of interests
Goals	• If there are several variants, find the one with the least resistance. • Low resistance strengthens the solution
Special features	Does not ask for consent but for resistance and thus has the least potential for conflict
Resources	Moderation
Duration	10 to 30 minutes
Section link	3.1
Source	Fink & Moeller (2018, p. 255) and Visotschnig & Schrotta (2005)

This decision-making process helps when there are several options to choose from. The charm lies in the fact that it is not asked which is the one correct solution. Rather, the different resistances to each proposed solution are asked. It is important that all members know the purpose and the procedure of this format. In addition, there needs to be a person who leads through the process and adheres to the process steps.

Direction

The first step is to clarify who this decision affects and who can and may decide. In principle, only roles or persons to whom two of the following three questions apply are invited: Am I affected? Will I be involved in the implementation? Am I responsible for this decision? Of course, other questions can also be added.

In the second step, common criteria are developed: Which factors should be considered in this decision? What is important to know and consider? Once the criteria are clear, the questionnaire can start. All proposed solutions are written down transparently for all to see. The last solution proposal is always a passive solution and this means maintaining the status quo and not adopting any of these solutions.

In the next step, one round starts per proposed solution. All eligible voters can assign 0 to 10 resistance points per solution in each round: 0 means "no resistance at all", 10 means "extremely high resistance". Before voting, it must be clarified how many 10-point ratings mean a veto and must be discussed.

When the first round starts, the facilitator tells each person to think about how many resistance points will be given for solution A. The facilitator then tells each person to think about how many resistance points will be given. After a short time, she counts to three and everyone raises their hands at the same time and shows the resistance points for solution A with their fingers. The points are added up and written down transparently for everyone. The same is done for solution B, C, D and the passive solution. The solution with the lowest resistance score is the best solution for the team.

5.2.3 Deciding in the electoral process

Purpose	Choose roles in a team or circle that are most appropriate from the perspective of the members
Goals	• Transparent choice • Ongoing updating of certain roles • Strengths of different people
Special features	• Is intended for specific Holacratic roles: Facilitator, Secretary, Rep-Link • Can also be extended to other roles
Resources	• Role facilitator consistently guides through the process. • The role of the secretary is visible and transparent for all. • Slips of paper for the election
Number of Participants	3 to max. 25 persons
Duration	30 minutes
Section link	3.1
Source	HolacracyOne

In this election process, the roles of facilitator, secretary and circle rep are chosen. The purpose is to elect the person into the role that is most appropriate at the moment and can energize it in the most meaningful way, with the aim of supporting the circle in its purpose in the best possible way.

Direction Preparations

The facilitator role opens the election and selects the order of roles to be elected. This role also determines how long the elected roles will fill them (sets the term) until there is a new election. Before voting takes place, the role of secretary displays the role description for all to see.

Electoral process

1. Each person in the circle gets a post-it and writes their own name and the person of choice on the post-it: "Barbara chooses Robert". It is important that no one sees what is written down so that they do not influence each other. By the way: You can also vote for yourself!
2. The role facilitator collects the slips of paper and sticks them visibly on a whiteboard and reads out loud the election proposals, which are also clustered immediately.

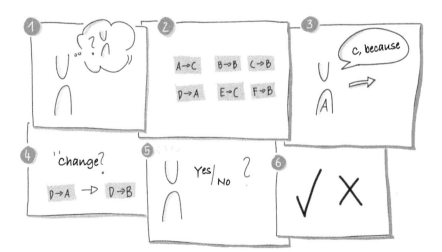

Fig. 5.1. Electoral process

3. Then each person in turn explains why that person was chosen: "I chose Karl because he has been working more deeply with Constitution for some time and he is certainly a good support for this circle here." Or: "I have chosen Renate because she is completely new and can get into our system so quickly and can deepen Holacracy and this circle quickly" and so forth.
4. Afterwards, the role facilitator asks: "After hearing all this, would anyone like to change their own voting process?" Any changes are recorded.
5. The facilitator role quickly evaluates who has the most votes and asks the nominated person: "Do you want to accept this election result?"
6. If the person answers "yes", he or she is immediately occupied in the IT system and takes over the new role at that moment!
7. If the person answers "no", a new election is held.

Special features and tips on the election process

This process has some aspects that we find particularly positive. On the one hand, it is a participatory process that integrates all circle members in filling roles. However, the much nicer thing is when those elected hear why their circle colleagues elected them. Many positive thoughts and assessments are shared and these individuals grow in the moment. We experience this part of the process as very invigorating. Additionally, it is also interesting to hear how other colleagues come to decisions. It is not uncommon to have good thought processes that lead to new decisions.

It should be noted that the person energizing the Circle Lead role may not be chosen as facilitator or Circle Rep. This is for two reasons: First, the Circle Lead role should be able to focus fully on the process in the circle. Secondly, it is important to distribute authority so that the person who has the Circle Lead role cannot be too distracting.

Many wonder why the role of Circle Lead is not also chosen in order to change power structures here as well. There are different reasons for this. First of all, Holacracy is not a democratic form of organization, but integrates democratizing aspects at certain points that strengthen the circles. Holacracy is based on the assumption that in group-dynamic decision-making processes the most suitable people are not always elected. An election process works well when the skills and tasks of a role are easy to assess, such as the role of facilitator. It becomes more complex when operational roles with different competencies and skills are needed. Therefore, the Circle Lead role decides who can best energize which role or circle at the moment, as the role is responsible for energizing the circle in the best possible way in terms of the purpose by filling roles with the appropriate people.

5.2.4 Patterns and beliefs

Purpose	Understanding awareness of one's own organizational culture and its operating principles
Goals	• Uncovering current patterns and beliefs operating in the organization • Sensitizing teams
Special features	Organizational members sharpen their view of non-formalized dynamics in the organization
Number of Participants	10 to 15 people
Section link	3.2
Source	Neuwaldegg practice

As already described, it is helpful in the agile transformation process to keep an eye on one's own culture and also the patterns and beliefs and to reflect on them continuously. These are constantly under observation and are always being supplemented, expanded and described in more detail. These patterns help to find hypotheses and thrust directions that can be alluded to through the decision-making premises of programmes, communication channels or/and personnel. One can do this exercise again and again with, for example, a core team or management team.

Direction

As a facilitator, really just briefly explain the systemic picture of culture. The image of the iceberg is usually most helpful here to get the exercise off to a good start. The first step is to form small groups, with everyone working on the same task: First, the questions and ideas need to be explored in depth and told to each other. It is best to visualize the most significant findings and results on a flipchart or elsewhere. Based on this discussion, find a metaphor that best describes the culture of your organization and draw it. Think of a skit that reflects a typical aspect and behaviour in your organization (can also be leadership).

We have the following questions on offer:

- When you tell a good friend what makes your organization tick, what do you tell them? What is typical?
- Imagine that your best friend starts working for you in the organization. What tips would you give her? What should she definitely not do?

- What are the secret rules of the game in the organization?
- Who is rewarded or punished for what?
- Who are the heroines of the organization and why? What do they do concretely? What do they get recognition for?
- What stories are told in the organization? What do you hear over and over again?
- What do you have to do to get kicked out of here?

This exercise can last up to 45 minutes. All results are presented and shown, starting of course with the sketches. Afterwards, it helps to have a dialogue in the whole group. If the group is larger, this can also be done in small groups. The following questions support this: What are the red threads that we recognize? What patterns and beliefs are at work here? What are our hypotheses about how these patterns and beliefs come about? What are these patterns and beliefs a good answer to? What purpose do they serve? Which are functional in the sense of transformation and which are dysfunctional? As a facilitator, make sure that you take notes and sort out the most important themes. Once a holistic picture has emerged, the next step can be taken. Small groups now describe which patterns and beliefs would be helpful for the future organization. How do the people then act? What stories do they tell? Who are the heroines then? What image emerges? Important: Existing patterns and beliefs are also important in this exercise. After this exercise, the findings are shared and discussed again. Based on this, the architecture, programmes, backlogs and prototypes are reviewed and new directions are also sought: Can something be adapted or changed? Does something additional need to be included? What would be a good next step? This exercise can be done again and again, in the best case adapted, and continuously feeds into the process.

5.2.5 Digging for insights

Purpose	Create awareness of one's own organizational culture
Goals	• Develop joint recognition of patterns, structures and mental models
Special features	Visual form of working on the theme of culture
Number of Participants	10 to 15 people
Section link	3.2
Source	Borget (2018, p. 65)

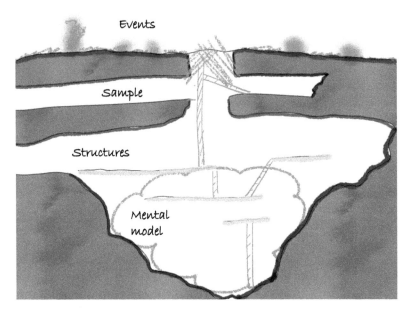

Fig. 5.2. Mine model based on Borget (2018, p. 64)

This exercise takes up another metaphor for the theme of organizational culture: A mine. The idea is that only the coal can be seen on the surface, but the real, essential work is being done underneath. Beneath this surface, trends and patterns can be identified if the system is observed over a longer period of time. One level below are informal structures that promote these patterns and events. These structures describe norms, rules, resources, informal networks, power relations, and so forth. These structures are based on assumptions and beliefs, also called mental models. In principle, the deeper you go, the more you learn. You can find this metaphor in Fig. 5.2. The idea when working together with teams is to use this metaphor playfully and thereby learn more about the organizational culture in order to be able to continue working in a looping way afterwards.

Direction

If you are facilitating this cultural analysis, explain this model in advance, which is best displayed on a large pin board or other medium. Explain what each level stands for. Each team member receives a post-it to answer the following question on it: Write down an important event that has a significant effect on your organization. Important: Please describe exactly. Once this is done, the participants stick the post-its over the mine. Afterwards, these events are discussed and deepened in order to find out together which patterns are connected to them. As a facilitator, write the patterns and trends found on post-its and stick them in the patterns area. It is important that the team has a common picture about this and agrees.

The next step is to find the structures behind it: What are the norms, rules and values that cause these patterns? Record these too and stick the findings in the space provided. Now it's the turn of the mental patterns, which also need to be uncovered. A question that supports this is: What different ways of thinking could be at play here? Here it helps to formulate rather hypothesis-oriented: "It could be that …; I believe …". If many beliefs arise, these can be evaluated by the team members: Which ones are most likely to work from my point of view.

In the last step, the findings are used in the current team: What beliefs, patterns and structures are at work here? What is helpful and what is dysfunctional? What of this do I observe in myself? What have we learned about our system today and what do we want to deduce?

5.2.6 Culture soundings

Purpose	Gaining patterns and beliefs through group exercises for agile transformation
Goals	• Capture cultural expressions • Capture different perspectives • Involve and thereby value members of the organization
Resources	• an armchair circle for the participants • a minute taker
Number of Participants	6 to 8 persons
Duration	2 to 3 hours
Section link	3.2
Source	Neuwaldegg practice

Culture soundings give the opportunity to put an ear to the organization to find patterns and beliefs. It is important that these are as multi-perspective as possible, across departments and hierarchies. We have good experience with three to four groups covering different perspectives of the organization: leadership, staff, divisions, and so on. It is important that the facilitator provides a structure, but at the same time acts flexibly and responds to the topics of the participants. The focus is on listening, asking questions and wanting to understand.

Principles

Allow an opening round with a short introduction.

- Ask *open questions* and avoid justifying yourself.
- Invite participants to *open discussion*, especially to understand even better whether statements made by individuals are only individual opinions or group opinions.
- *Avoid "question & answer" rounds.*
- Ensure *good documentation of* the statements made and results for further processing.
- *Share your personal impressions and insights in a timely manner.*

Direction

The introduction serves as an orientation by clarifying the purpose and the participants get to know each other. Confidentiality and the type of documentation are also discussed.

The first step is to start with an exercise that enables the participants to easily get in touch with the current topic. You can lay out picture cards from which each person chooses a card that from their point of view best underlines the following statement: "This picture describes our organization in its peculiarities because …".

In the second step, the participants delve deeper into the topic of culture by you as a facilitator explaining what patterns, assumptions, and beliefs are. The iceberg model helps here to get a better idea of what this means. Then pairs are formed to discuss and add to the following statements:

- The following secret rules of the game shape our culture …
- The heroines of our organization are those who do the following …
- Our organization ticks …
- Prohibitions and commandments in our company are …
- A metaphor or image that best describes our organizational culture …

These questions can first be worked on in pairs or groups of three and then taken to the whole group. The results are worked on in dialogue, with the facilitator taking notes of the most important statements.

The next step is mainly about additional and new suggestions: Now that I have deepened this topic, I would like to add the following suggestions. I would experience this as real progress. Finally, participants are given time to reflect on what they themselves have learned in this short time and what they take away for themselves. This mood is picked up during a check-out.

5.2.7 Purpose-quest with the Ikigai

Purpose	Finding and formulating the purpose for organizations and teams
Goals	• At the start of a transformation, after the strategic corridor and also one's own life path in the organization have been worked on • For teams that want to equip and reposition themselves in the context of change • Sharpening one's own identity and "what for"
Special features	• Additionally sharpens vocation, profession, passion and mission • Is a dialogical intervention • In an organization, you look for a diverse composition of members
Number of Participants	8 to max. 30 people
Duration	4 hours
Section link	3.3
Source	Developed on the basis of the model itself (Buzanich-Pöltl)

The Ikigai comes from Japanese culture and means to strive for what is worth living for and focuses on meaning and purpose.[10] This model is the starting point for the Ikigai process and supports teams and also organizations in deepening their own meaning and purpose.

---

10 More details at https://de.wikipedia.org/wiki/Ikigai#cite_note-1 (call date: 14.06.2020).

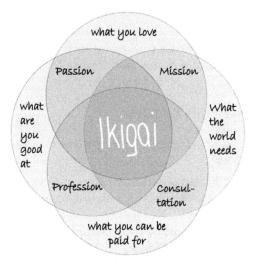

Fig. 5.3. Purpose quest with the Ikigai

Direction

As a facilitator, you first explain the purpose of purpose (see Section 3.3) and introduce the model of Ikigai. After everyone knows why this step is being taken, the group process starts.

Four groups are formed to work out the individual fields in about 20 minutes, each based on a question: What do the world, our environment, our clients need? What are we recognized and needed for? What are we really good at? What do we love to do? Each group presents its own results in plenary.

Now the next step is to form four groups that are mixed as much as possible so that ideally all the previous perspectives are present in the next elaboration. The group members now "intersect" the following fields in about 20 to 30 minutes and visualize their results:

- Group 1: Find the intersection of "What does the world need" and "What are we needed for" and thereby formulate the vocation in one sentence or in keywords.
- Group 2: Intersection of "What are we needed for" and "What are we really good at?" and thereby formulate the profession in one sentence or in keywords.
- Group 3: Find the intersection of "What are we really good at?" and "What do we love to do?" and thereby formulate the passion in one sentence or in keywords.

- Group 4: Find the intersection of "What do we love to do?" and "What does the world need?" and thereby formulate the mission in one sentence or in keywords.

These results are shared with the group and sounded: What do these impressions and findings trigger? What questions do they raise? After everything has been clarified, it helps to take a walk in silence for 15 minutes and find a symbol that expresses for oneself the whole purpose in the current moment. This symbol is explained in the group with one sentence. After this round, the task is to form an editorial team, preferably again a maximally mixed group and the leader should also be involved. This group now has the task of finding a sentence based on the results and the discussions according to the following structure (Fink & Moeller, 2018, p. 96): "What contribution are we making, for whom (stakeholders), to achieve what impact (for what)?" As a facilitator, you support the editorial team.

While the editorial team works on the new purpose sentence for about 30 minutes, the rest of the group prepares a small party so that the editorial team can celebrate with the new purpose. When the purpose is presented, the event group takes care of the staging. The rest of the group learns how the sentence came about and adds thoughts and urgent objections, which are added if necessary. Pay attention to the tips in Section 3.3.2 on Purpose! We recommend that after a purpose quest there is a next step to operationalize the purpose and develop first prototypes, for example: Objectives in the first year, first principles for our cooperation, first measures or derivations for some roles.

5.2.8 Purpose connection—we want meaning!

Purpose	Connect the members of the organization with the Purpose to make it more effective.
Goals	• Experiential format so that members can understand the development process and the purpose process • Understanding and aligning with purpose
Special features	• Scalable format and can also be carried out in ward mode • Project team consists of members of the organization
Resources	Formulated Purpose, Internal Project Team, Purposer
Number of Participants	6 to max. 1000 persons
Duration	0.5 to 1.5 days
Section link	3.3
Source	Own development with customers (Buzanich-Pöltl)

The Purpose connection starts after the purpose quest has been carried out. It helps to establish a project team that represents different parts of the organization and at the same time has already been part of the quest itself. The central question is: How can the purpose be brought into the organization and experienced? This means that it is not about individual communication measures such as posters, T-shirts and intranet posts, but about experience and dialogue formats that also integrate the entire transformation process.

Direction

The Purpose connection team takes care of the following steps:

1. **Storyline and format:** What is our core story that we want to tell? What has particularly moved us in this process? What name should this connection be given? What fits our organization? One organization had decided on a station operation in the sense of a future exhibition, which was held in its own building. The name was "We want meaning". Another had decided on several large group events.
2. **Preparation:** How can we arouse the curiosity of our colleagues without giving away the sentence itself? Ideas we have already tried out: Going to the cinema together with films like "The Silent Revolution" including reflection afterwards and lots of popcorn. Or specific invitations with sayings on them that call for some purpose-oriented actions. Small messages on the intranet.
3. **Purpose connection:** The formats contain the following steps and are ideally co-moderated by the project team:
   - Purposers: We recommend that purposers (people who have experienced the process) are in the groups so that they can keep giving information.
   - Understanding the strategic corridor (60 minutes): In the form of stations, the individual aspects that move the transformation itself can be deepened. It is important that the key players who can also give answers are part of these stations. One organization produced audio guides with panels like in an exhibition, and afterwards the participants could ask questions.
   - Life path: The aim here is to consciously bring up one's own history, events and important people. A timeline is helpful, which the participants can add to. Some organizations also use this point to conjure up old objects or products and then add a quiz!

- Why Purpose and the Purpose Phrase: First, the concept of purpose is explained and who all worked on it. When everyone has understood why purpose makes sense, the purpose sentence is presented. ATTENTION: Here a tension is built up that almost always disappoints. Because we know this, we often introduce it as follows: "In the next step, we will show them the Purpose sentence … and we already know one thing: Most of them will be disappointed. Try to engage anyway …". After the participants have read the sentence, we say: "Maybe you think: They made such a fuss for that? Or: This is supposed to be the sentence? … I could have done that in ten minutes." These objections are justified! We pick that up quickly, and then we explain that this purpose sentence is only the end product and not the purpose itself. It has to be experienced. Today and in daily action. Therefore, we ask the participants to continue to be open to what is yet to come. And for this openness they can, for example, choose a picture as an anchor and share it with their colleagues.
- Experience the purpose sentence: Depending on the process that led to the purpose, we recommend repeating it with the participants. The results are collected in note form or drawn. The difference to the Purpose Quest: No sentence is formulated, but it is only shown. The motto is: This experience, these stories have led to this sentence. The participants enter into dialogue with this experience. The findings are usually: Much is repeated and similar. Slight differences lead to positive tension and constructive discussion. Afterwards, an analogue anchor of the purpose sentence is needed by asking what it triggers, or also what a before-after can look like, for example, in the form of collages, sketches, and sculptures.
- Translation to role and job: This step asks about the impact of the Purpose on one's own role or job. In individual work and then in pairs, the following questions can be reflected on: What guides me in my job? What makes me proud? What is my common thread in it and how does it become visible in my professional path? How is this related to the purpose of the organization? In the course of listening to each other, the partners add interesting aspects. Afterwards, a first rough draft of one's own purpose is formulated and written down, and it is considered what the first concrete next steps will be to fuel this purpose.
- Connection Agile transformation process: The connection to the overall process is deepened again at the end at the latest. This is also a good time to encourage individuals to participate. Here you use the power of the large group!

5.2.9 Learning journeys

Purpose	Generate new perspectives and be inspired to learn
Goals	• Getting to know the possible future • Getting to know processes and ways • Creating security in one's own process • Learning from other approaches
Special features	• Thinking along with good preparation and follow-up • Becoming aware of your own assumptions and letting them go
Number of Participants	at least 2 to "how many make sense"
Section link	3.3
Source	Neuwaldegg practice inspired by Learning Journeys by Otto Scharmer (www.presencing.org)

Learning journeys are particularly inspiring when the organizations you visit are different and already carry the future in some form. Don't just stay in your own region but look around the world. It is helpful to visit organizations similar to your own sector. You can also get good ideas and inspiration from other sectors: The main thing here is that they have experienced similar processes or are pursuing similar future concerns, perhaps in a completely different form. Remember: These could be your future co-creators.

Direction

There is a lot to think about with learning journeys. Again and again, we see that they do not have the effect they could have, in that hardly anything is used. We have also seen conclusions drawn that had little to do with what was observed. Therefore, it helps to consider the following steps:

1. *Good preparation is essential:* What do we expect? What do we want to observe or ask? What do we think makes these organizations tick? Then, when you are there, take a lot of notes and try to perceive as much as possible of what is! Try to resist the trap of observing only what you already know or want confirmed. Above all, pay attention to what is new and contradictory.
2. *Design a mix of roles:* Different expertise will see and ask different things. Therefore, it helps to integrate different perspectives: Management has an

overall concern, production will look at processes, R&D will look at innovation, HR will look at human resources, and so on. Sometimes it also helps to stagger the groups and arrange different/new dates. This way a lot of material comes together!

3. *Solid evaluation:* Take your time, document the findings and put them into an editable form. It is best for each group to do a joint evaluation immediately afterwards to record even the small things. In addition, interviews and people listening with specific focuses help. We have also had good experiences when we have invited employees to listen and ask questions during learning journey evaluations and discussions. In this way, new perspectives come in and are integrated in the sense of mobilization.

5.2.10 Stakeholder interviews

Purpose	See one's own work from the perspective of the stakeholders and satisfy internal customer needs well, formulate responsibilities or expected actions in the role profile accordingly.
Goals	• Greater clarity about how the team's work is valued from a stakeholder perspective and what value is added • Concrete suggestions for improving cooperation at the interfaces • Identification of obstacles in the cooperation and derivation of possible solutions • Deepening the (personal) relationship with stakeholders
Special features	Moderation
Number of Participants	3 to 25 persons
Section links	3.3, 3.9, 4.0
Source	Scharmer, Theory U Sourcebook (2020), further developed by Jeggle

Direction

Step 1: Identify your most important stakeholders/interfaces/"neighbouring circles": Which are your relevant internal customers and interfaces?

Step 2: Schedule interviews or an open dialogue session lasting 45-60 minutes. The idea is to go into a good and open exchange on specific topics: A current look at relationship, cooperation, the outcome of the work and expectations of future cooperation. This appointment works best if you create an open atmosphere where you really connect with your stakeholder and create the possibility to address all issues openly. Try to avoid discussions about right or wrong.

These questions will help you get the conversation going:

- What are your goals where the contribution, the support, the outcome of our department is crucial for you?
- What criteria do you use to assess whether our contribution to your work was successful or not?
- How do you currently perceive us?
  a) What are examples of excellent cooperation? What benefits have you gained from this cooperation?
  b) What are examples that you were not so happy about? Where would you like us to improve?
- If I could change two things in my area of responsibility within the next six months, which two things would bring the greatest added value and benefit for you?

Step 3: Summary and acknowledgement. Immediately after the interview, take time to reflect on the most important findings, record your most important thoughts in writing. Close the feedback loop: Send a thank you letter to your interviewer directly after each interview (within 12 hours).

Step 4: Process the findings. Use the summaries of all the conversations held to define your team's "purpose" and responsibilities accordingly. What is our performance that we provide for the success of others? For this, a workshop with the team is suitable to work on the common direction at the same time. In the best case, several colleagues have these conversations in parallel to get a comprehensive picture of the situation.

Step 5: Give feedback with "your portfolio". To close the circle, you should share the results with your stakeholders and present what you took away from the discussions and what you will and will not deliver in the future.

Tips on how to use this method based on experience:

- Interviews should be conducted face-to-face and in an environment where you have the opportunity to interact with the other person.
- Use the questions asked as a framework and stimulus and keep the goal in mind.
- It is less about writing down every word heard and more about summarizing the content or the essence of what was said. In our experience, starting by

not writing everything down ensures a focus on the connection and creates an open atmosphere to share the things that are important … and after a few minutes you can start writing.

Step 6: After the interview. Summarize the interview, offering a good condensed overview rather than a PowerPoint answer to every single point with every little detail.

- How did I experience the conversation/dialogue? What was different than expected? What was surprising, what was irritating?
- What positive feedback and reassurance have I/has my role/department received?
- What are the expectations of my stakeholder? What does she need more/less of in the future? What needs can I/my area/circle help well with?

5.2.11 Ongoing role reflection and feedback

Purpose	Reflect on and develop role design again and again
Goals	• Conscious reflection on different roles
	• Continuous transparency of progress
	• Integration of other perspectives through role feedback
Special features	This format can also be implemented well digitally
Resources	Online questionnaire
Duration	20 to 90 minutes, every 1 to 2 months
Section link	3.4
Source	Own development (Buzanich-Pöltl)

This format focuses on the development of roles: An institutionalized form so that roles are constantly reconsidered and reflected upon. In order for this to take place on an ongoing basis and to be easily integrated in terms of time, at Neuwaldegg we combine a digital format with analogue feedback.

Direction

Preparation: A digital self-reflection sheet that integrates different questions, for example. For us, it is important that the completion is manageable in terms of time. Questions for this could be: Which roles have I been particularly energized about in the last month or two and why was that? Which tasks and challenges have cost me particularly much time and energy and what are the reasons for this? From my perspective, which roles and tasks have contributed most to the purpose and whole of the team? On a scale of 1 to 10—how satisfied am I with my role design? What would I like to do more/less/same and how would I like to approach this?

- Step 1: The questionnaire is sent out to everyone with a short introduction and has to be completed by a certain date. After that, all role reflections are visible to everyone in the team.
- Step 2: The role reflections are put up at a meeting. The team members have the opportunity to go through them like in a gallery and write comments: Great, keep it up! I would like to see more/less! I see it differently. Another good idea …
- Step 3: Now is the time for individual, development-oriented feedback. In pair sessions, the individuals report back: "A real strength in your role performance …", "What I notice and would like to pass on to you …", "Thinking outside the box, that still occurs to me …", "A question you would like to ask me …". Depending on how much time is available, two to three conversations are held.
- Step 4: In order for everything to be processed, the people ask themselves what they would like to take away from this session. Important: These are always impulses, the people themselves evaluate what they take in and take out!

5.2.12 The role-free space

Purpose	Gain clarity as a person and in roles to find out which tensions are best to litigate and how.
Goals	• Create an informal space where own uncertainties about tensions and how to deal with them can be discussed so that learning can take place together.
	• Mutual support in the question of which tension can be processed further and how
	• Role bearers have clarity on how to bring in their tension
Special features	In this space, the tensions themselves are not clarified, but only what kind of tension it is and how to deal with it. Often the temptation is great to want to go straight into the discussion.
Duration	45 minutes
Section links	3.4, 3.5, 3.8
Source	Own development (Jantscher)

People experience different tensions in different roles. Often it is not clear what kind of tension it is and how it can be dealt with productively. The purpose of the role-free space is to support people to be clear about the nature of the tension and how they can deal with it in their roles or as individuals: This can be anything from feedback conversations with individuals to governance suggestions. The beauty of this format is that shared learning is at the forefront. There are no stupid questions because everyone contributes their lack of knowledge and together they go in search of what could be a good next step. An additional advantage is that all members are challenged to look for and contribute tensions and gaps so that learning takes place together. Especially in the beginning or for newcomers, this format is helpful.

Direction

As a facilitator, you explain the purpose of this format, similar to what has already been described. Start with individual work by reflecting and noting individually: When in the last few weeks had I discarded a tension that I actually wanted to address and clarify because I was not clear in which format it had a place? Were there moments in the last few weeks when I was not clear where to go with my concern/tension and if so, what were they? Were there times when I felt powerless because I did not know how to deal with a tension in a productive way?

After about 10 minutes, groups of three to five people are formed: Each member brings in his or her topics and questions and together they discuss in which form the person could solve his or her tension. When clarity has emerged, the whole team meets again. Together, the group exchanges the most important findings so that everyone can learn. Important: It is not about the tension itself!

5.2.13 Edge—belief in "growth": Fixed mindset and growth mindset

Purpose	Uncovering beliefs and situations that hinder or limit growth and development.
Goals	• Developing awareness of one's own mindset • Create awareness of one's own mindset in teams and at the personal level. • Promote growth mindset and development
Special features	• Pays off edge and focuses on developing and growing • Concept is scientifically and neurologically well researched

Number of Participants	1 to 18 persons
Duration	approx. 3 hours
Section link	3.5
Source	Dweck (2017, p. 253f)

Stanford professor Carol Dweck describes two mindsets in people: The "growth mindset", in which people have a dynamic self-image of themselves and others, are always developing and promote growth-oriented thinking and action logics. People with a "growth mindset" actively tackle challenges again and again and are constantly learning. The opposite of this is the "fixed mindset", in which people have a static image of themselves and others. This mindset includes beliefs such as: "I am the way I am", "He or she is just talented" or "You are like this or like that—you can't do anything about it!" Almost everyone has both mindsets, but moving organizations need members who are primarily committed to the Growth Mindset.

Direction

This exercise can be done alone or in pairs, with or without facilitation. When working in pairs, more aspects and insights are usually found. After the concept of Growth and Fixed Mindset is introduced, the exercise can be started quickly, working on each step separately:

1. **Exposing and learning to love one's own Fixed Mindset:** This process is about becoming aware of the fact that we humans carry both mindsets within us and act accordingly time and again. This is not a bad thing; it is a matter of recognizing and accepting it in order to be able to change our own behaviour.
2. **What are triggers for my Fixed Mindset?** In which situations do you hear voices like: "Maybe you just can't do it and I'm already curious when others will find out? It's far too exhausting and only frustrates me." Other questions are: In what situations do I feel like a failure? What happens to me when someone much better is next to me, in a similar field? How do I evaluate others after a test, a performance, a project? Do I attribute talents to others and what impulses do I set based on that? When am I no longer supportive but bossy and demanding? Find out under which circumstances your own Fixed Mindset appears and describe everything in detail.

3. **Persona for my Fixed Mindset:** Now is the time to give the "Fixed Mindset Persona" a name. From now on, this name describes your own share if you are in a Fixed Mindset. This persona is introduced to the whole group or to the partner. Everyone is allowed to get to know this persona and they can even talk to each other!

4. **Learning consciously with the Fixed Mindset:** Every time your Fixed Mindset persona appears from now on, greet her by name as well. Thank her for the advice, she just wants to protect you: From setbacks, fear, unpleasant feelings. You may want to go into a brief exchange and explain what you see as the next step and where the opportunities lie. Continually reflect on your experiences and progress in a team or with a learning partner.

5.2.14 Location and goal: Belief "better me + better you = better us"

Purpose	Promote personal development in the team by working on the belief system
Goals	• Take stock of the belief system and make it transparent and discussable • Describe concrete situations • Create a target image for this
Special features	Dialogical approach to attaching beliefs to concrete situations, and
Resources	Lego or other craft material
Number of Participants	approx. 15 people, is scalable
Section link	3.5
Source	Own development (Buzanich-Pöltl) based on Kegan & Lahey (2016)

The belief "better me + better you = better us" focuses on one thing above all: Permanent development as a premise for development in an organization—as a person, role, team, area and organization. But what about this belief in the organization or team? Does this premise apply?

Before different things are started, it helps to develop a common picture: Where do we currently stand? What are our strengths and what are our weaknesses?

The following questions support reflection to open up the perspective (Kegan & Lahey, 2009, p. 100):

- To what extent does your organization help you identify challenges that are important for you and the organization itself to work on and grow?
- Do others know your current growth threshold and is it also important to you?
- What form of support do you get to overcome your limitations and can you name this support?
- Do you actively experience and work on these challenges at least weekly and try to overcome these limitations?
- When you work to become a more efficient or better person, is it seen, recognized or celebrated? And when you have achieved this, are you given opportunities to grow?

Direction

As a facilitator, you make your participants aware of what this step is now being taken for and how it is embedded in the bigger picture. The three hours are about diving in and making the deeper beliefs about development visible. In the long run, it is about strengthening the team and the organization in this and also taking action. The first step explores the here and now in order to then find initial thoughts and images for the future.

As a first step, we recommend a self-reflection based on the above questions. Participants are given about 30 minutes to reflect and write this down. It is important that the results are supported by concrete examples. If a statement or feeling is unspecific and cannot be concretized, it should still be taken away. The group may find examples together. Depending on the size of the group, small groups can be formed to share and deepen their reflection together. At each step it is important to take notes so that the information is not lost. In the third step, we recommend a dialogue format that brings the different perspectives to the whole group. As a facilitator of the process, write down the most important red threads or statements so that the group itself can focus on the dialogue. The dialogue can last between 30 and 60 minutes. Make sure you don't stop after the first silence, usually the better ideas come after that.

Following this step in the process, it helps to form hypotheses (see Section 4.3): What are our hypotheses and assumptions that the situation is the way it is? These can be worked out in small groups and then presented and discussed in the group. Based on this information, it is now a matter of switching modes and drawing a kind of target picture: How does our team act when this belief set is 120 per cent effective? What do we do? How do we do it? What does everyday work look like? How would others describe us? We have had good experiences with using creative materials and methods such as Lego, handicraft materials or analogue representations in this development step. In this way, the pictures become more colourful and concrete. Finally, these pictures are concretized and condensed into one: This can be done in the form of a discussion in the group, by the leader, by a small team. Once the common picture has been created, this is a good starting point for the next directions, that is, to work out practices, principles and personal next steps.

5.2.15 FIS: Feedback—Impulse—Voltage

Purpose	Sensitize the team to different "formats of feedback" and communicate how team members classify their own tensions or what they can expect from another role.
Goals	• Clarity in communication through differentiation of different types of feedback • Avoiding discrepancies due to incorrect assessment of feedbacks • Addressing gaps in a structured way
Number of participants	2 people (one-on-one) to the entire organization (from one-on-one to meetings/workshops)
Section links	3.5, 3.8
Source	Own development (Jeggle)

Development of people and roles is a big concern for us at Neuwaldegg. We all try to slip into the development role. Therefore, we receive and give feedback several times a day. We share ideas or express fulfilled and unfulfilled expectations regarding cooperation. In our experience, all this is often summarized under the term "feedback". We have learned to differentiate more, because otherwise this leads to confusion, especially in the agile context with its clear roles and responsibilities. It is not always clear how feedback is to be understood and how best to deal with it.

That is why FIS was created. FIS makes it easier for senders to clearly differentiate a message and package it accordingly. At the same time, the receiver knows how to receive and classify this message and manages to question a framework of how feedback is to be understood.

• F stands for feedback: Feedback refers to the relationship and is always development-oriented.

I report the effect of a **person's** behaviour on me: What does this behaviour trigger in me? What do I wish for? What do I consider helpful?

After that, it is up to the feedback recipient whether he or she implements my feedback for him or herself.

Important: A discussion about mistakes or criticism is **not a** feedback discussion. We recommend that you do not use the term "feedback" for it.

- I stands for impulse: In every company there are clear roles with clear responsibilities. At the same time, each and every one of us has ideas and impulses that fall under the responsibility of another role. What else should this role perhaps consider? Which idea that you have picked up yourself should (in your own opinion) be taken into account by the role in any case?

In order not to compromise the autonomy of the role, there is the "impulse". An impulse is a suggestion or an idea without any claim to be "taken into account". The responsible role decides to take up or ignore this impulse.

In the case of the impulse, there is another "reinforced" variant: If one wants to emphasize the relevance of the impulse, one can "challenge" the role. Furthermore, the decision to implement lies with the role. We assume that each individual in the organization does their best for the organization anyway. Being bossy is, therefore, fundamentally out of place. Even an impulse-giver must accept if the role sets other priorities.

Examples: Impulses to the role of social media

1. Social media role: I have seen that the competition is intensively advertising on LinkedIn. I'd like to give you that as an impulse, I'll send you the link as well. Have a look at it!
2. I saw that in your social media role you posted something on LinkedIn three times on Monday and then nothing for four days. I would like to challenge you. Is this really useful or would it be more helpful to spread it out over the week or develop a posting plan?

Don't forget: An impulse still does not mean that I can expect the role to take action. However, if a role does not take up its responsibilities, then there is a tension. This should be processed as S for tension.

- S stands for tension: Tension in the FIS model refers to roles and the relationship between roles (rolation). Your perception is that a role is not or insufficiently fulfilling its responsibilities, or you have the feeling that "something is wrong". Important: Every feeling can be relevant information for a tension.

The first step in clarifying tensions is to determine whether this tension relates to an expected responsibility or task, so the role documentation is checked. Now there are two possibilities: Either the expectation is documented in the form of a responsibility in the role or it is not. Our experience shows that often presumed expectations are applied to roles without having checked them first. So: First verify responsibilities, then express tension, that is, ask why the responsibility is not fulfilled, demand a "next action" or a project of this role or bring it up in a meeting if this does not happen several times. If this responsibility is not documented and therefore not expected, the second possibility occurs: The future expectation must be litigated, in a governance meeting or other format, by clarifying roles and responsibilities.

Examples: Expressing tension with the role of social media

1. Dear Role Social Media, in your responsibilities (expected actions) it is stated: "Ensure inspiring communication in blog and social media". I have a tension: Posting a quote on LinkedIn only once a week does not result in enough readers becoming aware of my event!
2. Alternative: You raise your concerns in the meeting and request a "next action": The social media role should develop a procedure that ensures regular postings. The "how" remains the responsibility of the role, you can add the "what" (result).

5.2.16 Practising here and now to be playable

Purpose	Acting in the here and now
Goals	• Perceiving what is right now
	• Focusing one's own perception
	• Create a constructive state
Number of Participants	1 to 20 persons
Section links	3.5, 3.6
Source	Met by David Emerald (2016) and Lukas & Agnes Zenk

For members of moving organizations, it is becoming increasingly important to perceive the "here and now" and to act out of it in order to be continuously playable. The following exercises support this.

Direction FISBE

If you are leading this exercise in a group, you can do it as follows: "I am going to introduce a model called FISBE. No, it is not a Frisbee, but it is called FISBE.

Close your eyes for a moment and imagine an ocean. You yourself are on the beach, looking at the blue sea, which is pleasantly roaring. How are you feeling right now? How do you feel? Describe your state. Imagine further that you meet someone on your walk and have a conversation at work: How do you behave? What characterizes the encounter? ... You can now open your eyes again. You have just applied FISBE. You have established a 'focus' by looking at the blue sea. This has created a certain 'inner state' and made you calm, wide and relaxed. This in turn has led to a certain behaviour '**BEhaviour**'. Depending on what you focus on, this will trigger an inner state in you, which in turn will influence your behaviour." This exercise can be taken further by having people consider a different focus, for example, looking at a flower or a particular photograph (Emerald, 2016).

Directing Guide "Focus on me—Focus on you"

This exercise comes from improvisational theatre and practices playability in the here and now. The group stands in a circle and taps their thighs with both hands in a common rhythm, with everyone saying "base, base, base, …" in rhythm. Once the first basic rhythm has been practised, you as a facilitator introduce the next level of difficulty while everyone else continues to tap the basic rhythm. They take both hands, point to themselves and say: "Focus on me", and then they point with both hands to another person and say: "Focus on you". The person you have addressed takes over and does the same as you: Pointing their hands at themselves, "Focus on me", and pointing their hands at whoever else, "Focus on you". All this in a basic rhythm, over several rounds. Once this is well established, the third level of difficulty comes. The two neighbours of the person standing next to the focus turn to the person, say "support, support" and cross and open their arms at each word, so do this twice. Once this is also well established, one can get faster and faster. This exercise can be wonderfully evaluated with questions like: What was difficult and what was helpful? How tiring was the exercise and why? What were support mechanisms? How does one interpret "always being playable" now? What does "here and now" mean? (Learned from Agnes and Lukas Zenk.)

5.2.17 Practise self-differentiation

Purpose	Sharpening one's own boundaries in cooperation
Goals	• Raise awareness on an individual and team level
	• Generate individual derivation

Special features	Is an important part of the Clear Leadership Model and can be a good basis for shared learning in teams
Number of Participants	up to 30 persons
Section links	3.4, 3.6
Source	Own development (Buzanich-Pöltl) based on Clear Leadership according to Gervase Bushe

The aim here is to make people aware of and practise self-differentiation by testing their personal boundaries. First and foremost, the "I versus We" becomes perceptible in the extreme contours: On the one hand, total fusion in the We and on the other hand, total separation from each other. As Table 5.2 shows, fusion results in too strong a connection with other people. If people primarily separate themselves from others, there is hardly any togetherness. Self-differentiated people integrate the strengths of both continuums: They can separate themselves and connect with others at the same time. They are aware of their boundaries and deal with them consciously. They also consciously decide how to engage in interactions, taking an interest in what others are experiencing while remaining true to themselves. Practising self-differentiation means finding and testing their own healthy boundaries for themselves while focusing on the energy with the circle of people in the here and now.

Direction

As a facilitator, first briefly introduce the concept and then move relatively quickly into the experience. Make a big circle and discuss two roles one after the other: Role fusion and role separation and demarcation. What images emerge? What are these roles like? What characterizes them? Then count through in the circle to two: One, two, one, two. The ones take the role of fusion and the twos take the role of separation and demarcation. Each person goes around the room and has time to charge that role for one minute and go fully into that energy.

Afterwards, everyone is in the following situation: They are all at a team event in the evening and they talk to each other about the day already experienced and what will happen tomorrow. Everyone stays in their own role. This exercise is done for a few minutes. Then the roles are changed and done exactly as before until both roles have been experienced. Afterwards, there is a short exchange in the plenary about the differences and experiences.

Table 5.2. Comparison of fusion, self-differentiation and demarcation based on Gervase Bushe (2009, p. 80)

Merger	Self-differentiation	Separation and demarcation
Too strongly connected	Separated and connected	Too strongly demarcated
No limits	Optional limits	Rigid borders
Reactive in interactions	Conscious decision-making in interactions	Reactive towards people
Own experience based on the experience of other people	Want to know what others are experiencing and experiencing, while remaining true to themselves	Do not think about what others are experiencing and learning. Stay with yourself.

The third role, self-differentiation, is discussed with the group: It combines both qualities of the previous extremes. A new situation is created: A day has passed and the second team evening is coming up: "Miraculously, everyone has adopted the role of self-differentiation over the day." And the exercise starts all over again. After this exercise, it goes into reflection groups: What was experienced in the different reflection roles? What was easy, what was difficult? What feelings and thoughts were there? What was the body posture like? The learnings are shared and initial conclusions can be drawn. For the transfer it helps to start a self-reflection, preferably in pairs: When do I experience these different tendencies? What are my learning areas? How do others see this? What do I want to derive and try out?

5.2.18 Clear leadership: Using the experience cube

Purpose	Use language that promotes cooperation
Goals	• Separating observation and evaluation
	• Bringing differentiated clarity to one's own thoughts and language
	• Promote cooperation by being clear about the relationship
Special features	Consciously applying the language of Clear Leadership requires a willingness to engage in self-reflection and practice the approach on an ongoing basis.
Resources	Slips of paper as ground anchors
Number of Participants	up to 20 persons

Duration   one loop lasts approx. 40 minutes
Section link   3.6
Source   Learned from Liselotte Zvacek based on Gervase Bushes
                    Clear Leadership (2009)

We have already described the Clear Leadership Model in detail in Section 3.6. Here we want to practise the experience cube as a whole. Before you start, it helps to practise the individual aspects, observing, separating observing and interpreting, noticing your own feelings. Once these exercises have been done, it is easier to use the experience cube.

Direction

After the participants have tried out the first experiments and exercises and are familiar with the basic idea of "ownership of experience", present the Clear Leadership experience cube to your participants, ideally also in the form of a graphic:

- Observations: That which "objectively" an alien would also observe and describe.
- Thoughts: These are the interpretations and stories I make about it.
- Feelings: The feelings that this observation and my interpretation trigger in me.
- Want: That which I need out of that in order to be able to think or go further.

Once everyone has understood the differences in the experience cube, concrete situations are sought: A conversation with a colleague that has been pending for a while and is easy to moderately difficult (not something that seems hopeless or has already been tried out many times!). As soon as everyone has found a situation, pairs are formed. In teams, current topics can be worked on at the same time. Each pair is given four pieces of paper, on each of which a building block of the experience cube is written down, that is, four pieces of paper with one term each: Observation, thoughts, feelings, wanting. These are placed on the floor and serve as floor anchors to support the conversation and differentiated language. One person starts with his or her own conversation situation and tries to climb to the right experience building block in the conversation. So if I tell how someone does something, I go to the observation note. If I tell how it feels, I go to the feelings note, and so on. The other person supports in differentiating the language and also gives resonance. The exercise is done until both have had their turn. Every conversation and every experience is evaluated afterwards: How did it go? What was successful, what was not? What is challenging? Afterwards, it helps to form new groups and have a new conversation.

5.2.19 Clear leadership: Practising appreciative and curious self in extreme situations

Purpose	Practising staying in the appreciative and curious self
Goals	• Getting to know different ego states • Practising postures in extreme situations
Special features	If this exercise is done in teams, it already requires a higher level of experimentation and courage to face different issues.
Resources	Input and moderation
Number of participants	6 to 20 people
Duration	45 minutes
Section link	3.6
Source	Own development (Buzanich-Pöltl/Jantscher)

This exercise helps to practise the two ego states in challenging situations. The appreciative I is characterized by still finding something positive in what my counterpart is doing. The curious I is characterized by finding this situation or experience exciting and being open myself to what is coming and not judging or turning my judgment into curiosity.

Direction

Once the participants have understood what Clear Leadership is about, the ego states can be made tangibly clear. The idea is simple: Each person looks for a topic that has annoyed them immensely lately and that also represents a problem. This can be private or, even better, in a work context. Once each person has found a situation, groups of three are formed. One person starts, enters the case situation and begins to talk. The other two each take on a role: Appreciation and curiosity! From this position they react to this person and ask questions, make suggestions and/or listen. The case bringer responds in terms of the feedback as it comes to her. After about five to seven minutes, they stop and reflect on the first round: What was helpful? What was difficult? Where were one's own limits felt? What were the thoughts and feelings? Then it is switched until all three people have provided their own case.

At the end of the exercise, everyone comes together and the different experiences are exchanged. Common learnings can be derived and, if necessary, lead to agreements.

5.2.20 Curious me: Four levels of listening

Purpose	Sharpening listening skills to support the curious self
Goals	• Practice listening and perceiving • Be able to differentiate between different aspects
Number of Participants	1 to 20 persons
Duration	45 minutes to several days
Section link	3.6
Source	Neuwaldegg practice based on Otto Scharmer (2015)

One of the most important resources for grasping new things and remaining curious is listening. Otto Scharmer (2015) describes four levels for this by describing the listener's own starting point:

- First level is "downloading": I myself am in the centre of listening and hear what confirms or contradicts my current knowledge and judgments. I judge what is right or wrong. My horizon of experience and point of reference is my previous knowledge. We recognize downloads when we notice what the other person does not yet know, we judge, give advice, think of our examples and also pass them on, or when we evaluate our counterpart.
- Second level is "factual listening": I listen primarily on the factual level and take and explore what I do not yet know. Irritations are recorded and checked and objectively evaluated. This form of listening and taking in is well practised in many scientific disciplines. We recognize this level of listening when we learn something new and try to classify or add to this new information in our world view.
- Third level is "empathic listening": I fully engage with my counterpart and my perception moves from me to the place of my counterpart. I empathize and connection arises at the level of the heart. In such situations, we notice a

change: We forget our own plan and begin to see the world through the eyes of our counterpart.

- Fourth level is "generative listening": While listening, images of the future or new ideas suddenly emerge that were not there before. By being fully present and not having any thoughts of my own, potentials are recognized. This process is often also a co-creation process in which more is created together. With good coaches, such moments arise again and again: New things emerge that were not on the horizon before.

Direction

In a group, introduce the four levels of listening in the context of the curious self. The video by Otto Scharmer (2015) on YouTube can also be helpful here. Then pairs are formed who reflect on the four levels for themselves: Which levels do I know in different experiences? What distinguishes them? How do I recognize them?

In the next step, each participant looks for her own challenge that she is currently dealing with in the team and work context. Groups of three are formed, whereby there is always a case-bringer, an interlocutor and an observer (the observer is not absolutely necessary). During the discussion, the aim is to better understand the case-bearer and possibly find initial approaches towards a solution. It is important that the focus is on listening. After ten minutes, the small groups reflect on the different levels of listening and how this has contributed to the curious attitude.

Another variant of the exercise can take place individually by reflecting at the end of the day over several weeks on the levels experienced that day. If this is documented, experiences can be shared within the team.

5.2.21 From a deficit-oriented to an appreciative mindset

Purpose	Practising the appreciative mindset
Goals	• Shedding new light on challenging labour relations
	• Practising an appreciative attitude
	• Practise three process steps
Special features	Individual reflection and exchange in pairs in three process steps
Resources	Reflection partner
Duration	30 minutes

Section link	3.6
Source	Bushe (2009, p. 232)

A simple individual exercise to strengthen the appreciative self is to identify relationships that are not working well and reflect on them in three steps.

Direction

This exercise works particularly well when started during an individual reflection: Participants identify one person who is emotionally challenging. Then present the deficit orientation column and each person fills it in for themselves. Then this result can be discussed with a second person for five minutes. In the second step, you present the questions for the appreciation column. This is also filled in and the results are then echoed and adjusted with a reflection partner. Finally, next steps are defined. A reflection in the group shows different perspectives on how the appreciative I can be strengthened.

5.2.22 Describe experiences and do not judge

Purpose	Practising the difference between experience and interpretation/judgment
Goals	• Practise descriptive I • Feel and recognize differences • Train physical perception
Special features	Moderation
Duration	30 minutes
Section link	3.6
Source	Bushe (2009), Bourquin (2018)

Table 5.3. Exercise to strengthen the appreciative self

	Deficit orientation	Appreciation
1	What don't you like about this person?	What do you like about this person?
2	How do you think this problem can be solved?	Think about what you would like to have more of.
3	What are you doing to support this pattern?	How can you take responsibility with the help of this experience?

Stage directions Variant 1—Deflate

For this exercise you need a second person. This can also be your partner. This second person takes on the role of a person who upsets you to no end. You now talk to this person for five minutes and say everything that upsets you about this person: You judge and are now not in correctness mode. After five minutes, you reflect with your counterpart how this was. Then comes another five minutes in which you share your observations with this person. This time you describe the observations and make sure that you speak from your experience and, therefore, use I-messages. Now reflect again on how it felt, what was easy and what was difficult (Bushe, 2009, p. 165).

Variant 2—Cat Walk

This exercise is done in a group. As a facilitator, you guide the group to line up in a trellis. Now, as a facilitator, you are asked to go over the Cat Walk. Make sure there is something special about it. Now the participants are asked to report back their observations. Now walk the Cat Walk a second time, but in a completely different style. How are the observations described now? Reflect on the different observations and distinguish interpretations from real observations: For example, descriptions of happy, lustful, angry are already a judgment, whereas arms moving is not (Bourquin, 2018, p. 21).

5.2.23 Journaling

Purpose	Writing down one's own experiences and thoughts to raise one's awareness
Goals	• Conscious reflection on one's own experiences, feelings, judgments and wishes
Special features	Is effective when practised over a longer period of time
Resources	Writing pads
Duration	15 to 30 minutes per day
Section link	3.6
Source	Bushe (2009) and many other directions

The important thing in journaling is regularity: You write a certain number of pages every day, preferably always at the same time, for example, in the morning or evening. In these pages you reflect on what you have experienced and what is on your mind using the dimensions of the experience cube (see tool in Section 5.2.18). It is also helpful to write down everything that comes to mind at that moment and needs to come out. We have had good experiences with writing three pages per day, for example. At the same time, you can also integrate a gratitude question. This has a lasting effect on your own well-being! After some time, go through your notes and analyze your patterns: What moves you, what do you focus on, what is repeated or what is missing? By the way, this method is one of the most effective forms of self-reflection that has a lasting effect.

5.2.24 Noticing game

Purpose	Getting in touch with each other by putting into words what arises in the here and now in order to practise conscious I
Goals	• Quickly create awareness of the current state and be able to refer back to it • Finding words for this own perception • Getting in touch with each other • Be present
Special features	A good preliminary exercise for the experience cube in Clear Leadership (see tool in Section 5.2.18). Team members who are not used to face-to-face contact can be taken out of their comfort zone.
Resources	Moderation
Duration	15 minutes
Section link	3.6
Source	Own development (Jantscher) based on Circling Europe

Direction

As a facilitator, explain the purpose of this exercise. You can point out to the participants that the conversation may feel strange at first. The important thing is to simply get into trying things out. In the first step, two people sit down opposite each other at a comfortable distance. You make eye contact with each other, which can already be uncomfortable for some participants. This is a first test. In the next step, one person starts, for example, the person with the longer hair, the lighter T-shirt.

This person answers the question: "When I sit opposite you, I notice/notice that …". This person could put the following things into words: "… that my neck is tense, ... that I feel uncomfortable sitting so close to you and would like to have more distance, ... that you have beautiful earrings, ... that I am very curious about how you are doing right now ..." etc.

The second person listens and answers: "When you say that, I notice in myself that ...".

So this conversation goes back and forth all the time. In each moment, the participants are present and feel what is going on right now and express it in their own words.

Note: Here it is important not to drift into "chit-chat". The opportunity lies in being present! This could be shown, for example, as follows: A: "I notice that I am just feeling a resistance to following the exercise instructions. Actually, I would rather chat with you."—B: "When you say that, I notice that I am becoming unrelaxed. I feel this mainly through a pressure in my stomach. I realize that it is important for me to take this exercise seriously".

After about five minutes, the exercise can be stopped and a new conversation partner is sought. The following questions are useful for reflection afterwards: What differences did the counterpart make for me? What could have been the reasons for this? How long was I able to be present? What interrupted me? What was easy to put into words, what was not? How often did I find myself thinking about other things?

5.2.25 Status flexibility: Power in high and low status

Purpose	Sensing and flexibilizing different power qualities as a person
Goals	• Getting to know different statuses • Flexible use of more or less authority • Raising awareness of different status symbols
Special features	Interesting and fun experiment from improvisational theatre that quickly makes power and status tangible
Number of participants	up to 20 persons
Section links	3.6, 3.7
Source	Tried and learned by Lukas and Agnes Zenk. See also Schinko-Fischli (2018)

When it comes to accepting and relinquishing leadership and authority in roles, it helps to get to know this quality physically. On the one hand, to develop a sensorium for it, and on the other hand, to be able to use it actively. For this purpose, improvisational theatre uses the concept of status (Johnson, 1979). People can be either in high or low status. When people are in high status, they are characterized by the following observable criteria: They talk loudly, take up a lot of space, make themselves big, touch others, move quietly and prudently, approach others, maintain eye contact easily, stand mostly on both feet, stand shoulder width apart. In a strong state, politicians are a good example of this. If a person is in low status, the following can be observed: The person takes up little space, makes himself small, has a soft voice, is hesitant, keeps his distance from others, is publicly self-critical, is easily interrupted. Clowns or even reality shows show this status in its pronounced form. In everyday professional life, we experience this assignment of status in the form of hierarchy. As a rule, the higher the manager, the more pronounced the high status, and vice versa. In principle, it does not have to be this way, because both statuses are useful and helpful (Schinko-Fischli, 2018, p. 110). For the purpose of the exercise and getting to know these two statuses, it helps to paint in black and white. In reality, there are different gradations that can also be used specifically. More on this below.

Direction

If you are leading a group in this exercise, explain this concept in advance. The whole thing works even better if you use your acting skills. Then have the participants line up in a line: One side should go into high status, the other into low status. Take a minute for this and let the group slowly find their way into the role, for example, by saying: "Go slowly into your status, start at 1 and increase. On 2, on 3, … feel it, it gets stronger and stronger … 4, 5, … to 10." This helps to get into the roles well. Then the people should meet their counterpart and start talking to each other, body language is also important here. After two minutes there is a break, the roles are changed and the conversation is held again. In the second round, you can also walk around.

After this exercise, the group reflects on the experience: How was it recognizable, how did it feel, what was said, how was the counterpart reacted to. Often there are stereotypical messages or even examples from well-known people. In a next exercise, six people volunteer and draw a number from one to six, the rest are spectators. The actresses go to a cinema or a panel discussion, and each has a different status that the spectators do not know: 1 = lowest low status, 2 = middle low status, 3 = little low status, 4 = little high status, 5 = middle high status, 6 = highest high status. Now it is up to the participants to observe and guess who has which status. After some time, the participants break it up and reflect in the group on what produces what effect. And here comes the important learning: Each status serves a different purpose. If I am a little below my counterpart in status, it is easier to de-escalate conflicts or hand over authority to the other person. At the same time, I can clearly increase my status by standing up and being taller. And here's the kicker: Knowing this, I can adjust my behaviour depending on the context by giving others more space, giving them more authority and responsibility. At the same time, in my role as an expert, I can make it clear that I, in particular, am in charge by taking on more high-status. In moving organizations, it helps if people can flexibly shape their status. This is also meant with respect for expertise!

5.2.26 My power in my roles

Purpose	Recognizing one's own sources of power instead of reeling in fantasies of powerlessness
Goals	• Clarifying and de-tabooing the concept of power • Differentiation of different sources of power • Strengthening the competence to act in one's own roles • Application of power theory to a social system
Special features	This intervention should be integrated into a process. The exercise should be used in a hypothesis-based way to know what is to be achieved.
Resources	• Preparation for the topic • Moderation
Duration	2 to 4 hours
Number of Participants	2 to 15 participants, i.e. a group size to be able to follow each other's results, although it can also be adapted for larger formats
Section link	3.7
Source	Own development (Boos/Jarmai)

We developed this intervention for us in Neuwaldegg. The idea came up while writing this book, dealing with the topic of power and how it works internally in our organization. In terms of content, the starting point is Section 3.7, in which we clarify our view of power. Our hypothesis for Neuwaldegg was that different people and roles have different power and use it differently, also in the context of Holacracy. The exciting question for us was which parts of power are in the informal, what is formally decided and which frames are used or unused. *Note:* We want to emphasize here once again that power in itself is nothing negative. In agile organizations, it is more about distributing power consciously, which is why formal power is more explicit in our view than in classic organizations. At the same time, there is still an informal share of power!

Direction

The staff members are invited by the facilitator for a sequence of almost 2.5 hours. It starts with an attunement in pairs: How am I here? What gives me strength? What gives me a headache? Then it goes into individual work by listing all the individual roles in the organization. Once this step is done, an impulse on the topic of power is presented: Power systemically seen and Power and control in the zones of uncertainty.

After this stimulus, further individual reflection takes place by deciding which one or two roles in this exercise should be examined in more detail for power resources. These roles are examined in more detail: What power resources do I have in this role? What would change if I fully utilized these power resources? After this individual reflection, each member briefly shares a statement of where they are in this reflection. After this information, pairs are formed to share their reflections for 15 minutes.

Now two groups (possibly subgroups) are formed to deepen the following question for half an hour: How can we use these insights and support each other? The first group focuses inwards and integrates the internal roles and barriers into these questions. The second group focuses outwards in connection with the clients. In our case these are the counsellors. Our experience is that the internal perspective is more intensive and also requires the courage to address taboo topics. After this exchange, everyone comes together in the plenum and shares their experiences. Joint next steps are determined.

5.2.27 Team and role diagnosis: Force field analysis

Purpose   Improve the performance of teams and roles by making
                      it possible to discuss supporting and pulling forces

Goals	• Identify current situation in teams and circles Create a basis for continuous team development
Special features	• Two sides of the same coin • Making obstacles explicit • Strengthen strengths and make them conscious
Number of Participants	4 to 20 persons
Section links	3.6, 3.8
Source	Own development (Buzanich-Pöltl/Jantscher) based on Gantt & Agazarian (2018) and Kurt Lewin (1963)

A good method that helps to increase the performance of roles and teams is the advanced force field analysis based on Kurt Lewin (Gantt & Agazarian, 2018, p. 7f): The forces and behaviours that drive the goal and the purpose are identified as well as those that work against it. This is exemplified by the role of a team leader in identifying the specific behaviours and thereby creating a behavioural map. Lewin has shown that it is more helpful and effective to reduce the hindering energies than to increase the supporting ones. By reducing obstructive energies, supportive forces are automatically supported. This method is used to diagnose different social systems and can be used to good effect.

Additional questions help with the diagnosis for teams and are suitable as an assessment when starting out (Gantt & Agazarian, 2018, p. 22):

• What is the relevant system hierarchy for this objective?
• What is the purpose and target system for the planned change?
• How much of the communication is personalized or context-driven?
• How clear, goal- and context-oriented are the roles?
• How adequately permeable are the boundaries between departments, teams and working groups?
• How clear and transparent are the boundaries that contain the work of the individual departments?
• How high is openness in communication in which contexts?
• When and where is the flow of communication restricted?
• Which borders are open and which are closed?
• Is the boundary adequately permeable to the objective of the context?
• How are differences dealt with?
• How high is the level of innovation in this company and team?

Table 5.4. Force field analysis of a team leader role according to Gantt & Agazarian (2018, p. 8)

Role of the team leader	
Driving forces →	← restraining forces
Clarify the goal →	← Be vague about tasks
Interrupt to get back to the task → Interrupt to get back to the task → Interrupt to get back to the task.	← Introducing volatile topics
Ask for ideas →	← Disrupting ideas, monopoly position

- How high is the emotional intelligence of the organization?
- How much intuitive knowledge is supported?
- Which phase of system development is characteristic for the company? And for the departments within the company?

Direction

After a detailed check-in round, it is explained to the team members what the approach to the force field analysis is and what the assumptions behind it are. After this is clear, groups or individuals consider what are supportive and restraining forces in the team. The questions serve as support. Then these forces are collected from the whole group on two different areas and clustered. In this phase, clarifying questions can be asked if something is not understood. A discussion does not take place and opinions of others are not yet discussed. In the first step, it helps to look at the supporting forces and to consciously perceive them. In the next step, the most important restraining forces are addressed, for example, in the sense of subgrouping (see Section 3.8.2). At the end, it is useful to develop a goal and record it: When we meet in a year's time, how will we know that we have really developed! Based on this, the first concrete measures are derived. The force field analysis is used and further developed on an ongoing basis.

5.2.28 Immunity to change: Overcoming personal obstacles in a team-oriented way

Purpose	Work on personal changes that are aligned with the common team goal.
Goals	- Identify individual behavioural contributions that pay towards the common goal. - Uncovering which individual behaviours are obstructive - Identify development paths so that individuals can work on themselves

Special features	• First of all, there needs to be a jointly developed purpose or goal in the team that everyone can align themselves with.
	• Individuals are strengthened and supported in their own transition (especially leaders).
	• This is an ongoing process that is accompanied over approximately 6 months to 1 year in the form of coaching or learning partner sessions.
Resources	Immunity to Change Columns
Number of Participants	approx. 12 to 20 people, is scalable
Section links	3.5, 3.6, 3.7
Source	Neuwaldegg practice based on Kegan & Lahey (2009)

When it comes to learning and reflection in teams, it is also important to work on our own obstacles and challenges. We all have behaviours that prevent us from fully supporting the new. This is for different reasons and is rarely because we don't want to: Something is preventing us from getting better in some aspects for a non-apparent good reason. This usually harms several people: The team, the family, friends and oneself. We don't like to peddle these behaviours because they are also associated with shame. Even if we like to hide them, one thing is quite clear: Others can easily name and point out this weakness. Often others are already talking about it. It's more like a white elephant: No one talks about it officially and yet it tramples around. The difficulty is that everyone has at least one such white elephant.

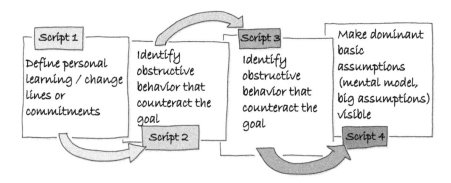

Fig. 5.4. Immunity to change: Overcoming personal obstacles in a team-oriented way

And now imagine how many elephants are trampling around in a team (Kegan & Lahey, 2009).

That is why we support individuals in teams and organizations that are strongly affected by change with the Immunity to Change Map. The principle is relatively simple and has the motto: "Let's face it, even if it's uncomfortable for a moment!" Experience has shown that this encourages continuous development and feedback. It helps individuals not to be left alone with the change. The process runs in four steps, as Fig. 5.4 visualizes.

Direction

When you facilitate such a process, you and the participants already have a picture of what the team or group wants to do in the future. The basic question in the Immunity to Change process is: What is the one thing that I as a person can do better in my behaviour so that we as a team or group achieve our goal and purpose? This question hovers over everything in the whole process. Once everyone understands what this process is for, how the process works and what exactly is behind the four steps, we can get into the content. We are describing a team process here; for other group configurations, adapt the procedure accordingly.

We start with development-oriented feedback sessions. Depending on the number of people and the time budget, these can last 5 to 15 minutes per person. The questions are: What do I appreciate about you? What do I see as your strengths? What weaknesses and areas for development do I see in relation to our common goal? What change in your behaviour will really bring us a big step forward as a team?

On the basis of these feedback discussions, all members independently identify their current field of development that makes a major contribution to the joint project—their white elephant. It often helps if people reflect on and sharpen this development goal in advance with a second person. Then the development goal is made transparent in the team and each team member gives appreciative feedback on this proposal: What is considered good, where could it be sharpened, to what extent does this contribution help the whole. Based on this feedback round, the development goals are sharpened and presented again in the second step. The next step is to work on the first two pillars of these four pillars, which are described with examples in Table 5.5:

- Pillar 1: deals with mutually agreed and future behaviour that is intended to contribute to the whole.
- Pillar 2: describes in detail the obstructive behaviours that work against the goal.

- Pillar 3: addresses the hidden motives behind these behaviours.
- Pillar 4: goes one level deeper and explores what basic assumptions, mental models, values and beliefs underpin these motives.

Once the team members have worked on these two pillars, they are shared again in the team. These steps sound simple and logical, yet they are quite a challenge to work through together: The people show themselves vulnerable, which is why a trusting containment needed, which is repeatedly and attentively established. In our experience, something new emerges: Trust increases, the people see themselves from a different perspective and have the feeling that they are really pulling together more and more.

Afterwards, everyone works individually and processually on their field of development, ideally with coaches who know this form of process. The difference to classic coaching is the focus on the team goal and the fact that everyone

Table 5.5. Immunity-to-change pillars based on interview with R. Kegan (2014)

1. my improvement goal What do I want to change?	2. my behaviours that prevent me from achieving my goals in Pillar 1	3. my hidden motives (which cause/trigger my behaviour in Pillar 2)	4. my dominant basic assumption(s) (big assumptions)
Criteria	Criteria	Criteria	Criteria
• Coherent for me	• Behaviour (not	• Fear-driven	• Shows how
• Concerns myself	feelings)	• Self-protection	immunity is
• Has potential for	• Counteracts Pillar 1	• Shows the logic why	maintained
improvement	• Not: Why or what	Pillar 2 behaviour	for fear of
• Important for me	I should do about it	makes sense	threatening
		• Feels "strong"	emotional
			consequences
Examples:	Examples 1:	My fears:	Examples:
• I resolve to do this	• I eat too much when	• If I implement my	I
or that better …	I'm frustrated.	goals in Pillar 1,	• am a wimp
• I resolve to change	• I eat too much	I fear that	• lose face
this or that …	sweets.	• I feel bad,	• Be criticized
• I want to be	• I eat snacks	• I am unfair, rude to	• make a fool
braver in	between meals.	others.	of myself
situation X, Y …	Examples 2:	These lead to	• being humiliated
• I resolve to	• I get loud when I'm	behaviours	• Appear
show more civil	emotional.	(engagements) that	incompetent
courage …	• I do not listen to my	compete with Pillar 1	• must be
• etc.	counterpart.		ashamed
	• I enforce my opinion.		

keeps aligning themselves with it. From now on, the Immunity-to-Change process is an ongoing team process: Progress and regress are worked on continuously and transparently.

Background info: The assumption behind this process is that it is not about learning a simple technical skill that can be solved quickly and easily, but about adaptive change. Problems are addressed whose solutions are not yet known and which, in addition to changing behaviour, also bring about a change in thinking patterns and set fundamental things in motion. The advantage in the transformation process is that this creates an extreme focus in teams on the new and the behavioural patterns. Especially in top management teams we experience a strong impact when it comes to individuals, their role and their contribution.

5.2.29 Check-in exercises in teams: Shaping the transition of people and members

Purpose	Create transition for people so that they can arrive well in the current context
Goals	• Letting go of past and future thoughts and distractions • Establish focus on the current context and topic • Connect with the other members
Special features	Continuously find out and adapt what fits well for the respective members and context.
Number of Participants	up to 15 persons
Section links	3.5, 3.8
Source	Neuwaldegg practice with different sources of inspiration

Check-ins are like shoehorns: They are designed to help individuals let go of the weekend, the previous client meeting or the future conflict meeting so that these individuals can become full members of the current situation. When there are no distractions, each individual can fully engage with the current context and make a meaningful contribution in terms of the task and the team. This is also the reason why these check-ins are not only for workshops, but are also useful in meetings, conversations and at the beginning of the day. What takes a little time at the beginning has a positive effect on the meeting: The results are of better quality, the people more focused and the whole thing more effective. The following aspects play a role in check-ins:

- **Distractions:** Everyday life, what has gone before and what is yet to come, distracts many people's thoughts. It often helps to address and talk about these distractions so that they can be let go.
- **Me as a person:** The individual is important, especially in teams. That's why it's good to know where the other person is at the moment and how that person is doing. This can be professional and private! At the same time, each person also bears responsibility for the whole, which is why everyone gets a turn!
- **Connect:** In order for me to make a good contribution to the whole in this team and in the current meeting, it is also about connecting with the others so that the formula "a better me + a better you = a better us" can also work.
- **Focus:** It is important to create an active awareness of what is important in this context and what purpose and goal should be pursued.
- **Atmosphere:** The check-in is the beginning. That is why the way the check-in is organized often determines what happens next. Positive psychology in particular shows that, for example, gratitude and a focus on positive events have a positive effect on cooperation.
- **Adequate and connectable:** The design can be very different. What is important is that it is coherent for the respective team in the long term: In terms of time, socially and in terms of content.

Not all aspects can always be considered in one check-in. We have had good experiences with switching these over and over again in some contexts, especially when there is more time. In virtual meetings and also in other short meetings, our check-ins are always the same. We present a few variations here that you can use depending on the purpose.

Direction Check-in with two to three impulses or questions

One to three impulses are sensibly combined by the facilitator. In addition, it is determined how much time each has so that the total time is well in view. Before starting, it can be helpful to introduce the agenda and the purpose. The participants respond in turn:

- In order for me to be fully present, I have to let go …
- For today, it is important to me that …
- A beautiful private and a beautiful professional moment of the last two weeks …
- To make this a successful day, I will contribute …
- I am grateful to "Name" from this team because …

- Share something you are grateful for …
- Share something you did well last week and something you struggled with….
- A magical moment in this company was …
- That's what's on my mind at the moment …
- A strength that I would like to bring to bear today …
- We have taken a big step when …
- My intention for today is …
- On a scale of 1 to 10: This is how present I am today …. This is what is still holding me back …
- A metaphor for my condition today is …
- That's what I want to learn today …

Check-in with a small exercise

Starting again and again with a small exercise can be varied and surprising. We always start with guided mediations or an exercise like FISBE (see exercises in Section 5.2.16 "Practising here and now"). In addition, the start can also be used for people to get into a certain mood and talk about certain topics. Here are a few selected exercises from our everyday life:

- Speed networking: The idea here is that different people always come into contact and exchange views on different questions. In three rounds, in groups of three, people exchange views on three questions. Each round is swapped. If necessary, the facilitator asks what was discussed.
- Staging a motto: The day and the room are placed under a certain motto by decorating it accordingly. Here are two examples:

  1. **summer holiday theme**: For example, we once had a summer holiday theme with a picnic blanket, fruit, tropical fruit juices and cushions instead of armchairs. Summer music was played. As facilitators, we explained that we were at a lake in summer and were spending time together here. The colleagues had the task of talking to each other in half an hour and exchanging ideas about the company and their everyday life: What is successful? What is challenging? How are things otherwise? What do they see coming up in the future? What is important for today? Of course, any other question can be asked!

  2. **motto "Enjoy"**: We placed scented plants everywhere to smell and distributed fine chocolate to eat. Then people could meet and talk about the following questions: What have I been able to enjoy lately professionally? What privately? When was the last time I was pampered, also professionally? What has touched me in the last few weeks?

- Motion Flow: Small groups keep to themselves for the questions. After three questions, they have the task of presenting a three-second movement to each other in front of everyone and then explain the most important points.
- Nourish PERMA: From Positive Psychology we know the PERMA model: Five ingredients that strengthen our life satisfaction. Start the day with your participants to nourish and align themselves with these ingredients by each writing down for themselves: What positive experiences do I want to have today? What strengths will I bring to the table today? What relationships do I want to strengthen? What meaningful contribution will I make—in small and large ways? What do I want to do today to feel my self-efficacy—what hackles do I want to make? Afterwards, you can exchange briefly or bring in the whole check-in (Ebner, 2019).
- Distraction exercise (Agazarian, 2018, p. 73): This is about connecting and resonating with team members. This exercise and language is also a good basis for subgrouping and is best explained beforehand. Everyone checks in individually:

  1. what distracts me on the outside? Formulate facts and describe them precisely. Important: As a facilitator, be careful to distinguish between facts and feelings: Describe facts precisely; feelings are about the experience of the feelings and not about what I think about them.
  2. feel the feelings: How do you feel about this experience?
  3. bring the feelings into the relationships and go into non-verbal resonance through eye contact: Go around and look into the eyes of the people here in the room. Bring your distraction into the relationship with these people. Choose for yourself which duration of eye contact is appropriate: In terms of closeness and distance.
  4. Check your energy level: After looking everyone in the eye, check if your energy is more in the here and now than before.

5.2.30 Creating a map

Purpose	Making inner images of agile transformation visible and discussable
Goals	• Identify differences in the joint process and derive thrust directions
Special features	Interactive map that makes inner attitudes visible with individual designations from the organization

Resources	• Map
	• Metaphors and landscape descriptions
	• Moderation cards
	• A moderation
Number of Participants	5 to 25 people
Duration	0.5 to 1 day
Section links	3.8, 4.1
Source	Own development (Lauchart-Schmiedl)

"Create a Map " helps to uncover thematic areas, patterns and internal core competencies that are relevant in the context of agile transformations. Based on this, strategic thrusts and interventions can be derived to initiate a next loop in the overall architecture. At the same time, the different images of the people become discussable and critical points can be taken up. This method is well suited for starting in the context of the strategic framework and also in challenging the current development in the transformation process.

Direction

Preparation: You need a map that is two by two metres. We at Neuwaldegg have developed a tarp for this. In addition, many inspiring names are needed for the landscapes, describing both the outer and the inner situation: Emsig Church, Summit of Lonely Decisions, Voting Meadow, Forest of Possibilities, and Highway of Change.

First, it is important to create a content and organizational framework so that the metaphor of the map can be introduced as a description for the organization. Once you as a facilitator have introduced the participants to this metaphor, unroll the map in front of the whole group on the floor or a large table. If the group size is over 12, simply form four small groups and quarter the map.

The participants can now choose from the different landscape names and metaphors. It is helpful to provide blank pieces of paper so that terms can be added independently. Now the landscape is given different meanings with the names: What is working in our organization? What best describes this agile transformation right now? What roads are there in our organization? What valleys, mountains and groups of people? Where are they moving? Where are they going? and so on.

Fig. 5.5. Create a map

If several teams have worked separately, the maps are presented in plenary and the stories associated with them are told. Then the focus is on the whole: What stands out? What is surprising? What are the similarities and differences?

The next step is to open up design possibilities: Now that we see it this way, is there something that can be better/easier/more meaningful? What would that look like? The group starts to change the map (Attention: Take pictures beforehand!) and in doing so create the future and make other names and distances. After some time, when nothing is moving any more, the next steps and directions are to be derived from this: Which concrete steps and measures will lead us from today to the future? From *now* to *then*? The agreements and ideas are recorded, prioritized and roles and persons are assigned.

5.2.31 Meeting mastery based on the four rooms

Purpose	Establish effective meetings in organizations that are the engine for common progress.
Goals	• Introduce meetings differentiated by purpose • Focused meeting time
Special features	This form of meeting demands a lot of discipline from the individuals, as it involves common agreements
Resources	Moderation
Duration	Several rounds of different duration
Section link	3.8
Source	Own development (Buzanich-Pöltl)

Agile teams already know that they work in four different spaces: Operational, organizational, interpersonal and intrapersonal. All three spaces need to be addressed, and a meaningful meeting structure is one of the biggest levers for teams and organizations. We find it helpful if the purpose and responsibilities of the team are clarified in advance and the roles of the team are sharpened and made explicit.

Direction

The whole team will deepen their common purpose and responsibilities as a team. The aim of this session is to design a meeting structure along the four rooms that will be tested in the coming months. In addition, each meeting is to be designed in detail so that they can be tried out immediately in the next step.

As a facilitator, give the group members the following overview:

1. The operational space includes everything that is important in daily activities. This includes coordination meetings, stand-ups, tactical meetings with current KPIs and project updates; creative prototyping of products and services is also central. This is where roles move.
2. The organizational space creates the framework to clarify the framework and rules of the game. This includes strategic directions, role development, governance meetings, purpose questions. Here we clarify what is needed in the game itself.

3. In the interpersonal space, the focus is on the shared relationship, which is why feedback is given to each other on a personal level, cooperation is reflected on together, learning spaces are created in order to grow together.
4. In the intrapersonal space, it is mainly about the person him/herself: Self-reflection, own development in the organization, further training.

In the next step, four groups can be formed along these spaces. Each group is given the following assignment:

- Consider which formats can fill this space well—in terms of purpose and responsibilities.
- For each format, describe the purpose, the resources it requires and a possible process including timings.
- Please make it as visual as possible so that others can easily imagine it.
- Make a recommendation on how often this format can make sense.

This step takes on average 45 to 60 minutes. The small groups present to each other what proposals they have worked out for the rooms. Afterwards, there are two variants for the next step: In variant 1, the manager or expert takes over the next concretization step. In variant 2, the team itself develops proposals for concretization. The motto: This is a prototype that can be adapted at any time. The following parameters and questions should be worked out and understood before concretizing (can also be done beforehand):

- Where will decisions be made in the future and how do you want to do it (for this it is helpful if decision-making formats are known)?
- Which formats can be virtual, where is personal presence important?
- Some meetings can be subdivided again.
- Make sure that there is a moderation and documentation role in each format.
- What behaviours do you want to encourage or change?
- What rules of the game do you want to give yourself?

Based on these results and frameworks, the individual prototypes can be sharpened by small groups working on them and presenting them again.

Table 5.6 shows an example of a management team outcome that was jointly developed and supervised, especially at the beginning.

Table 5.6. Example of a management board result

Frequency	Name and purpose	Procedure

• 1 × week
• 30 minutes, virtual
• 30 minutes time reserve afterwards
	Stand-ups
	Important ongoing updates from the areas; then role-based deepening, if necessary
		1. Check-in 5 minutes
		2. Everyone gives 3.5 minutes update
		3. 1 minute for comprehension questions per area
		4. Check-out
		5. Hint:
		  - Moderation changes
		  - The 30 minutes afterwards are important because the people are very busy and difficult to grasp spontaneously. This way, topics from the stand-ups can be clarified right afterwards.

• 1 × month
• 3 hours, live and in case of emergency virtual participation
	Steering meeting
	Make decisions that are evidence-based and generate a common picture on cross-cutting issues.
		Frame:
		  • Part 1: Update KPIs and projects (1 h)
		  • Part 2: Deepening and deciding on steering-relevant topics (2 h)
		6. Check-in
		7. Check List Items (Check or no Check)
		  - I am prepared
		  - I have done all the ToDos
		  - Status of the last meeting communicated
		  - I gave feedback to someone in this team
		8. KPIs
		  - Dashboard by area
		  - Comprehension questions
		  - Resonance
		9. Projects
		  - Update
		  - Comprehension questions
		  - Resonance
		10. Short break
		11. Deepening the content and decisions
		  - Presentation of the topic
		  - Comprehension questions
		  - Clarification of what is needed (resonance, info, decision …)
		  - Resonance (or input to be able to move forward)
		  - Decision after objection query or role responsibility
		12. Check-out

Table 5.6.   Continued

Frequency	Name and purpose	Procedure
• Every 2 months • 1 day, live	**Reflection meeting** Joint look at the development and adaptation of rules of the game and roles	With external support. Important building blocks: • **Person check-in:** People can talk in detail about how they are and what is on their mind at the moment. • **Reflection on roles and rules of the game:** Roles and rules of the game are consciously gone through, tensions are collected in order to work on them afterwards. • **Decision-making mode:** Objection check. In case of multiple options, systemic consensus. • **Reflection on cooperation:** Feedback sessions, working through strengths and challenges, making new agreements.
• 2 × per year • 2 days	**Strategy meeting** Strategy check and adjustment of thrust directions	With external support. Important building blocks: • Evaluate the current strategy including data analysis • Systemic loop with focus on whole organization • Organizational sample check • Stakeholder management • Derive measures and priorities for the individual areas and the whole • Operationalization plan

5.2.32 Role marketplace: Aligning team and roles with purpose

Purpose	Sharpen and continuously strengthen roles in the team
Goals	• Establish role-based working • Identify roles in the team in a differentiated way • Create transparent responsibilities and tasks • Strengthen liabilities • Detect interfaces and overlaps
Special features	Sometimes it's exciting because it becomes visible what someone feels responsible for.
Resources	Flipcharts and Post-it; Team-Purpose, Moderation
Duration	1.5 days
Section links	3.4, 3.8
Source	Neuwaldegg practice

We have already tested this method in many teams. The prerequisite is not a Holacratic organization and circle structure. Every team can use this method to describe and sharpen the current roles—also along the current profiles. This makes responsibilities clearer and over time these roles can become more and more differentiated. In the long term, it makes sense to also think about which roles can change or are also filled more than once. The long-term goal is to think and work more in terms of roles and to handle them more flexibly. The process for this can be established over time. We describe the starting point here.

Direction

In your facilitation role, you clarify in advance the purpose of this step and roughly what to expect. After that, it's time to get started:

- Step 1 Collect roles: Each person should first write down headings for their own roles in individual work: One role per post-it. Often it helps in the first step to use only one's own job title. After five to ten minutes, the roles are presented in plenary and clustered: Are there duplicate roles, single roles, and so forth.?
- Step 2 Describe roles: Once the role headings have been clarified, they are divided into small groups and/or individuals and worked out in depth. Each role is described as follows (for details see also Sections 2.3.2 and 3.4): Name of the role, Purpose of the role, Accountabilities, Optional Domains (we do not recommend this in the first step because it tends to contribute to "allotment" thinking). It is best to visualize each role on a flipchart. The credo is: What can be expected from this role from our point of view. Tip: It helps individuals emotionally to describe their own roles, as this is very exciting and exhausting anyway. Therefore, plan enough time for it and don't rush!
- Step 3 Role communitization: First, it helps to do a gallery walk and read everything. Participants go from one flipchart to the next. Post-its can be used to add comments: Fits great! What is missing here is …! I see it differently! Attention interface! Afterwards, it is helpful to discuss the individual roles together and, if necessary, to decide already: Objection or no objection. The IDM is also helpful here, but it must be clarified in advance with the team (and should be introduced). In addition, this is also the time to identify missing roles: What has not been written down or what roles do we still need, such as a feel-good manager or an after-work role?
- Step 4 Role adaptation in the future: The next step is to clarify how the roles will be further processed in the future and how they will be transparently documented (see Section 5.2.31 "Meeting mastery" and Section 5.2.34 "Governance meeting").

- Step 5 Operationalize roles: Now there is still time to make the first deductions, preferably in individual work: How do I energize my roles in the near future? What will be my next steps? Which of my strengths do I want to contribute? Where do I need support?
- Share in the group and write it down!

5.2.33 Tactical meeting

Purpose	Serves the quick coordination of teams (synchronization)
Goals	• Reconcile agreements quickly and make them visible • Aligning important projects • Coordinate operational issues • Develop and distribute next steps • Learning together
Special features	• Needs good facilitation and discipline from all involved • Is very unusual in the initial phase • Can also be used outside Holacracy structures • Tensions, that is, the difference in the here and now and what is possible in the future, are processed • Is also possible virtually
Resources	13. Role Facilitator consistently guides through the process. 14. The role of the secretary is visible and transparent for all. 15. Laptop include projector so that everyone can watch.
Number of Participants	4 to max. 25 persons
Duration	60 to max. 90 minutes
Section link	2.4
Source	HolacracyOne

Direction

1. **Check-in:** The purpose is for members to be present and free themselves from distractions. We often ask the question, "How am I here today and what do I need to let go of so that I can be fully present?" It is important to talk in turn and not discuss!
2. **Go through checklists:** The defined check-list items are asked. Everyone says "Check" or "No Check". The questioned roles answer in turn. Check list items

can be: The completion of certain tasks, such as whether ten customers have been contacted or the billing has been done. The aim here is to encourage behaviour by regularly asking the check-list item and being transparent about the contribution of the roles in the group. It can also be topics like: "Gave direct feedback to five roles on … Gave feedback". Asking or discussing is not allowed in this round. This would be a tension that can be noted and brought in at a later time (triage).

3. **Metrics review:** The current, relevant and necessary figures are called up and viewed together. Questions of understanding can be asked. The focus here is on updates and monitoring within the circle: Circle members receive an overview of the latest developments and are informed.

4. **Project updates:** This step is about getting a quick overview of the current projects, which are all a contribution to energizing the Circle Purpose. Each role is asked individually if there have been any developments since the last meeting. The role holders either say "no update" or bring in their most recent updates. Questions of understanding are allowed at this step, but no discussion.

5. **Form agenda:** In this step, a "flying" agenda is formed. Each person calls out only one or two words to the role of the secretary, who then writes down this point and the person for all to see. Important: Nobody has to understand the title (max. two words) of the tensions. Therefore, some points can also be called the same. The role of facilitator is now to work through the agenda points in the next step of the triage with the circle. Depending on how many agenda items there are, it can be asked whether some of them should be prioritized. In addition, the time frame and duration of the items should be clarified with the circle so that the facilitator role can plan the time well. The goal is basically to get everything through.

    Tip: The best way for the roles to come prepared is to collect their tensions and thus bring them in easily. However, tensions can also be introduced that have only arisen at that moment, later in the triage or in the previous steps of the process.

6. **Triage of tensions:** This is the core of the meeting. Now the individual points are worked through. Each tension or point is dealt with individually. The focus is always on the person bringing the tension. That is why this person is always asked: "What do you need?" Depending on how much time is available or how much time is needed (the role of facilitator has sovereignty over this), the role of facilitator makes sure that the tension is released. The tension-bringer can invite others to join in the discussion, ask for feedback from a few, pass on information, ask for something, and so on (see above). Ideally,

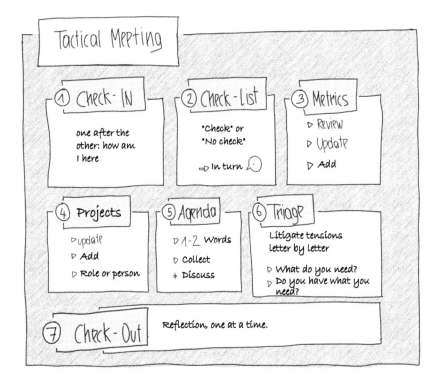

Fig. 5.6. Tactical meeting based on HolacracyOne

there is always a next action that is assigned to a role. This ensures that there is always something going on. At the end, the facilitator role asks: "Do you have what you need?" Sometimes this can be just a small step forward. Then it's on to the next tension. In contrast to conventional meetings, no one can join in the discussion without being asked. The role of facilitator focuses only on one person's tension. All others are to be put on hold for this moment. No discussing, bringing in other information unless asked. The advantage: There is no talking out of turn. The challenge: Not everything that each individual wants to say or contribute is relevant at that moment. This is a learning process in the beginning.

7. **Closing round:** At the end, each person in turn shares a short reflection. We like to ask: "What was successful today and what can we do better next

time? In this way, everyone has their say again and learning takes place together.

This meeting format has helped us to work through many more points in our meetings and not get stuck at certain points again and again. In addition, everyone has a good feeling of where the respective circle is at the moment and where things are getting stuck. It is challenging to always keep a good eye on the time and also that the process sometimes feels very mechanical. The purpose here is not to make everyone feel good. The point here is to work through things quickly. And that is certainly one of the biggest differences to the meetings that are usually held in organizations. This meeting is one of the more sporting ones and is clearly played fast: So everyone should also be well warmed up and ready to go! The facilitator acts as a referee and makes sure that everything that is needed for the meeting is done.

Tips for practising a tactical meeting

- It is better to bring in more tensions than less. The role of facilitator supports you in the process of clarifying where tensions belong.
- If clarifying a tension is important to you in this meeting and you are given the opportunity to prioritize it, use it.
- Keep a list where you collect all tensions and edit it regularly. If you use the Glassfrog platform provided by HolacracyOne, there is such a function in the app. But a normal list will do as well.
- Always start with "In my role as …", then the others know their way around.
- Address others in their role: "In your role as …"
- We recommend an implementation time of one to a maximum of one and a half hours. In the beginning you need longer!
- The type of agenda building and triage is also very useful in other meeting formats.
- Remember: You can fully engage in their tension release process; your facilitator accompanies you through the process.
- At the same time, do not forget: The role of facilitator acts in such a way that the whole circle gets the most and the best out of it in terms of the purpose and the meeting format of "synchronizing".

5.2.34 Governance meeting

Purpose	Serves to develop, edit and clarify rules, roles, responsibilities, teams, domains, policies and agreements.
Goals	Clarifies decision-making powers and responsibilities according to a specific process and with defined rules of play <ul><li>The course of the meeting is clearly defined</li><li>Clarifies diffuse issues and formalizes them, which can be exhausting at times.</li></ul>
Special features	<ul><li>Great potential to quickly design many structures</li><li>Needs commitment in the team/circle that this is the only way to proceed.</li><li>Everyone knows the procedure of the Integrative Decision-Making (IDM) process (cf. Section 5.2.1)</li></ul>
Resources	8. Role facilitator consistently guides through the process. Role secretary writes transparently for all to see. 9. Laptop include projector so that everyone can watch.
Number of Participants	2—20 persons
Duration	60 to max. 120 minutes
Section link	2.4
Source	HolacracyOne

Direction

1. **Check-in:** One by one, people check into the meeting. Another possible question can be: "In these roles I am here in this circle today and in order for me to be fully present, I still need to leave the following behind …". The focus is on getting the meeting off to a good start.
2. **Administrative concerns:** Facilitator asks if there are any important organizational concerns and issues. At this point, for example, we have people who have to go to their kids say that they have to leave at a certain time. This helps the circle members and roles to plan the time well and everyone knows their way around. Also the total time duration for the governance meeting is made clear here so that focus can be established.

3. **Form agenda:** This point is the same as in the Tactical meeting (see Section 5.2.33). A "flying" agenda is formed by the role of the secretary writing down one or two words and the corresponding person noting them down. The role of facilitator has the task of working through the agenda points in the next step with the circle and at the same time pays attention to the resource of time. As always, the goal is to get through with all the points. However, this is strongly related to the complexity of the proposals and also how much of it still needs to be understood.

4. **Process agenda items:** The procedure in this step is always the same. The facilitator role's mandate here is to clarify the tensions and proposals with the respective role and guide them towards a usable and meaningful path.

   a) **Present a proposal:** The role introduces its own tension and suggests how the issue should be addressed in the future. All possibilities such as policies, role expectations and purpose sharpening are available for this. The role facilitator supports the formulation and sharpening. Only the person proposing is in focus.

   b) **Questions of understanding:** Now everyone has the opportunity to ask questions. The energy is that of a curious child: I want to understand more! Each member sits here both in role and as a person. In this respect, everything can be asked. The role of facilitator takes care that there is no discussion and that no hidden opinions are conveyed. If in doubt, let the question be asked so that the process flows!

   c) **Reaction round:** Here everyone is allowed to express their opinion on the proposal. It is important that people do not refer to each other and that everyone gets a turn. The idea behind this is that the person making the suggestion gets more ideas for improvement and is encouraged at the same time. In addition, anger or concerns can also be expressed. Experience shows that it is helpful to give space to negative energies as well. It is important that the person making the suggestion is not intimidated or withdraws the suggestion. This is what the role of facilitator looks at, especially in the next step!

   d) **Adjustment and clarification:** Now the proposal can be adjusted or sharpened. The facilitator role points out to the proposer that this does not need to be done as there are further steps. Everything that is relevant takes place in the objection round and the integrative decision-making process.

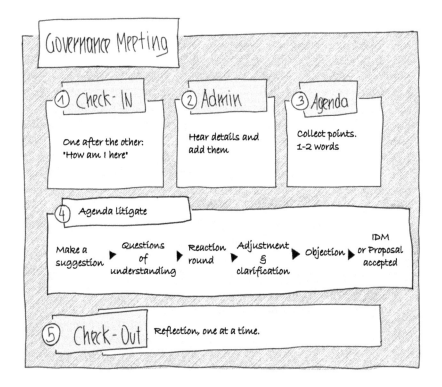

Fig. 5.7. Governance meeting on HolacracyOne

e) **Objection question:** Here the role facilitator asks all circle members the same question and each circle member answers with "objection" or "no objection". The question is: "Do you see any reason why this proposal could set us back or cause harm? Objection or no objection?"

Depending on how the members respond, the process continues. Objections are dealt with in the Interactive Decision Process (see Section 5.2.1). If there are no objections, the proposal is accepted and is recorded in the IT system (Glassfrog in our case) as new governance and a short celebration mood strengthens! Then it is the turn of the next agenda item.

5. **Closing round:** As in the tactical meeting, reflections are shared here. The role facilitator can ask a focused question. It is important that there is no discussion.

Governance meeting tips

- In this process, the attitude of all circle members that more personal impulses lead to better proposals is particularly helpful! This suddenly creates an energy of co-creation. This energy is sometimes not so easy to create, because some proposals evoke different or diffuse emotions. This is where the role of facilitator is most important: Both to create this state with one's own attitude and to let it flow into the meeting format. We observe and experience the opposite again and again: The role of facilitator is often perceived as the defender role of the person making the proposal, who has to be fought against.

- In this format, too, the following applies: Encourage and allow tensions and objections. It is better to have more than less. This helps everyone to get into the game together.

- Facilitators are guardians of the process. They make sure that everything runs according to the agreed rules of the game and accompany the circle in the two meeting formats. Therefore, anything that underlines this is helpful. For example, holding the Governance or Tactical card (available at HolacracyOne) symbolizes: "Hey look, I'm sticking to the process just like you!". Others may also have such cards, or the process steps may be posted in the room. The announcement in the process steps is also helpful here: "We are now going to the third step…".

- Out-of-governance proposals: There is also the possibility to process governance proposals outside the meetings. We do this with the tool Glassfrog. This is how it works for us: I enter my tension and also my new proposal in the tool. In doing so, I select the circle and also the nature of my proposal, for example, a new responsibility and task for the role of advisor. Everyone receives an email and sees the proposal in their profile if it concerns them. Everyone can now vote online for seven days: "I have an objection" or "Escalate to meeting". If there is no objection after seven days, the new governance applies. In our view, this form is suitable for organizations that already work well with Holacracy and are very disciplined. It sometimes happened to us that there were so many suggestions that hardly anyone came along and the suggestions were not heeded. After seven days, there were proposals that no one had looked at. We then found the following practice: We tracked how many people looked at the proposals. In addition, we introduced a policy that everyone takes time briefly per week and escalates more in meetings so that we can exchange on this.

5.2.35 Virtual on-focus meeting

Purpose	Focused work—especially in a virtual context
Goals	• Low-distraction collaboration in the virtual setting • Making one's own tasks transparent • Dealing efficiently with stress patterns • Establish focus on the current context and topic • Connect with the other members
Special features	Can also be implemented "non-virtually" or with unknown people from the internet
Number of Participants	2 to max. 5 persons
Section link	3.8
Source	Own development (Meier) inspired by focusmate.com

Especially in virtual work, it is difficult for some people to keep the focus on the important tasks. This is also due to the fact that one notices less of other members of a project because transparency is more easily neglected. Additionally, working in a virtual setting offers a lot of potential for distractions and multitasking. Focus meetings help a team to spend time together virtually, to work in a concentrated way and to create transparency about their tasks. Another benefit is that people are less easily distracted in stressful situations.

Direction

In preparation, think about how long the appointment should last. We recommend at least 30 minutes and a maximum of three hours. It is important that all team members receive an invitation and are technically well equipped. Each prepares a work package that is to be worked on in the chosen time period.

   Implementation: At the set time, all participating team members meet online in a virtual meeting with all webcams on. One participant takes over timekeeping and then the meeting can start:

• *Personal goal:* All participants state to each other the goal they would like to achieve within the set meeting time, for example, "This is what I would like to achieve in the next sixty minutes." It is important that there is a fixed end. (This step should take a maximum of five minutes.)
• *Visibility:* Webcams stay on (this works particularly well with two screens), sound can be turned off if needed and everyone starts working individually on

their respective work package. This simulates the physical presence of others and increases the commitment to work in a concentrated way.

- *Update milestones:* Participants keep each other informed via chat or in exchange with audio when they have reached important milestones in their chat (or are also distracted by phone calls, etc.).
- *Check-out status quo:* Five minutes before the end of the meeting, everyone finishes their work and shares what they have achieved. Successes are jointly rewarded, if it was not achieved, one can briefly reflect together on what the reason could be—for example, are there dependencies, for example, waiting for input from others, what can be done to be less distracted: Best practice sharing.
- *Follow-up:* Ideally, the next appointment for a further session is arranged immediately, so that entire projects can be worked on together.

Variants: This is of course also possible face-to-face.

Special variant: As an individual, find a person online whom you don't know at all or who comes from a completely different field and hold a meeting. Like co-working, only in the virtual world. Surprising, but it works!

5.2.36 Team agreements for virtual cooperation

Purpose	Enable well-coordinated virtual workin the team
Goals	• Adapt existing team agreements for virtual collaboration
	• Or: Re-working team agreements for virtual settings together
Special features	Can of course also be developed in a face-to-face setting and then implemented virtually
Resources	If created virtually: Ideally digital whiteboard for collection and clustering
Number of Participants	Depending on the size of the team
Section link	3.8
Source	Own development (Meier), inspired by Work Together Anywhere (Sutherland & Janene-Nelson, 2018)

Virtual teamwork requires different arrangements than face-to-face collaboration. There are more or different aspects that need to be considered. This can be done either virtually or in a face-to-face workshop.

Direction

In the preparation, make sure that existing team agreements are taken into account and form the basis for further work. Send an invitation to all team members including a short briefing scheduled for two to three hours. Also plan for a break!

When you meet the participants in the virtual space, you create a framework for the workshop with the usual conditions (e.g. check-in). Then the team agreement starts, which can be developed as follows:

- Collecting already existing team agreements (e.g. virtual rule meetings)
- Collecting wishes on undefined topics
- If applicable, collect frequent ambiguities and/or conflict issues in virtual collaboration (if the team has already worked virtually or is currently working virtually).

Depending on the size of the group, the points are collected on virtual moderation cards on demand or in small groups and presented in the virtual plenary. It is recommended to cluster the topics as follows: Technology and media, cooperation and "we as a team", information and communication. After clustering, the individual pieces of information are processed and worked on in the workshop using common moderation methods (consensus versus consensus, majority decision, etc.). In the facilitation, you can choose from this list of questions to open up further perspectives:

- Information, communication
  - What meetings do we want to have, with what regularity, with what participants, with what structure and what content?
  - What level of preparation is required and expected before which meeting?
  - What information do we want to share and how promptly (especially relevant for leadership roles)? Through which medium?
  - What goals do we set ourselves and how? What milestones do we use to measure success?
  - How can we distribute tasks? How do we know what everyone is currently working on?
- Technology/Media
  - What technical equipment is required for each team member? What additional resources are still needed?
  - What response time do we expect on which medium? (This can vary for, e.g. chat, email, telephone, …)
  - What information and training is necessary for safe use of all media?

- What preferences do we have to be reached?
- Cooperation/"We as a team"/Social interaction
  - How do we make decisions (consensus vs. consensus)? Who has the authority to make which decisions?
  - How do we want to deal with conflicts?
  - How will we give each other feedback? To what extent?
  - How do we celebrate success?
  - How and when can we exchange informally?
  - How do we make sure we feel like a team when we don't/rarely see each other face-to-face?

5.2.37 Virtual tribe space in virtual space

Purpose	Strengthen team cohesion in project teams
Goals	• Mapping tribe space virtually • Make informal exchange explicit • Maintaining connection between team members • Have fun in a team
Special features	Webcam necessary
Number of Participants	2 to 20 persons
Section link	3.8
Source	Own development (Jeggle)

Teams working together in one place can exchange and coordinate informally with relative ease. Short conversations at the coffee machine, in the canteen or in the lift serve to synchronize and quickly clarify. At the same time, social exchange takes place and the relationship between team members is cultivated. The brief exchange about the weekend or one's state of mind makes it easier to assess what colleagues are saying or commenting on. Tribe space happens "by the way", so to speak, and almost by itself.

The situation is quite different for global change teams and agile project teams that work in different locations or depend on working (partly) from home. The question arises as to how team cohesion can be guaranteed. It is important to make this informal exchange "in between" explicitly virtual. Our own team was challenged in the Corona pandemic in spring 2020 to keep our team of 15 counsellors and office staff together for several weeks. What felt strange at the beginning quickly became the highlight of the week, which was created in turn.

Ideas for the virtual tribe space/social space

1. **Chat in the meeting room/virtual coffee & virtual apero**
   The simplest way to strengthen informal exchange is to consciously reserve time for it. For example, open the virtual meeting room five minutes early and invite everyone to dial in five minutes early for chit-chat and "stories from the home office". You can also call a virtual coffee 15 minutes, ask everyone to meet on Friday for a virtual apero with a cold drink, or, or, or. It is important that you specifically allow space for this exchange. Alternatively, you can ask team members to meet virtually for a one-to-one coffee.

2. **"Anyone who …" question round/warm-up**
   It is important that all participants have their camera switched on and that all camera images are shown on a screen. The idea of the game is to learn more about the colleagues in a playful way.

Gameplay

All participants cover their camera with their hand or with a post-it.
- The facilitator asks any question that can be answered with "yes" or "no", such as:
  – All those who have managed to be offline (email and mobile) for 12 hours at a stretch, show yourself now!
  – Anyone who has ever slept in straw now reveals themselves!
  – Anyone who still used a dial phone now reveals themselves!
  – If you've ever texted while walking and almost fallen, show yourself!
  – If you've never Googled yourself, show yourself now!
  – Anyone who has already completed a bungee jump, now reveals themselves!
  – If you like watching funny YouTube videos, show yourself now!
- Those who have taken the piece of paper, tell a short story about it.
- The first person to show up asks the next question. In this way, the group itself controls the intensity or intimacy of the questions. There are no limits to creativity, each person decides for him- or herself when to show him- or herself!

This procedure is also suitable for quick coordination within the team.

3. **Guess who is sitting where?**
   – Ask all participants to send you a photo of their home office in advance of the virtual meeting.
   – Select three to five images for the planned virtual meeting, depending on how long you plan to spend on this activity.

- At the beginning of the virtual meeting, show photo after photo and let the participants guess which team member each photo belongs to.
- Perhaps you can have the person briefly report on their own home office.
- Alternatively, you can ask your participants to send in a photo of an object that has a special meaning beforehand and have them guess it. This can lead to good conversations about the respective team members afterwards.

4. **Send in children's pictures**
   - Ask all participants to send you a child's photo in advance of the virtual meeting!
   - Place the photos on a whiteboard or transparency and number them consecutively.
   - Now let the participants guess which photo belongs to which team member, alternatively you can also use a voting tool for this.
   - When the puzzle is solved, have each team member briefly tell the context in which the photo was taken.

5. **Draw a team member**
   - The facilitator assigns one person in the team to each participant beforehand.
   - In the virtual meeting, the facilitator gives a signal and then everyone has one minute to draw the assigned partner on a piece of paper, alternatively on an online whiteboard.
   - Afterwards, the individual pictures are shown and guesses are made as to which team member it is.

6. **Who is this …? A nice story about a colleague**
   - Ideal for a positive start to a meeting
   - The facilitator asks (possibly in advance) who would like to tell a story, incident, personal characteristic ("always positive with a wink") about a colleague. The others then guess.
   - Examples:
   - The team member I'm referring to gets a sweet kick after lunch and eats a whole pack of Mannerschnitten within minutes!
   - The team member I'm referring to likes to listen to loud pop music in the car!
   - With the team member I am referring to, I had the following situation with the client …

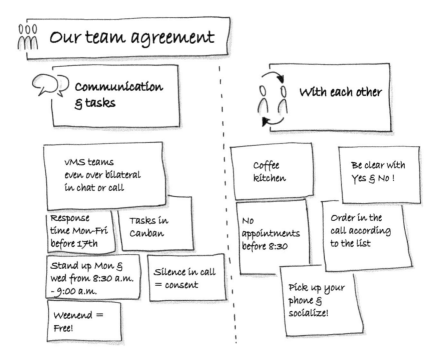

Fig. 5.8. Team agreements for virtual cooperation

7. **Common movement "Touch an object"**

We sit in front of the computer all day, so a little exercise is good. That's exactly what this energizer is for:

The facilitator asks everyone to touch something as quickly as possible on "go". Examples:
– Touch something made of metal!
– Touch something round!
– Touch the nearest door!
– Trying to get to the ceiling (with aids)
– ....

8. **End of the week with praise and thanks**
   – Ring in the weekend together and share the "beautiful stories of the week".
   – At the end of the week, hold a virtual meeting of about 20 minutes in which you briefly highlight the successes of the week and then open the space for praise and thanks:

- Who would like to say thank you to whom for what?
- What did we do particularly well this week?
- At the beginning, this seems unusual and accordingly a round starts hesitantly. Once the ice is broken, you will probably have to stop it sooner.

5.2.38 Retrospective in teams

Purpose	Promote self-optimization in the team and develop a corresponding mindset
Goals	• Review • Learning for the future • Promote growth mindset
Special features	Moderation
Number of Participants	Team from 5 to 20 people
Section link	3.8
Source	Own development (Jeggle)

The retrospective is a constructive, trusting and open reflection on cooperation and serves a team to learn from the past, to address social dynamics at an early stage and to derive measures for improvement. The central question is what went well and what went less well, and what the team can learn from this. We recommend conducting them as needed or every four to eight weeks. Regular retrospectives help the team to continuously develop. In addition, it is important to keep developing and to create a Growth Mindset.

Central rules

- Shared understanding that everyone did the best they could and retrospective looking forward in a solution-oriented way. It is not about finding culprits.
- Openness requires an atmosphere of trust, that is, what is said with personal reference remains in the room.
- Each individual has the right to his or her own truth and perspective; reality emerges in joint dialogue.
- The whole team is involved and the retrospective does not refer to individuals but to the result or the social dynamics in the team.
- Based on the retrospective, concrete measures are derived at the end that contribute to improvement.

- The topics discussed are relevant to all present.
- The retrospective lasts between 1 and 2.5 hours, depending on the size of the team, and is best conducted by a neutral facilitator.
- Clear time limits (time boxing) for the individual phases and the retrospective as a whole. Experience: The team learns over time that the time limits are "meant seriously" and adapts to the length and importance of statements.

Five steps in retrospective

1. **Framing (5–10 minutes)**: Check-in, objective of the retrospective, explanation of the format and the rules of the game.
2. **Gather information:**
   a) **5–10 minutes:** Ask team members individually or in small groups to collect facts and feelings about working together on moderation cards.
   b) **15 minutes:** Results are brought up on the wall and clustered.
3. **Gaining insights (20 minutes):** What is the overall picture? Is there a clear trend? Do some causal research, why is it the way it is, what are the hypotheses? Also look at what is going really well that is often overlooked. If there are many issues, have them rated with points.
4. **Deriving actions (10 minutes):** Decide what the team will take away together from the retrospective. What two to five agreements are made? The central question is, what do we need to agree on and do to become better?
5. **Check-out (5-10 minutes):** Review of the retrospective, for example, what was good, what should be different next time or how helpful was this retrospective for you on a scale of 1 to 5 and how do you go out?

Possible retrospective formats

To keep this format interesting in the long term, it helps to alternate different methods. Here are a few suggestions:

- Starfish method: Dividing a flip chart into "less", "more", "keep", "stop" and "start".
- 3-corner method: Start, Stop, Continue or in German: Anfangen, aufhören, weiter so.
- Quadrant of 4: What was good, what was bad, what ideas exist, derived actions
- Timeline with feeling line (see Fig. 5.10): First, the most important events since the last retro are collected on the timeline. Then each person draws a feeling barometer, telling why the feeling line was like that.

5.2.39 Twin Star—Reteaming®

Purpose	Develop cooperation in teams and strengthen psychological safety
Goals	• Improve team spirit and the atmosphere • Solve problems in cooperation • Establish solution-oriented cooperation
Special features	Simple approach that can be integrated on an ongoing basis
Resources	Moderation, input
Duration	1.5 hour to 1.5 days
Section link	3.8
Source	Furman & Ahola (2014)

The Twin Star maps two sides of a team: Crucial factors for the positive development of cooperative behaviour and problems that endanger psychological well-being in teams. Positive experience and cooperation are strengthened through appreciation, fun, participation and shared successes. Psychological well-being is promoted by inadequate handling of problems, criticism, slights and setbacks.

All eight factors can be worked on together in a team. This method can be carried out by counsellors as well as by managers themselves. If there is little time available, 45 minutes per factor is sufficient.

Direction

First, the Twin Star itself is presented with all its factors. The team members now have the opportunity to rate each dimension for themselves: On a scale of 1 to 10, how well do I rate this factor in our team? Afterwards, the team members exchange ideas in pairs. The different pictures can also be carried into the group. Afterwards, it helps to prioritize by asking for points: Which factors do I find particularly important at the moment? It may be helpful to always ask about one factor from both dimensions. The dimension with the highest number of points starts and is deepened first.

Then the respective dimension is explored in more depth. The questions listed below help with the discussion. From our experience it makes sense to start with small groups. They are given up to 45 minutes to work out the questions for themselves. One person writes down the most important issues. In addition, each group chooses a representative who then represents the small group.

After the small groups, a fish bowl is started. The representatives are in the inner circle, an empty chair is also in the inner circle. The outer circle listens and, if necessary, individuals can express their opinions on the empty chair. The aim of the fish bowl is first to get into an exchange and then to derive initial measures towards the end. The facilitator makes sure that the fish bowl process is well observed and that the results are recorded at the end.

Depending on how much time is available, the prongs can be worked on using different methods. Other variants are a dialogue or a world café in which several prongs are worked on at the same time.

At the end of the exercise, each person still takes time to derive concrete insights and individual actions. It also helps to share these publicly. At the next meeting, where the next prongs are worked on, the implementation of the derived measures is reflected on first.

Questions for the factors

- **appreciation** (Furman & Ahola, 2014, p. 37):
  - What kind of appreciation evokes a particularly good feeling for you?
  - How can you ask for positive feedback if you don't get it any other way?
  - How can each in her own way contribute to making colleagues feel that their work is valued?
  - How can you tell that your performance is appreciated if it is not explicitly communicated?
  - What does the saying "If you don't sing your own praises, no one will" mean?
  - Why does positive feedback sometimes cause embarrassment?
  - How many compliments does it take to find the courage for new activities after criticism and reprimand?
- **fun** (Furman & Ahola, 2014, p. 47):
  - Why are humour and fun so important in the workplace?
  - What positive effects do humour and fun have?
  - Why should people who work hard also joke hard?
  - Where are the boundaries between harmless and hurtful jokes?
  - Making jokes about the misfortunes of others demonstrates unacceptably bad taste. Can you think of any other kinds of hurtful or malicious humour?
- **success** (Furman & Ahola, 2014, p. 57):
  - Why should one have the attitude from the beginning that the project will succeed?

Fig. 5.9. Starfish method

- Why is it worth considering even small successes as important?
- How do you celebrate your successes?
- Why is it sometimes not possible for others to rejoice with you over your successes?
- Why does "We got it done." sound much better than "I got it done."?
- Why should we analyze success and why do we do it so rarely?
- Why should we spend at least as much time discussing successes as we do discussing setbacks?
- Why can it look like bragging when you tell others about your successes?
- **sympathy** (Furman & Ahola, 2014, p. 71):
  - What are implied by the expressions "sympathy" and "paying attention to each other"?
  - Do people naturally care about other people, or does this depend on habits and behaviours that can be changed?
  - What do other people need to say or do to make you feel genuine sympathy?
  - In what ways can you offer your help to someone so that they can easily accept it?
  - How can you tell that someone actually cares about the others—apart from their words?
  - What should you do if you think a colleague has a serious problem?
  - When do you consider others' interest in you to be genuine sympathy and when just annoying snooping?

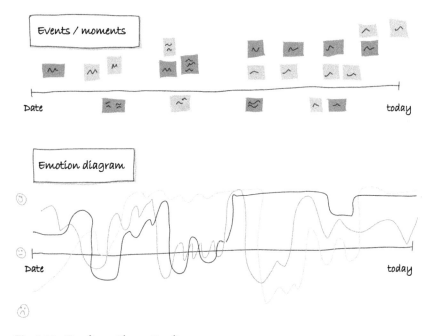

Fig. 5.10. Timeline with emotion line

- In what way can you ask the other about his well-being if you want to know how she is out of genuine interest in her, and not just to satisfy the usual form of politeness?
- What or what would you like to be asked about more often by others?
- **problems** (Furman & Ahola, 2014, p. 88):
  - Why do people like to avoid talking about problems?
  - Why does the joint analysis of a problem so quickly turn into mutual accusations?
  - Actually, you should be able to talk openly and honestly about everything, and yet you don't always succeed. Why?
  - How can you talk about problems without getting everyone upset?
  - When can trying to solve problems be an obstacle rather than a help?
  - What word could you use for "problem" to make it easier for you to talk about this issue?
  - Why does talking about problems alone not lead to finding the best solution to the problem?
  - How can you create an atmosphere in the company in which it is easy for employees to solve problems?

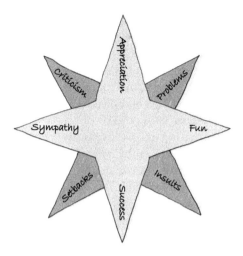

Fig. 5.11. Twin Star according to Furman & Ahola (2014)

- **offending** (Furman & Ahola, 2014, p. 102):
  - Why do mutual slights occur so easily?
  - Can offenses be avoided at all?
  - What should you do if you think you have offended someone?
  - What should you do if someone else has offended you?
  - What should you do if someone tells you that you have offended them?
  - Why are people generally reluctant to admit that they are offended and how can you address hurtful situations so that you can be sure that the other person will not immediately go on the defensive?
- **setbacks** (Furman & Ahola, 2014, p. 113):
  - "What do we mean when we say: "It was just a stupid coincidence", "What doesn't kill us makes us stronger" or "There is something good in everything"?
  - Why are we humans afraid of making mistakes or committing errors?
  - How should a good manager deal with the mistakes of her employees?
  - Why can some people overcome setbacks more quickly than others?
  - What role do the views and attitudes of others play when someone is trying to get over a setback suffered or a mishap?
  - What role does humour play when you look back on distant failures and misfortunes?
  - Why is it often better for your well-being to talk about your failures and mishaps with others than to keep them to yourself?

- Sometimes you have to analyze failures to find out their exact causes. Some other failures you should just leave behind and forget. But how do you know which category a failure belongs to?
- What attitudes should one adopt towards one's failures and mishaps if one wants to be tormented by the memory for a long time to come?
- How can you help someone get over their failures?
- **criticism** (Furman & Ahola, 2014, p. 133):
  - What kind of criticizing is particularly offensive?
  - What kind of criticism can be called "constructive"?
  - In which situations is it best not to criticize?
  - You don't want to criticize someone but would like them to change their behaviour. What can you do instead?
  - It is much easier to accept advice and wishes than criticism. Why?
  - How should we generally react to critical feedback, reproaches and rebukes?
  - Why do many people find it difficult to accept and embrace criticism?
  - Why is it relatively easy for one to accept critical feedback, while the other finds it difficult?
  - What kind of criticism can each rightly ignore?

5.2.40 Strengthening feedback and cooperation between teams

Purpose	Strengthening cooperation between teams
Goals	• Derive feedback to strengthen cooperation
	• Reflect on critical situations in the cooperation
	• Address irritations early on and avoid conflicts
	• Establish safe space for open dialogue in cooperation
Resources	Moderation, input
Number of Participants	Ideal for 2 to 3 teams that work together regularly, also for clarifying cooperation of internal-external relations or cooperation partners
Section link	3.8
Source	Own development (Jeggle)

Direction

As a facilitator, start by having all participants form a large circle while standing and quickly check in. Then have the respective teams get together and form a group. Group 1 starts talking positively about the others for three to five minutes: "What were the highlights of working with the other team in the last few weeks?" The other group listens. Then they switch.

Now send the two groups to separate rooms or corners of the room and give them the four questions below. Give the groups about 30 minutes to answer:

- What do we appreciate about working with the other team? What should they continue to do?
- What irritated us in the cooperation? What should the other team do (more/less)?
- What should the other team additionally do or start doing?
- What do we offer the other team for successful cooperation?

Come back to the plenary and let the groups take turns to present the results in about 15 minutes per group. This works best standing on two prepared walls with the question categories as headings. Make sure that at the end both groups, preferably well mixed, are in a large circle and then encourage an open dialogue between the teams. For this, introduce rules on how the dialogue should take place. As a facilitator, decide which core results you want to record and which evaluation criteria are to be derived, against which both teams want to be measured with a time interval of, for example, eight weeks.

Bibliography

Agazarian, Y. (2018): *System-Centered Therapy for Groups*. New York.

Allen, D. (2019): *Getting things done. The art of stress-free productivity*. New York.

Argyris, C./Schön, D. (1974): *Theorie in Practice*. San Francisco.

Baecker, D. (2003): *Wozu Kultur?* Berlin.

Baecker, D. (2007): *Studien zur nächsten Gesellschaft 2007*. Frankfurt/M.

Baecker, D. (2017): *Agilität, Hierarchie und Management. Eine Verallgemeinerung*. Unveröffentlicher Artikel: Universität Witten/Herdecke.

Beedle, M./Schwaber, K. (2001): *Agile Software Development with Scrum*. Upper Saddle River.

Boos, F./Fink, F. (2015): Vom Wissenden zum Lernenden – wenn Organisationsberater sich selbst verändern. Die Beratergruppe Neuwaldegg im Changeprozess. *Organisationsentwicklung. Zeitschrift für Unternehmensentwicklung und Change Management*, 1. Jg., 2015, S. 54–60.

Boos, F./Mitterer, G. (2019): *Einführung in das systemische Management. 2. Aufl.* Heidelberg.

Boos, F./Fink, F./Tobeitz, G. (2017): Wenn Krisen Krisen folgen. Die Beratungsgruppe Neuwaldegg im Changeprozess, Teil 2. *Organisationsentwicklung. Zeitschrift für Unternehmensentwicklung und Change Management*, 1. Jg. 2017, S. 48–54.

Borget, S. (2018): *Unkompliziert: das Arbeitsbuch für komplexes Denken und Handeln in agilen Unternehmen*. Offenbach.

Bourquin, P. (2018): Der Laufsteg. In: Lockert, M. (Hrsg.): *Perlen der Aufstellungsarbeit: Tools für systemisch Praktizierende*. Heidelberg, S. 21.

Brown, B. (03.01.2011): *Ted Talk: The Power of Vulnerability*. https://brenebrown.com/videos/. (Abrufdatum: 01.12.2019).

Bushe, G. (2009): *Claer Leadership: sustaining real collaboration and partnership at work*. Boston.

Crozier, M./Friedberg, E. (1993): *Die Zwänge kollektiven Handelns. Über Macht und Organisation*. Frankfurt a. M.

Denyer, D. (2017): *Organizational Resilience: A summary of academic evidence, business insights and new thinking*. BSI and Cranfield School of Management.

Dominik, G. (29.01.2020): Stolz am Boden. *DIE ZEIT online* (6). https://
www.zeit.de/2020/06/boeing-dave-calhoun-737-max-flugzeughersteller
(Abrufdatum 20.05.2020).

Dörner, D. (1989): *Die Logik des Misslingens.* Hamburg.

Dweck, S. C. (2017): *Minset: Changing the way you think to fulfil your potential.*
New York.

Ebner, M. (2019): *Positive Leadership. Erfolgreich führen mit PERMA-Lead: die
fünf Schlüssel zur High Perfomance.* Wien.

Edmondson, A. (2020): *Die angstfreie Organisation: Wie Sie psychologische
Sicherheit am Arbeitsplatz für mehr Entwicklung, Lernen und Innovationen
schaffen.* München.

Emerald, D. (2016): *The Power of TED: The Empowerment Dynamic.* Bainbridge
Island.

Epstein, S. (1990): Cognitive-experiental Self-theory. In: Pervin, L. (Hrsg.):
Handbook of Personality: Theory and research. New York, S. 165–192.

Fink, S. (2002): *Crisis Management. Planing for the Inevitable. 2. Aufl.* New
York.

Fink, F./Moeller, M. (2018): *Purpose Driven Organizations. Sinn –
Selbstorganisation – Agilität.* Stuttgart.

Fischer, J. (2004): *Macht in Organisationen. Zu einigen Aspekten des
Verhältnisses zwischen Individuen, Strukturen und Kommunikationsprozessen.*
Münster.

Förster, v. H./Pörksen, B. (2008): Die Wahrheit ist die Erfindung eines Lügners.
Gespräche für Skeptiker, 8. Aufl. Heidelberg.

Frankl, V. (1977): *... trotzdem Ja zum Leben sagen.* München.

Fröhlich-Gildhoff, K./Rönnau-Böse, M. (2019): *Resilienz.* 5. Aufl. München.

Furman, B./Ahola, T. (2014): *Twin Star – Lösungen vom anderen Stern.
Teamentwicklung für mehr Erfolg und Zufriedenheit am Arbeitsplatz.*
Heidelberg.

Gantt, S./Agazarian, Y. (2018): *SCT in Action: Applying the System-Centered
Approach in Ogranizations.* New York.

Gebauer, A. (2017): *Kollektive Achtsamkeit organisieren. Strategien und
Werkzeuge für eine proaktive Risikokultur.* Stuttgart.

Geisbauer, W. (2018): *Führen mit neuer Autorität: Stärke entwickeln für sich und
das Team.* Heidelberg.

Gester, P. W. (1992): Warum der Rattenfänger von Hameln kein Systemiker war. Grundlagen systemischer Gesprächs- und Interviewgestaltung. In: Schmitz, C. G. (Hrsg.): *Managerie. Systemisches Denken und Handeln im Management. 1. Jahrbuch.* Heidelberg, S. 136–164.

Glasersfeld, E. (2006): Einführung in den radikalen Konstruktivismus. In: Watzlawick, P (Hrsg.): *Die erfundene Wirklichkeit.* 11. Aufl. München, S. 16–38.

Grawe, K. (2004): *Neuropsychotherapie.* Göttingen.

Heitger, B./Doujak, A. (2014): *Harte Schnitte – Neues Wachstum. Wandel in volatilen Zeiten.* München.

Hochgerner, J. (2013): *Soziale Innovation in Zeiten wie diesen.* Zentrum für Soziale Innovation, Vortrag vom 08.02.2013. https://www.fh-ooe.at/fileadmin/user_upload/linz/fakultaet/aktuelles/forum-sozialmanagement/docs/fhooe-linz-workshop-hochgerner-2013.pdf (Abrufdatum: 14.06.2020)

Hsieh, T. (2010): *Delivering Happiness. A path to profits, passion, and purpose.* New York.

Hübschmann, W./Nagler, C. (2015): Captain Potentialanalyse. In: Brand, M. et al. (Hrsg.): *Handbuch der Persönlichkeitsanalysen.* Offenbach a. M., S. 138–163.

Hüther, P. G. (28.11.2017): *Quantenphysik und Kommunale Intelligenz.* https://www.youtube.com/watch?v=RzVoat6K-zQ&feature=youtu.be (Abrufdatum 02.02.2019).

Imai, M. (1992): *Kaizen – Der Schlüssel zum Erfolg der Japaner im Wettbewerb.* 6. Aufl. München.

Johnson, K. (1979): *Improvisation und Theater.* Berlin.

Kegan, R. (2014): Interview mit R. Kegan: Wie wir uns selbst im Weg stehen. *ZOE Zeitschrift für Organisationsentwicklung, Nr. 1,* S. 51.

Kegan, R./Lahey, L. (2009): *Immunity to Change.* Brighton.

Kegan, R./Lahey, L. (2016): *An Everyone Culture. Becoming a Deliberately Developmental Organization.* Boston.

Kelly, K. (2011): *What Technology wants. Technology is a living force that can expand our individual potential – if we listen to what it wants.* London.

Kirchgeorg, M./Meynhardt, T./Andreas Pinkwart, A./Suchanek, A./Zülch, H. (2019): *Das Leipziger Führungsmodell: Führen und beitragen.* Leipzig.

Kline, P./Saunders, B. (1997): *Zehn Schritte zur lernenden Organisation.* Paderborn.

Klinkhammer, M./Hütter, F./Stoess, D./Wüst, L. (2015): *Change happens: Veränderung gehirngerecht gestalten.* Freiburg.

Kotter, J. (2011): *Leading Change. Wie Sie Ihr Unternehmen in acht Schritten erfolgreich verändern.* München.

Kühl, S. (2011): *Organisationen: Eine sehr kurze Einführung.* Wiesbaden.

Kühl, S. (2015): Gesellschaft der Organisationen, organisierte Gesellschaft, Organisationsgesellschaft. In: Apelt, W. (Hrsg.): *Zur Zukunft der Organisationssoziologie.* Wiesbaden, S. 73–91.

Kühl, S. (2016): *Organisation gestalten. Eine kurze organisationstheoretisch informierte Handreichung.* Wiesbaden.

Kühl, S. (2017a): *Arbeit – Marxistische und systemtheoretische Zugänge.* Wiesbaden.

Kühl, S. (2017b): *Laterales Führen. Eine kurze organisationstheoretisch informierte Handreichung.* Wiesbaden.

Kühl, S. (2018): *Organisationskulturen beeinflussen.* Bielefeld.

Laloux, F. (2016): *Reinventing Organizations.* Zürich.

Lewin, K. (1963): Geplante Veränderungen im Dreischritt: Auflockern, Hinübergleiten und Verfestigen eines Gruppenstandards. Gleichgewichte und Veränderungen in der Gruppendynamik. In: Lewin, K.: *Feldtheorie in den Sozialwissenschaften.* Ausgewählte theoretische Schriften. Hrsg. v. D. Cartwright. Bern.

Lewin, K. (2012): *Feldtheorie in den Sozialwissenschaften. Ausgewählte theoretische Schriften.* 2. Aufl. Bern.

Lewrick, M./Link, P./Leifer, L. (2018): *Das Design Thinking Playbook.* Zürich.

Luhmann, N. (1976): *Funktion und Folgen formaler Organisation.* 3. Aufl. Berlin.

Luhmann, N. (1984): *Soziale Systeme. Grundriss einer allgemeinen Theorie.* Frankfurt a. M.

Luhmann, N. (1990): Kommunikationssperren in der Unternehmensberatung. In: Königswieser, R. L. /Hrsg.): *Das systemisch evolutionäre Management. Neue Horizonte für Unternehmer.* Wien, S. 237–250.

Luhmann, N. (1994): Zweck – Herrschaft – System. Grundbegriffe und Prämissen Max Webers. In: Luhmann, N. (Hrsg.): *Politische Planung. Aufsätze zur Soziologie von Politik und Verwaltung.* Wiesbaden, S. 90–112.

Luhmann, N. (1997): *Die Gesellschaft der Gesellschaft.* Frankfurt.

Luhmann, N. (2000): *Organisation und Entscheidung.* Wiesbaden.

Luhmann, N. (2002): *Die Religion der Gesellschaft.* Frankfurt a. M.

Luhmann, N. (2012a): *Macht.* 4. Aufl. Stuttgart.

Luhmann, N. (2012b): *Macht im System.* Berlin.

Luhmann, N. (2014): *Vertrauen. Ein Mechanismus der Reduktion sozialer Komplexität.* 5. Aufl. Stuttgart.

Masten, A./Reed, M. (2002): Resilience in development. In: Snyder, C. R./ Lopez, S. J. (Hrsg.): *Handbook of positive psychology.* UK Oxford, S. 74–88.

McGregor, D. (1982): *Der Mensch im Unternehmen. (The Human Side of Enterprise.).* Düsseldorf.

Meynhardt, T. (02 2020): *Purpose ist kein Gutmenschentum.* https://heft. harvardbusinessmanager.de/digital/#HM/2020/2 (Abrufdatum: 05.06.2020).

Moore, M. (2013): *Recognizing public value.* Boston.

Moser, M. (2018): *Vom richtigen Umgang mit der Zeit. Die heilende Kraft der Chronologie.* Berlin.

Oesterreich, B./Schröder, C. (2016): *Das kollegial geführte Unternehmen: Ideen und Praktiken für die agile Organisation von Morgen.* München.

Parsons, T. (2012): *The social system.* New Orleans.

Pink, D. (2011): *Drive: The surprising truth about what motivates us.* New York.

Pinner, D./Rogers, M./Samandari, H. (2020): Addressing climate change in a post-pandemic world. *McKinsey Quaterly,* April, S. 1–6.

Ries, E. (2019): *Lean Startup. Schnell, risikolos und erfolgreich Unternehmen gründen.* 6. Aufl. München

Robertson, B. (2016): *Holocracy – Ein revolutionäres Management-System für eine relative Welt.* München

Rosa, H. (2019): *Resonanz. Eine Soziologie der Weltbeziehung.* Berlin.

Rudolph, E. (2017): *Wege der Macht. Philosophische Machttheorien von den Griechen bis heute.* Weilerswist.

Ruether, C. (2018): Soziokratie, Holakratie, S3, Frederic Laloux' »Reinventing Organizations« und »New Work«. Online verfügbar unter: https://www. soziokratie.org/wp-content/uploads/2018/07/buch-soziokratie-holakratie-laloux-2018-zweite-auflage.pdf (Abrufdatum: 03.08.2020).

Scharmer, O. (2015): *Theorie U – Von der Zukunft her führen. Presencing als soziale Technik.* 4. Aufl. Heidelberg.

Scharmer, O. (25.11.2015): *Otto Scharmer on the four levels of listening.* https://www.youtube.com/watch?v=eLfXpRkVZaI (Abrufdatum 12.12.2019).

Scharmer, O. (2020): *Theory U Sourcebook.* Von https://www.presencing.org/resource/tools (Abrufdatum: 05.06.2020).

Schein, E. (1999): *The Corporate Culture Survival Guide: Sense and Nonsense about Culture Change.* San Francisco.

Schein, E. (2017): *Organization Culture and Leadership.* 5. Aufl. New Jersey.

Schinko-Fischli, S. (2018): *Angewandte Improvisation für Coaches und Führungskräfte.* Berlin.

Schumacher, T./Wimmer, R. (2019): Der Trend zur hierarchiearmen Organisation. Zur Selbstorganisationsdebatte in einem radikal veränderten Umfeld. *ZOE – Zeitschrift zur Organisationsentwicklung, 2*, S. 12–18.

Seligman, M. (2014): *Flourish – Wie Menschen aufblühen: Positive Psychologie des gelingenden Lebens.* 2. Aufl. München.

Senge, P. M. (2011): *Die fünfte Disziplin. Kunst und Praxis der lernenden Organisation.* 11. Aufl. Stuttgart.

Simon, F. (2018): *Einführung in die systemische Organisationstheorie.* 6. Aufl. Heidelberg.

Sparrer, I./Varga v. Kibéd, M. (2009): Ganz im Gegenteil. Tetralemmaarbeit und andere Grundformen systemischer Strukturaufstellungen – für Querdenker und solche, die es werden wollen. 6. Aufl. Heidelberg

Sutcliffe, K./Vogus, T. J. (2003): Organizing for Resilience. In: Cameron, J. E. K. S. (Hrsg.): *Positive Organizational Scholarship*: San Francisco, S. 94–110.

Sutherland, L./Janene-Nelson, K. (2018): *Work together anywhere: A handbook on working remotely –successfully – for individuals, teams, and managers.* Den Haag.

Taleb, N. N. (2010): *Der schwarze Schwan. Konsequenzen aus der Krise.* München.

Taleb, N. N. (2012): *Antifragile. Things that gain from disorder.* New York.

Ulrich, H./Dyllick, T./Probst, G. (1984): *Management.* Bern.

Visotschnig, E./Schrotta, S. (2005): *Das SK-Prinzip*. Wien.

Visotschnig, E., Schrotta, S./Paulus, G. (2009): *Systemisches Konsensieren*. Holzkirchen.

Watzlawick, P. (2006): *Die erfundene Wirklichkeit. Wie wissen wir, was wir zu wissen glauben?* 11. Aufl. München

Weick, K./Sutcliffe, K. (2016): *Das Unerwartete managen. Wie Unternehmen aus Extremsituationen lernen*. 3. Aufl. Stuttgart.

Weingardt, M. (2004): *Fehler zeichnen uns aus. Transdisziplinäre Grundlagen zu Theorie und Produktivität des Fehlers in Schule und Arbeitswelt*. Bad Heilbrunn.

Williams, K. Y./O‹Reilly C.A. (1998): Demography and diversity in organizations. A review of 40 years of research. *Research in Organisational Behavior, Vol. 20*, S. 77–140.

Wilson, J. Q./Kelling, G. L. (1982): Broken windows. The police and neighborhood safety. *The Atlantic Monthly*, March, S. 29–38.

Witzel, M. (2012): *A history of management thought*. London.

Zirkler, M. (2019): H.O.P.E. as the framework for the Positive Organization. *IBA Journal of Mangement and Leadership, Vol. 10(2):* 15–22.

Links

https://www.holacracy.org/ (Holacracy Constitution)

https://mural.co/about-us

https://positivepsychology.com/growth-mindset-vs-fixed-mindset/

https://sociocracy30.org/

https://de.wikipedia.org/wiki/Ikigai#cite_note-1

https://www.youtube.com/watch?v=RZWf2_2L2v8

https://www.zukunftsinstitut.de/dossier/megatrends/

The authors

Dr Frank Boos has been an organizational consultant for over 35 years and is a managing partner of the Neuwaldegg Consulting Group, which co-founded systemic consulting. Through the design and development of Beratergruppe Neuwaldegg, he has been able to learn a lot about organizations.

He is motivated by working with people who want to shape organizations and make them a better place. Organizations have always excited him. For him, they are an exciting "crime scene" where important things happen—for people, for the economy and for society. They must move and touch people and actively shape their relationship to the common good (purpose). He wants to contribute to this, because it is important—today more than ever—to work with organizations and not only in them.

For Frank Boos, it is a great pleasure to be able to share his experiences, which he does successfully on the one hand in further training courses, and on the other hand through his regular publications. It gives him great pleasure to link the practical with the theoretical in such a way that it is also applicable to others. For him, the only way to halfway understand today's complex world is through good theory.

www.neuwaldegg.at, www.moving-organization.com

Barbara Buzanich-Pöltl is a managing partner of the Neuwaldegg Consulting Group. She has many years of experience in organizational development and leadership. In recent years, she has focused on agile transformations, self-organization and cultural development in a wide range of sectors with female teams and managers. In addition, she strengthens organizations in pushing gender equality in an impact-oriented way.

The way organizations function fascinates her anew every time: Incredible things emerge as if by a miracle—in the positive and also in the negative. She sees her mission in uncovering strengths for change, developing ease in change and at the same time tackling difficulties clearly and consistently. It is always about the next step.

For Barbara Buzanich-Pöltl, the book title is also part of what drives her. She is a person who is always on the move to promote development and growth. This is her purpose and generates energy, which she brings into cooperation, into further education programmes and above all into her family. Her motto is: Have fun and reach out!

www.neuwaldegg.at, www.moving-organization.com

The co-authors

Anna Jantscher, MHR, lives in Vienna and is a managing partner of the Neuwaldegg Consulting Group. As a business economist, she worked in human resource management for many years before she started to work as a facilitator and systemic consultant for organizations and people. She is currently working intensively on the question of how the transformation of organizations, teams and individuals towards self-organization, agility and purpose drive can succeed. Together with Nicole Lauchart-Schmidl, she is working on a book about the development of resonant organizations and resonance-generating leaders.

David Max Jeggle is a consultant at the Neuwaldegg Consulting Group and an experienced organizational developer and change expert. He combines the worlds of classical management consulting with systemic organizational development. As a consultant, he has accompanied organizations in their agilization since 2005 in order to master the challenges of digitalization and disruptive dynamics. His special focus is on agile organizational design, innovative governance formats and the empowerment of managers and team members. In his work, he surprises clients time and again with his clarity and innovative designs and interventions.

Nicole Lauchart-Schmidl, MSc, lives in Vienna and is a consultant at the Neuwaldegg Consulting Group. She has been advising and accompanying people and organizations in change for more than 20 years. Her focus is always on the further development of the entire organization, the sustainable success of the company and the successful interaction between all those involved. She worked in human resource management for many years, starting her professional career in psychosocial counselling for people with complex traumas. Familiar with the challenges of organizations and people in change, she accompanies managers and experts in the design of successful transformations. Together with Anna Jantscher, she is working on a book about developing resonant organizations and resonance-generating leaders.

Insa Meier is a trained organizational developer, trainer and coach at the Neuwaldegg Consulting Group. She has been working internationally as a management consultant since 2006 and accompanies organizations with a focus on leadership development. She is intensively involved with group dynamic processes, improvisation and leadership, especially also in the context of virtual cooperation and leadership. She was able to put this experience to good use for her clients during the Corona crisis and the "back to new normal", for example, in designing innovative digital learning journeys.

Gregor Tobeitz is an expert in complex transformations and an executive coach. He has been advising and supporting companies in an international context in change processes for many years. His focus is on the design and support of agile and digital transformations as well as the topic of innovation. He is particularly interested in the interaction of new technologies, organizational forms and collaboration models.